a two-hundred-million-dollar renovation by Selldorf Architects; the Met, seventy million dollars poorer but one twinkly Michael C. Rockefeller wing richer. 2025 is no anomaly. In 2015, the Whitney moved to a new four-hundred-million-dollar Renzo Piano building; in 2019, MoMA reopened after a years-long, block-darkening, four-hundred-fifty-million-dollar expansion, its third in as many decades. COVID paused the growth for a while but did nothing to challenge the trustees' confidence that growth is good. The rest of the 2020s will add fifty thousand square feet of waterfront property to the Tampa Museum of Art (a little ominous, given the state of the Atlantic, but hopefully Florida knows what it's doing), a hundred thousand square feet to the Portland Art Museum in Oregon, sixty thousand to the Portland Museum of Art in Maine. Upward and outward they swell: palaces of art covered in endless pricy lifts and implants and transplants, not so different from the kind the sponsors lavish on their own bodies.

If you want a clear x-ray of an era, every triumph and delusion crisply rendered, you can always study its art. In the case of the United States in 2025, however, it might be more revealing to study its art museums. Such anxious, blustery things! By the time a new renovation has hatched, a successor is already pecking through the shell. The final products slant and shift their weight as though aware that there is nothing final about them: not a chance in a society that relishes moving fast and breaking things, including itself.

Is it ungrateful, in Trump Part II Year One, to be skeptical of the art museums that have managed to keep expanding, thanks to billionaire largesse? The American system of private cultural philanthropy has a lot to answer for, but at least it provides some cushion from POTUS 47's whims. The better question might be: given the rain-or-shine ballooning of these buildings, and the municipal taxes that help make them possible, and the unaffordable restaurants, and the thirty-dollar tickets, and the shady land rights deals, and the write-offs, and the walls covered in donor names so that your eyes start to burn well before you reach the paintings, and the gift shops of deluxe crud, and the gentrifying neighborhoods that make the restaurants look affordable, and the galas — given all this, what, exactly, does museum expansion have to do with art?

The concept of growth, I am not the only one to notice, is having a rough twenty-first century. Blame the housing bubble, the overextended American empire, the mallification of urban centers, the net worth of the plutocracy, the greenhouse gas emissions, or all of them, since they may be symptoms of the same sickness. At least among people without summer houses, growth is reckless, boorish, decadent, cancerous, inherently suspicious; growth is the needle tower that could wipe out homelessness but stays empty fifty-one weeks of the year; growth is the rising tide that exclusively lifts yachts. Even its cooler friend, sustainable development, may only be growth with a better PR agent.

In the midst of this, museum growth seems to enjoy something like the benefit of the clergy. Not always, and not all museums — many journalists have wondered how much of 53rd Street MoMA will swallow before its stomach stops growling — but an expanding American art museum is still innocent until proven guilty, as an Amazon headquarters or a McMansion is not. In the clash between love of art and skepticism of growth, love triumphs. Art museums are sacred spaces where many visitors have the closest thing to a religious experience they will ever feel. What could be wrong with making room for more worship?

Start with the simplest justification for museum expansion: structural necessity. Some of these places are a century old, and nobody can worship if the walls crumble. All big buildings require repairs: ceilings blotch, plumbing and heating fritz. They are the kinds of problems that irk every museum, and, traditionally, they are the kind trustees have no interest in paying to fix. Upkeep is as important as it is unglamorous — no ribbon-snipping ceremony welcomes the new roof tiling, and nobody wants their name on a radiator, though to be fair I did see a named fire escape on a recent visit to MASS MoCA. It is a curious side-effect of tycoon psychology that a museum director may have an easier time scraping together fifty million for a new building than half a million for new toilets: vanity being vanity, unnecessary expansion is one of the shrewdest ways of funding necessary repair.

Who cares about necessity, as long as the results are beautiful? Some of the recent museum growth in New York, where I live, certainly is lovely. The cantilevered staircase that connects the two floors of the Frick has an elegance that doesn't overpower; the Breccia Aurora marble somehow splits the difference between the flowery Bouchers upstairs and the pale chill of the Reception Hall below, so that transition rivals either destination. I have heard sniggers about the Gilder Center at the Museum of Natural History, but I think its oozy granite interiors are built to last in the most important sense: while other, more self-consciously tasteful buildings are doomed to look more like the 2020s with each passing year, the Gilder will go on looking like itself.

For every triumph, though, there are multiple museum makeovers that inflame my inner Peggy Lee. *Is that all there is?* I thought this when I visited the new Whitney a decade ago. The design was far from terrible; an outright terrible building would have been so much less perplexing. The eastern façade resembled four or five façades stacked together while their architect, recently dubbed "our Brunelleschi" by one of America's leading magazines, decided where to put them. The western side, facing the Hudson, resembled a ship with a white sail, if the sail was a hunk of Styrofoam and the ship was sinking. North had lots of exposed pipes that somebody must have found pleasant to look at, and south was so utterly, breathtakingly *okay* it could only have been the work of a renowned architect dozens of museums deep in his career.

And for everything that goes up in a city this snug, something else must be knocked down. The Frick's Music Room was one of the most ravishing places in New York before Selldorf's renovation scrapped it to make way for temporary exhibitions (some excused the act by saying the venue was too small, as though this wasn't half the charm of the Music Room, not to mention the rest of the building — architectural victim-blaming). In 2014, as an *amuse-bouche* before its next meal, MoMA chewed up the American Museum of Folk Art, having bought the building and decided that Williams and Tsien's bronze façade disagreed with its house style of grids, glass, and more glass. That the world's most influential modern art museum has taken to junking work that stands too far outside the aesthetic norm is a sick joke I will leave hanging.

Who cares about beauty, as long as the results are bigger? At least in press releases, the rationale for museum expansion is fiercely utilitarian: more space equals more wall area, which allows for the display of more art and a greater bang-for-buck for the common museumgoer's eyeballs; more space also means more floor area and elevators and stairwells, which work together to relieve congestion. All very sensible on paper — funny, though, how the tiny museums that would benefit most from additional acreage cannot afford any and the museums that already own football fields of it seem to get more congested with growth, as any MoMA visitor knows. But only a fraction of the new layout goes to art, and the total amount may go down — at the moment LACMA is wrapping up a new six-hundred-fifty-million-dollar building by Peter Zumthor with ten thousand *fewer* square feet of galleries.

Even when the new space is bigger and one hundred percent art-devoted, it is unclear why a mega-museum gets intrinsically better with more stuff on the walls. "One cannot enjoy a pure aesthetic sensation," Kenneth Clark terrifyingly put it, "for longer than one can enjoy the smell of an orange." The purpose of going to the Met should not be to huff every orange on the tree, nor should it be the Met's duty to pelt visitors with as much citrus as possible. In point of fact, large museums never come close to displaying everything they own and instead rotate their permanent collections in and out of storage. The Met's collection includes close to two million works, only about five percent of which fit in the building; for MoMA, the number is somewhere around ten percent; for the Guggenheim, three. Making room for everything will always be a quixotic cause — besides, if given the choice between a shinier museum with marginally more on the walls or an already massive museum that doesn't cost a family a hundred dollars to visit, which one would our mythic common museumgoer choose?

The question is theoretical, needless to say. One of the tartest ironies of this era of nine-figure art museum philanthropy must be how little of the money reaches the consumer: across America, pay-what-you-can entry has been scaled back to free weekends, free weekends to seasonal free weekdays, and seasonal free weekdays to free parking. With every hundred-million-dollar expansion, free museum admission looks more like a weird twentieth-century fossil. Administrators cite study after study proving that cheaper tickets have no measurable effect on the size of museum audiences, and so — ah, terrible shame! — they might as well charge twenty or thirty dollars. I am less interested in the studies than I am in why free admission is now posed as a question instead of a right, economics be damned. Had the same stern, penny-pinching scrutiny been applied to the hundreds of new wings and annexes of recent years, I wonder how many of them would exist.

Fear not, though: museum expansion is of debatable value to the visitor but of enormous value to somebody else. If there is a central reason why museums keep growing, it may be that the donors like a guarantee that their gifts will remain on permanent display and not be buried in storage — more space, more guarantees. (Philip Guston's daughter Musa Mayer, for example, made the Met a present of 220 of her father's works on the condition that at least half be on display at all times.) When done right, philanthropy pets the ego and pads the wallet. There is the psychological reward of knowing your art collection will be ogled long after you are dead, plus the charitable tax deduction, plus all the ancillary ways of pocket-lining. A high-end museum drives up property values, attracts tourists, fills up hotels and department stores, and generally enriches the sort of people who populate museum boards to begin with. Conflicts of interest are, of course, discouraged — why else would it say so in the code of ethics? Gentlemen, I'm shocked, shocked to find that profiteering is going on in here!

Still, reasons only take you so far. Follow utilitarian logic through to the end, usually, and you arrive at some humorless "well . . . *because*." Few multi-millionaries and billionaires are famous for the practicality of their wants; probably not even they know why a rising tide delights them so much. Why have America's museums kept getting bigger, then? To fit a few thousand more artworks next to fifty thousand others, certainly. Fundamentally, though, museums expand because expansion does not need a reason: to the people who make the decisions, it justifies itself, like life or happiness or, for a few hopeless fogeys, art. For a long time now, the signature style of the contemporary art world has been something like real estate aestheticism — growth for growth's sake.

Even though I'm the other kind of aesthete, my first instinct is to say, let the tycoons do what they want. There are worse things to do with money than burn it, and every million dollars spent on a modern art wing that nobody likes is a million dollars not spent on predatory loan marketing or the reelection of some moussed, drooling climate change denier.

If museum expansion warped buildings and buildings alone, I could laugh it off, but it has a way of warping what's inside them, too. Make a quick list of the glitteriest art careers of the past twenty years or so, and you find a few genuine talents and a rollcall of mediocrities with a gift for ritzing up the vast gray interiors in which museums increasingly abound: Ai Weiwei, scatterer of porcelain seeds at the Tate Modern; Yayoi Kusama, wallpaperer of the same institution and dozens of others; KAWS, whose giant brown dolls I am doomed to pass every time I find myself in the lobby of the Brooklyn Museum. The first task for these people is to fill up lots and lots of space, and at this they succeed brilliantly, since their work consists of a few simple elements (seeds, dots, dolls) that can babble on to whatever degree is required of them. When museumgoers walk in and *ooh* at the dots disappearing into the distance, they are *ooh*ing at the giant space that hosts them, handsome in its bright new costume. Space is boss, and art does what it says.

The premier filler-upper artist of the decade so far must be Jeffrey Gibson, the MacArthur genius and proud occupant of the American pavilion at last year's Venice Biennale. With the help of a stable of assistants, he assembles hundreds of thousands of rainbow beads into sculptures, paintings, and costumes, none of which exhibit the slightest grace or facility with color, unless turning on the entire spectrum full blast is your idea of chromatic wizardry. Glance one-eyed at a Gibson and you absorb the whole thing along with most of the others. The best test of this is the impressive forgettability of his work — not long ago I spent a while in *POWER FULL BECAUSE WE'RE DIFFERENT*, his installation at MASS MoCA. I am still pondering that fire escape, but today I would be hard-pressed to say if *this* dress was bright yellow or bright blue, if *that* bit of wall was bright orange or bright pink, or much else beyond the fact that the room was big and everything was bright. But this would seem to be part of what museums love about Gibson, and why at the time of this writing his beads are being slobbered over from sea to shining sea: they dress up anywhere because they don't say too much of anything. Like Kusama's dots, there is something superficially innocent about them that gives the most bloated museum hangars a sweet glaze of populism.

Bloat and populism are having spectacular twenty-first centuries. It seems strange that both should be doing so well simultaneously, but here we are. Bloat won economics, while populism seems to have won aesthetics some time ago. (Politics is the usual tug o' war between them.) Peacocking displays of wealth are so common that our senses have numbed to them, but "elitist" has been one of the filthiest words in the English language for as long as I have spoken it. Nobody gets in trouble for selling out anymore, but the idea of making art that might alienate some of its audience has become vaguely impolite, to the delight of some and the horror of others. (The inevitable Mark Fisher quotation:

"The assault on cultural elitism has gone alongside the aggressive restoration of a material elite.") Nowhere do bloat and populism clash with such matter-antimatter explosiveness as they do in museums: the new spaceships to nowhere are for everybody, and they are toys and tools for billionaires. The harder they strain to seem down-to-earth, the more bloat they hide.

The art historian András Szántó bottles the bloat and the down-to-earth-ness and the rest of contemporary arts administration culture in *The Future of the Museum*. A collection of twenty-eight interviews with museum directors, all conducted in the early months of COVID, the book is a quietly amazing compendium of the ways in which art people — but not artists — think about art. I read and reread it like a novel. There are twenty-eight main characters, half men and half women and all fluent in their regional dialects of bureaucratese. (The fungal creep of the word "immersive" in the last decade or so has spared few museum directors.) Their institutions are scattered across fourteen countries in every continent but Antarctica. Together they preside over some seven million objects and an annual budget of nearly a billion dollars. Their average age is forty-nine. Many studied art history in college, though one is an ex-Louis Vuitton executive and another is an ex-child star. Part of the pathos and the comedy of this novel is that nobody is allowed to say what's really on their mind, but sometimes they are so determined not to say *X* it is clearly *X* and nothing else that they are thinking.

The first thing I noticed, reading *The Future of the Museum* in this bumper year of buildings, was that nobody fesses up to wanting a bigger museum. In hindsight, at least some of these people were speaking to Szántó in between frantically rescheduling the new sculpture wing, yet the subject of expansion goes all but unmentioned for three-hundred seventeen pages — like the dog in the Sherlock Holmes story, it doesn't bark because it recognizes its master. Instead of growth, museum directors would like to talk about community. It would be impossible for me to overstate how badly they would like to do this. The executive director of the M+ Museum in Hong Kong believes in the importance of community. So does the director of the Garage Museum of Contemporary Art in Moscow. So does everybody — "the term 'community' is bandied about too much," says the director of the Brooklyn Museum after bandying it about too much. Not that anyone can really be *anti*-community, but the tic-like repetitions suggest a guilty conscience. The more I read the word "community," the more vividly I pictured a big concrete slab named for a Sackler. And it is strange to see communities praised on page after page with so few mentions of what they are communities *of*.

To put it another way: this is a book of conversations with twenty-eight of the world's most educated and powerful arts administrators in which almost nobody speaks with passion, or even much warmth, about art; in which everybody remembers to praise community but nobody rhapsodizes about a painting or a sculpture or a film or a tapestry or a drawing. At times, some of these people seem almost sheepish about managing such flimsy things. One director does speak at length about the value of his museum's collection, but he is talking about their cash value, which apparently is five billion dollars. ("The conversation about how the liquidity trapped in artworks can be used has been a very unnuanced one.") In the book's most touching and depressing moment, the Brooklyn Museum's director confesses that she wonders if she should have gone into politics instead.

These interviews were conducted in a pandemic year, to be fair, and perhaps it struck Szántó's subjects as insensitive to extoll Rembrandt in dark times, though it might have struck them that in 2020 some of us needed Rembrandt, who lost his lover to plague, more than ever. Americans consider art "a luxury rather than a necessity," as the poet and one-time NEA chair Dana Gioia wrote in 1991, well before the pandemic or the dismembering of the NEA. By "Americans," Gioia meant people who have not chosen to devote their lives to art, but this book made me wonder if some art bureaucrats are hiding the same sneer. If you didn't believe paintings to be of vital importance during the COVID-19 pandemic, you don't really believe them to be of vital importance at all.

To understand a tribe, anthropologists say, it is not enough to pay attention to what the tribespeople talk about. Truth lies also in what they are not talking about: all the thoughts they consider too self-evidently absurd to mention. The big unspoken subject in *The Future of the Museum*, even bigger than museum expansion, is *pleasure*. Museum directors differ in their attitudes toward retail or political neutrality, but on pleasure, and the possibility that a museum might afford its visitors some, they sing the same silent song. Twenty-eight times Szántó asks what a museum is for, and almost every interviewee replies with something about education or activism or building community — all admirable goals, but lifeless when the central one goes missing. The director of the de Young in San Francisco says in four words what everyone else in this book says in zero: "We are not entertainment."

His grimness would have amused Alfred Barr, MoMA's first director, who felt his museum's purpose was to help people "enjoy, understand, and use the visual arts of our time." We can imagine what would happen if the art museum directors of the early twenty-first century had to agree on their own definition, though actually we don't need to imagine anything: in September 2019, the International Council of Museums determined that museums "are participatory and transparent, and work in active partnership with and for diverse communities to collect, preserve, research, interpret, exhibit, and enhance understandings of the world, aiming to contribute to human dignity and social justice, global equity and planetary well-being." A revised version appeared three years later, with "enjoyment" tossed in at the end like a pack of gum in the checkout line. I have nothing against planetary well-being, and you may quote me as saying so. How bizarre, though, to hold entertainment, one of a handful of things that makes this planet bearable, in such low esteem, like an opera house that proclaims its commitment to justice but forgets to mention music.

The final twist of *The Future of the Museum* is that it *is* full of odes to the power of the image, just not the kind of image you would expect museum workers to praise. There are millions of people who will forgo sleep, sex, sun, water, and food to keep staring at screens, and clearly arts administrators have taken envious notice. Things go from bizarre to sinister here: the museum directors of the early twenty-first century look at the red-eyed consumers and the companies selling their own dopamine back to them and think, "How can we be more like *that*?" "How can we better understand the motivations and intentions of the kinds of experiences that people are seeking through online games," wonders the director of Singapore Art Museum, "so that we may use these as a way to steer them toward, as well as complement and enhance, the experiences museums can offer?" "This idea of the museum as photo backdrop arrived here early," adds another director; "We spend a lot of time thinking about how to turn this inexorable urge into something productive." (Notice he doesn't say, "Something pleasurable.") "People love serialized content," the nuanced liquidity guy opines. "Imagine if museums found a way to have each program build off the previous one, and if we figured out a way to distribute that through digital media in a way that was binge-worthy. That is a digital future I would like to imagine."

Binges and gamifications and inexorable urges — behold the museum directors' glorious dream! What disturbs me more is that they claim to be dreaming in our names.

Pleasure, you have surely noticed, is having a spectacular time of late, and a terrible one. Some audiovisual thrill is always available, provided your devices stay charged, but if you have never felt the ache of all this bottomless fun, bully for you. There are whole clinics clotted with people who got such a kick out of online games or porn or other pixelated delights that they no longer feel much of anything; and their undiagnosed kin absent-mindedly run the world. It is telling that the concept of the guilty pleasure has almost disappeared from the culture — now there are only different pleasures for different folks. Neuroscience concurs, cheapening the feeling to a chemical squirt.

Some dour economic principle seems to be at work: mint too much pleasure too fast and it is devalued into the merest itch. As though to keep its stock trading high, meanwhile, fine art gets cashed in the stabler currency of community or duty or self-improvement or self-advancement — "something productive," as that wise museum director might put it. Hence all the books insisting that the function of great literature is to make us nicer (Céline? Hamsun?); hence all the op-eds my grandfather used to mail me about how a humanities degree could help me get a job at McKinsey.

There is something I have not yet mentioned but should. I get enormous pleasure from art museums, not only the underfunded ones, but also the gray lugs I have been complaining about. And not only the art that hangs in them; I mean also the lines, the selfies, the gross kid-friendly installations in the lobby, the humid elevators of tourists, the tour groups, the wall texts written in something that somewhat resembles English. Of course I also get sick of every one of these things, but I believe that any real love for the exhilarating, exhausting art museum involves some irritation, a healthy mix of *because* and *in spite of* that is stronger than *because* alone. The kind of pleasure I get from museums, I suppose, is the kind I get from communities (we shouldn't let the art bureaucrats ruin the word), and from art, and from almost anything else that is intrinsically worthwhile.

The question with which I began was not all rhetorical: what does museum expansion have to do with art? Very little, but also everything. Unless you happen to be wealthy enough to buy masterpieces yourself, to experience art means to experience it with a pack of strangers in a shiny new room named after people you couldn't stand much more than they could stand you. The people who make such places happen seem to think of museumgoers as dopamine junkies, utility maximizers who will of course want to see more things since more things equal more dopamine. You can, if you like, play along with this and try to binge as you might binge on serialized content. You can also slow down, choose a handful of works, and go swimming in them. I recommend option two, not because I have any illusions that it measurably alters the world but because I believe that real pleasure exists outside measurement, and because I believe that real pleasure needs no reason to exist. If you require one, though, might I suggest the satisfaction of not acting like the sheep that art bureaucrats would like us to be? If we need help, we can always consult artists.

The artist Johann Zoffany has been of some help to me, even though I can't always convince myself that he really existed. His work hangs in the Tate, and the ZOFFANY, JOHANN (1734/5–1810) entry in my edition of *The Oxford Companion to Art* is respectably long. Still, ask yourself, does this sound like a person or a literary character? Born Johannus Josephus Zauffaly near Frankfurt, he moved to Rome at seventeen and reinvented himself as Zoffani. In his twenties he got himself a court painter gig in Wurzburg, but three years later he ran off to London, leaving his wife behind. In Georgian London, he changed his name to Zoffany, took a mistress whom he passed off as his wife, and befriended the greatest actor of the era, David Garrick. For a while he had the favor of Queen Charlotte, but by the 1780s he was cash-strapped and resolved to sail to India to start again yet again. On the voyage back to England he was shipwrecked on the Andamans and, he claimed, ate a sailor to survive. I have no idea why someone would say this if it weren't true. I have no idea why someone would say it if it were. Start self-mythologizing as a teenager, I suppose, and you never stop.

"Indifferent artistic merit" is what the *Oxford Companion* has to say about Zoffany's work. I'm not so sure myself, and neither, for that matter, is the *Oxford Companion*, which gives Zoffany's *Tribuna of the Uffizi* pride of place on the front cover. I have an odd relationship with this image, having never seen the original at Windsor Castle but glancing at the little ink reproduction most days for the last five or six years. Ordinarily, I would not write about a work of art I had never seen with my own eyes, but given that the Queen instructed Zoffany to travel to Florence in order to paint the most important room in the city's most important museum, cramming his canvas full of tiny reproductions of works she had never seen with *her* own eyes, it seems forgivable somehow.

Zoffany spent six years doing the cramming, and it shows: every kind of image and sculpture can be found floating somewhere in this swollen gut of a painting. It is true that museums before the twentieth century displayed art frame-to-frame, but even by this standard the Uffizi that we are shown by Zoffany is a mess — compare it with a calmer gallery interior like Samuel Morse's *Gallery of the Louvre*, completed a few decades later, and you see how far Zoffany is overstepping the curatorial rules of his own era, not just ours. More is more, and still not enough. Works that ordinarily hung elsewhere in the Uffizi were rushed into the Tribuna for the Queen's delight. So were works that ordinarily hung in other museums. There are so many things here that some cannot fit on the walls and need to be carried or dumped on the floor: Rubens' *Consequences of War*, a sculpture of baby Hercules, Titian's *Venus of Urbino*, an Etruscan urn, a Holbein, a Correggio, a few Raphaels . . .

Charlotte hated it. She had expected a Tribuna overflowing with paintings and sculptures; instead she got one overflowing with paintings, sculptures, and people. These are tourists, in the original sense of the word: educated and wealthy men hitting the last stop on their Grand Tour of the European continent. We can imagine the Queen's anger at this unsolicited reminder that mere *gentlemen* had been to the Uffizi and she had to be content with copies. This is a particularly bovine bunch, too — "a flock of traveling boys," Horace Walpole thought, "and one does not know nor care whom." Look how they swarm and gawk, sticking their noses and fingers where neither belong. The painter Thomas Patch pokes Titian's *Venus* but doesn't look at it — he is too taken with the homoerotic *The Two Wrestlers*. Zoffany himself makes an appearance on the painting's left: he is the one grinning too widely as he holds up Raphael's *Niccolini-Cowper Madonna*, to the fascination of everyone around him. Even Pietro Bastianelli, the Uffizi's curator, seems unenlightened by his daily exposure to the sublime: he's got his greasy digits on the Titian, too.

But to look at *The Tribuna of the Uffizi* a quarter of a millennium later is to breathe easier and, dare I say, to believe in art slightly more. If he was anything at all, Zoffany was a skilled copyist. His miniature Rubens preserves the meaty writhe of the original, and, adjusting for superficial things like clothes, he more or less copied the feel of any big museum in the twenty-first century, too. There are few problems with the contemporary art world that were not also problems in the 1770s. Hopeless commercialism? Zoffany added paintings to *The Tribuna of the Uffizi* because his friend was trying to sell them to George III. Congestion? You can barely scratch your cheek in this room. Distractable tourists? Mr. Patch cannot keep his eyes on a Titian. The cheapening of artworks into lifestyle props? The only reason most of these posh yahoos are here is because the Grand Tour is an experience that they are supposed to collect — a pretty accessory for a life of foxhunting and gout. Art only matters because someone looks. The more renowned the art, the greater the number of clueless lookers, joyless collectors, donors in search of tax breaks, and steroidal museums. It's the muck that clings to most worthwhile culture. It is not going anywhere, and neither is art.

We are all in the muck, to slightly paraphrase a writer who was serious about pleasure, but some of us are looking at the stars. One of the few figures in *The Tribuna of the Uffizi* who shows some glimmer of life in his eyes is a young man toward the painting's left side whom the professors identify as the painter and politician Charles Loraine Smith. He is one of the few people in the scene who is seated, which would seem to mean he intends to be there a while, and he is the only one who is *making* something — sketching on a little pad — instead of gulping things down. Not his face but his whole body points at an ancient sculpture of Cupid and Psyche, and one imagines him taut with his own fervid staring. A cloud of contagious distractions hangs over his right shoulder, but somehow he is immune: Zoffany and his friends could walk away, but Charles would keep sketching. A grenade could go off and he wouldn't wince. But the bigger miracle is the boy hunched behind Charles: given the choice between the loud, louche circle and the artist quietly sketching, the boy chooses the artist. He squats, trying to feel whatever pleasure keeps Charles seated — the grenade might not startle him, either. Under the right conditions, attention can be more contagious than distraction.

DAVID GREENBERG

The Nonsense of 'Neoliberalism'

A Conceptual Trash Heap

Toni Morrison was wrong when she intoned that language is violence. But let's give her this: the reckless use of words can do violence, idiomatically speaking, to clear thinking and therefore to political analysis. Slinging about words whose meaning is muddled, misleading, or tendentious — or whose usage is meant to oversimplify or to inflame — makes it impossible to think rationally, coherently, and productively.

It is a tall order in this age of slogans and shibboleths to select one word to expunge from our political vocabulary, but if asked to do so I would nominate "neoliberalism." A coinage of the late 1970s and early 1980s, the term remained fairly limited in its use for two decades, gaining currency at first in academic circles and then exploding in popularity after the financial crash in 2008 and Bernie Sanders' rise to celebrity. Then, just when it was fading from overexposure, it surged back into fashion. Critics, scholars, consultants, and commentators now finger neoliberalism as the reason for practically all our political problems, especially the Democrats' failure to keep the presidency out of the hands of Donald Trump.

"What Trump is attacking is neoliberalism. Economic neoliberalism underpins the past seventy years of Western economic and cultural order," declares America's most overrated senator, Chris Murphy, who alleges that neoliberalism has bequeathed a "very real epidemic of American unhappiness." (Struggling with his cognitive dissonance over a concept he doesn't quite understand, Murphy added: "Though it contains the word *liberal*, neoliberalism was devised by libertarian-conservative economists.") Ro Khanna, another ambitious, out-of-his-depth operator, calls for "the rejection of neoliberalism. For forty years, we made a mistake. Frankly, it was both parties." (Forty? Wasn't it seventy? But what are a few decades among friends?) The Hewlett Foundation, which bankrolls efforts to replace neoliberalism with something else — the left hates billionaires except when they fund the left — defines neoliberalism as "free-market fundamentalism" and "the free-market, anti-government, growth-at-all-costs approach to economic and social policy." Search the horizonless steppes of the internet and you will find countless pundits, politicians, and even ostensibly knowledgeable policymakers invoking the bogeyman of neoliberalism to explain where the Democrats and America went wrong.

The promiscuous use of the word "neoliberalism" has plagued our discourse since well before Trump. Over the years several intrepid explicators have pointed up its semiotic bankruptcy. Back in 2009, in an academic article titled, "Neoliberalism: From New Liberal Philosophy to Anti-Liberal Slogan," the political scientists Taylor Boas and Jordan Gans-Morse concluded that "*neoliberalism* has become a conceptual trash heap capable of accommodating multiple distasteful phenomena without much argument as to whether one or the other component really belongs." A decade later, the fine intellectual historian Daniel Rodgers warned that "the success of 'neoliberalism' is a measure of its substantive hollowness" and noted "four distinctly different phenomena" that fly under its banner: an economic theory; a set of economic policies; the capitalist economy itself; and — take a breath — "the hegemonic force of the culture that surrounds and entraps us." The journalist Jonathan Chait meanwhile traced how "neoliberal" morphed into an off-the-shelf slur used to denigrate regular Democrats. "The ubiquitous epithet is intended to separate its target — liberals — from the values they claim to espouse," he shrewdly observed. "By relabeling self-identified liberals as 'neoliberals,' their critics on the left accuse them of betraying the historic liberal cause." In his Substack newsletter, Matthew Yglesias continues valiantly to puncture what he calls "anti-neoliberal" thinking. Yet for all these debunkings, the term has only gotten more popular, leaping out of academic tracts and leftist polemics and into the vernacular.

As it is used today, "neoliberalism" contains at least three assumptions that its users hope to promulgate but which are, in fact, wrong. The first concerns what historians call periodization: reliance on neoliberalism as a historical framework depends on the flawed premise that in or about 1980, with the election of Ronald Reagan, the American ethos changed. Second, the invocation of neoliberalism incorporates a critique of liberals and Democrats, who, it is insinuated, supinely acquiesced in Reaganism, creating a "Washington consensus" by jettisoning the party's historic commitment to using government to better people's lives. Third, the neoliberal mantra implies that the economic policies pursued by Democrats when they had power were an economic, political, and even moral failure.

Each of these ideas may contain kernels of truth. But none holds up as an overarching and empirically demonstrable proposition. If we want to understand liberalism and liberal governance over the last half century — and there is no denying that it is now facing a crisis — we should start by euthanizing this unenlightening word. The sooner we clarify our thinking about our recent economic and political history, the more intelligently we can debate what should come next.

The Origins of Neoliberalism

To understand where "neoliberalism" came from, we must return to the 1970s, when American voters were repudiating liberalism — known ominously in those days as "the L word" — in droves.

By the late 1970s, the enormous achievements of Lyndon Johnson's Great Society had become clear — but it was no less clear that they had failed to stanch the spread of social maladies such as divorce, out-of-wedlock births, drug use, and violent crime. The civil rights movement had secured formal equality for black Americans and invigorated efforts to do likewise for women, gays, and other groups, but liberals suffered when they counseled more intrusive governmental measures to guarantee not only political and legal equality but also economic and social equality. Keynesian policies that had fueled prosperity since World War II proved powerless to combat the beast of stagflation, and the rise of a post-industrial economy — which had shifted away from heavy manufacturing and toward white-collar jobs that demanded a college education for the new hordes of "symbolic analysts" — triggered a long series of painful geographic and professional dislocations. In foreign policy, the Vietnam War stained the luster of liberal internationalism, leaving many Americans leery of wielding power abroad and voters leery of trusting the Democrats as a younger generation of leaders slouched toward isolationism.

The political wreckage was immense. During the presidency of Richard Nixon — who, though loathed by liberals and already tainted by Watergate, cruised to reelection in 1972 — the Democratic Party hemorrhaged support from key constituencies, including white Southerners, blue-collar workers, Catholics, and the intellectuals soon to be known as neoconservatives. Watergate allowed the Democrats a brief reprieve, but Jimmy Carter's hapless White House sojourn propelled more voters rightward. In 1980 and 1984, Ronald Reagan twice routed the Democrats, while the Republicans also seized the Senate for the first time since the 1950s. Between 1968 and 1988, Democrats lost every presidential election but one, almost all in landslides. "Unless they recover their partisan energies and intellectual vigor, the Democrats could enter a long historical passage of declining influence and relevance," warned Lance Morrow of *Time* magazine in 1980, "becoming the political equivalent of some of the decaying cities of the Northeast, once flourishingly productive, the exuberant places where the modern Democratic Party originated."

Projects arose to ask where the Democratic Party had gone astray. Politicians and analysts drew up new strategies and policies that they hoped could restore confidence in an affirmative if more realistic vision of government's capacities. These efforts are commonly described as designed to steer the Democratic Party to the political center. Exhibit A is the founding in 1985 of the Democratic Leadership Council, a group led by Southern moderates aiming to win back Reagan Democrats by stressing values such as patriotism, religion, work, discipline, and responsibility. But the call for internal reform did not come only from centrists; it was heard across the center-left spectrum, urged by liberal stalwarts as well as middle-of-the-roaders. In the late 1970s, Edward Kennedy, the liberal lion, took up airline decontrol and criminal sentencing reform, breaking with recently enshrined left-wing orthodoxies. In the 1980s, his aide Paul Kirk, as Democratic Party chairman, implemented a platform emphasizing "traditional values." Barney Frank, another quintessential liberal, wrote a book called *Speaking Frankly* urging Democrats to swallow their unease about brandishing their patriotism or condemning criminals. The civil rights hero John Lewis, elected to Congress in 1986, prodded his fellow Georgian Sam Nunn — maybe the most conservative Democrat in the Senate — to run for president in 1988. Lewis also attended DLC events, offering the insurgent group advice on forging biracial coalitions. Notwithstanding its sobriquet as the "Southern White-Boys Caucus," the DLC included many pragmatic dyed-in-the-wool liberals who, like Lewis, wanted to build a big tent in order to win again — including prominent African Americans such as Tom Bradley, Maynard Jackson, Kurt Schmoke, Andrew Young, Mike Espy, Floyd Flake, Bill Gray, Doug Wilder, and Ron Brown. Refashioning the party's public philosophy, in other words, was a goal pushed by Democrats of all stripes.

This crisis was what gave rise to the impulses that came to be known as "neoliberalism." Apart from the DLC, the most prominent group of reformers in these years were those who hoisted the neoliberal flag. (The DLC included some neoliberals, such as Al Gore and Dick Gephardt, but the two groups were not identical.) The word itself was invented around 1979 by Charlie Peters, majordomo of the *Washington Monthly*, a scrappy little policy magazine and popularized by Peters and Randall Rothenberg, who wrote a defining article and book on the topic. (Peters' and Phillip Keisling's *A New Road for America: The Neoliberal Movement* and Rothenberg's *The Neoliberals: Creating the New American Politics* are the ur-texts for understanding the phenomenon.) Even then, the meaning was vague. No hard-and-fast set of doctrines united neoliberals. "There are no meetings, no dues, no constitution," said Gephardt, a Missouri congressman who was among those tagged with the label. Voting patterns in Congress revealed neoliberals to be no more conservative than other Democrats.

Despite the lack of a membership roster, the same people typically appeared in discussions of the movement: officials such as Gephardt, Gore, Gary Hart, Bill Bradley, Paul Tsongas, and Bruce Babbitt; academics such as Lester Thurow, Robert Reich, and Amitai Etzioni; and the journalists trained by Peters at the *Washington Monthly*, including James Fallows, Nicholas Lemann, and Michael Kinsley. The *New Republic*, then a weekly magazine at the center of Washington debates, published neoliberal policy proposals alongside critiques of the movement. Of course these people often disagreed about policies, candidates, and even principles. But a few commonalities among the neoliberals could be discerned.

For the most part, neoliberals focused not on cultural issues or foreign policy or judicial fights but on economics. Reacting to the crises of the 1970s, they called for policies suited for the emerging post-industrial landscape centered on technology and information. In the 1970s, many on the left had hailed an "age of limits" and called for relinquishing the hope of ever-rising living standards. Neoliberals, without forsaking the goal of economic fairness, reemphasized growth as a cornerstone of their agenda and message.

Neoliberals also extolled efficiency. They excoriated bureaucracy, public and private, and allowed themselves to defy their allied interest groups such as government workers, unions, public-interest lawyers, and pro-regulation lobbyists. They favored investments in education and research and development. Many championed what was clunkily called "industrial policy," or having the government select up-and-coming sectors of the economy for support. Technology captivated them, giving rise to the phrase "Atari Democrats." They foresaw that high-tech innovation could help maintain America's global competitiveness. They were far-sighted, too, in acknowledging the tightening interdependence of nations — a condition that spawned the word "globalization," a close cousin of neoliberalism — and the need to adapt. In the 1970s, in deference to the unions, congressional Democrats had begun discarding liberalism's traditional commitment to free trade; but most neoliberals, underscoring the folly of protectionism, countered that lowering trade barriers and opening markets would help both the United States and its international partners.

The philosophy just described bears scant resemblance to the caricatures proffered by Chris Murphy, Ro Khanna, and their ilk. Contrary to current mythology, the neoliberals were not libertarians, conservatives, free-marketeers, supply-siders, rampant deregulators, Reaganites, Thatcherites, Friedmanites, Hayekians, or enemies of the New Deal or the welfare state. More than other liberals, they saw a role for markets in their new policies, but they rejected the axiom that the market was all wise. "First of all — and most important of all — we are liberals," Peters explained, noting "large areas" of policy in which neoliberals scarcely differed from other liberals. "We criticize liberalism not to destroy it but to renew it." Babbitt defended the "welfare state" from the Republicans who would gut it, calling for sustaining "an activist federal government in areas such as environmental matters, health, and entitlements." Morton Kondracke of *The New Republic* in 1980 called neoliberalism "an attempt to combine the traditional Democratic compassion for the downtrodden and outcast elements of society with different vehicles than categorical aid programs . . . or new federal bureaucracies." Neoliberals sometimes derided their liberal forbears: "We are not a bunch of little Hubert Humphreys," Gary Hart famously railed. But more often they affirmed the values and the principles that had animated twentieth-century liberalism — coupled with a desire to devise new ways to meet the demands of a new economic reality. Far from Reaganites, neoliberals were practical-minded welfare-state anti-Reagan liberals seeking to adjust their means to meet their traditional ends. Neoliberalism was a revision that took place *within* the liberal tradition. This may be why many of the detractors of neoliberalism on the left and the right are really just old-fashioned enemies of liberalism.

So why do so many people misunderstand neoliberalism? Why is it now equated with what we normally call economic conservatism? For that, as we shall see, the fault lies, at least partly, with Michel Foucault.

A Little Knowledge Is a Dangerous Thing

By the early 1990s, as Bill Clinton emerged as the Democrats' standard-bearer, the word "neoliberalism" took a backseat to a more capacious label: "New Democrat." Clinton had not often been listed among the neoliberals and didn't quite fit the bill. He appears in neither Rothenberg's nor Peters' books. In the Democratic primaries in 1992, on economic issues Clinton ran *to the left* of his closest rival, the card-carrying neoliberal Paul Tsongas, contrasting his own pledge to protect Social Security with Tsongas' dour fixation with trimming entitlements. Some Clinton aides, such as Robert Reich and Ira Magaziner, were called neoliberals, and as a governor and a presidential candidate Clinton had found promise in neoliberal ideas about growth, high-tech investment, government reform, and globalization. But he balanced his technocratic side with a visceral economic populism and a critique of Reaganomics for catering to corporations and the rich. Clintonism was a synthesis of several strands of liberal reformism, of which neoliberalism was only one. A chairman of the DLC, Clinton stressed the values of community, opportunity, and responsibility. He also captured the loyalty of a diverse mix of other groups: the black community, the nation's governors, assorted academics and intellectuals. During his presidency, Clinton's program was described not as neoliberal but as that of a New Democrat or, starting in his second term, as a "Third Way" — a label also used by center-left leaders in Britain and Germany.

In short, Clinton's ascent rendered "neoliberalism" obsolete as a taxonomic category. A different strain of updated liberalism — call it Clintonism — now held sway. Yet just as Washington journalists were retiring "neoliberalism," it got picked up, by sheer coincidence, by European leftists — people who had no familiarity with the legislation once bandied about by Bradley, Gephardt, Hart, and the others; who were not well-versed in American policy debates about military reform or education reform or "reinventing government"; who hadn't read the neoliberal books and journals. Some of them probably had not even kept up with the decades-old shift in the meaning of the word "liberalism" itself, which in the nineteenth century had meant an assertion of individual rights, including economic rights, against the state, but in the Progressive Era had also come to encompass a belief in an active governmental role in the economy. Tethering liberalism to its former and now-antiquated meaning, these left-wing European academics thus felt none of Chris Murphy's addlement in applying a word rooted in liberalism to a non-liberal philosophy.

These European academics glommed onto "neoliberalism" to name a school of conservative or right-of-center economic thought that they traced back to the 1930s. It turned out that neoliberalism — or more precisely the French *néo-libéralisme* — had been fleetingly applied in 1938 to a group of intellectuals who attended a conference in Paris called, charmingly, the "Colloque

Walter Lippmann," which debated the ideas in the American journalist's book *The Good Society*. Like Lippmann, the convener of the conference, a French philosopher named Louis Rougier, hoped to develop an "essentially progressive" alternative both to rigid nineteenth-century *laissez-faire* doctrines and to socialism. To this end, Rougier invited twenty-six thinkers, ranging from the liberal humanist Raymond Aron to the free-market economists Friedrich Hayek and Ludwig von Mises, for a long weekend in Paris in late August. But Rougier's dreams went unrealized. The discussion in Paris "remained vague and broad," according to the historian Angus Burgin's well-researched account, "because of both the relative brevity of the individual contributions and a general sense of uncertainty about whether . . . [to] focus on a reexamination of foundational principles or . . . practical policies." A follow-up symposium the next year was canceled after Hitler and Stalin invaded Poland. So much for *néo-libéralisme*.

Enter Foucault, four decades later, who appears to have been the first European to misapply the resurrected term "neoliberal" not simply to the Paris conferees of 1938 but specifically, and inaccurately, to the *conservatives* in attendance — Hayek, von Mises, and their intellectual allies. Foucault did so in a series of lectures from 1979, published in 2004 as *The Birth of Biopolitics*, which included an account of the Colloque Walter Lippmann. (Biopolitics describes the — inevitably sinister — workings of political and governmental power upon the body and organic life more generally, as states manage their populations through policies relating to reproduction, sexuality, public health, and the like.) Foucault's core point was a reasonable one: that unlike the nineteenth-century apostles of pure *laissez-faire*, who had theorized a weak state, these economists of the 1930s believed that governments had to take an active role in underwriting any market-based system. "The problem of neo-liberalism," Foucault argued in one of his lectures, "was not how to cut out or contrive a free space in the market within an already given political society, as in the liberalism of Adam Smith and the eighteenth century. The problem of neo-liberalism is rather how the overall exercise of political power can be modeled on the principles of a market economy." His blunder in choosing the label "neoliberal" — which was just then coming into circulation in the United States with a categorically different and indeed nearly opposite meaning — can be understood when we recall that he was resuscitating a forgotten French term and was surely unaware of neoliberalism's contemporary American meaning.

Foucault's application of this appellation to twentieth-century free-market economists such as Hayek, Ludwig von Mises, and (later) Milton Friedman was historically ignorant — and triply so. First, Foucault seemed not to have known that, as Burgin tells us, neoliberalism as "a formal designation" for the ideas at the Lippman Colloquium was "raised and rejected" at the time. Second, the Hayekians in fact did not call themselves neoliberals; those who had briefly flirted with that name were those on the center-left, like Lippmann and Rougier, not those on the right. Finally, for most of the century nobody else called these conservatives neoliberal either. Foucault's was thus a highly peculiar and misleading usage. Yet just as with some of his other dubious theories, he got away with it.

It took time for this weird use of "neoliberalism" to catch on and still longer for it to reach American shores. By the 2000s, books by the eccentric British Marxist geographer David Harvey, the barrister Daniel Steadman Jones, and then Angus Burgin, along with a zillion academic articles and conference papers, had fused the idea of "neoliberalism" to market-based economics — and specifically with a genealogical narrative centered on Hayek, von Mises, Friedman, and their kind that ran from the Lippmann colloquium to the Mont Pelerin Society of the 1940s (a Switzerland-based hub of conservative thought) to the University of Chicago in the 1960s and 1970s. Interestingly, there were a few superficial points of overlap between *Washington Monthly* neoliberalism and Mount Pelerin pseudo-neoliberalism. As the historian Kevin Schultz remarks in his new book, *Why Everyone Hates White Liberals (Including White Liberals)*: "Both prioritized economic growth. Both hated excessive government intrusion. Both were attempts, in rhetoric at least, to expand individual freedoms. But the Democratic 'neo-liberals' were more welcoming to social welfare programs, national allegiance, and government intervention to assist people." More importantly, the Foucault/Harvey/Steadman-Jones/Burgin conception of neoliberalism had no actual historical or intellectual connection to the standard meaning of neoliberalism in American political analysis. That the same word was used for both was a deeply confusing coincidence.

Yet perhaps unavoidably, the two *were* confused, and conflated and commingled. That commingling created a conceptual error that has since warped our discourse. Imagine dusting off the old meaning of "filibuster" — originally from the Dutch word for "freebooter," used to refer to eighteenth-century pirates in the Caribbean — and concluding that today's speechifying U.S. senators are all sword-swinging buccaneers. Or merging two meanings of "gay," so that all happy people are deemed homosexual or all homosexual people are deemed happy. A half-knowledgeable Washington observer could see the absurdity of saddling a genuine neoliberal such as Gary Hart with the views of Milton Friedman. But the Europeans and academics bruiting about the label were not knowledgeable, or even half-knowledgeable, about these matters. And after 2000, the political climate made the merging of the two meanings of "neoliberalism" irresistible to some. Cursory understandings of the concept allowed left-wing critics to brand Obama as a neoliberal because he had bailed out the banks. Clinton's support for the North American Free Trade Agreement (even though it was negotiated by his predecessors) and his repeal of the Glass-Steagall Act (enacted in 1933 to separate commercial banking from investment banking) were cast as pivotal moments when Democrats surrendered to market forces and set us on a path to where we are now. The misnomer stuck.

The leftist academics who tossed about "neoliberalism" almost always used it as a pejorative. As it bled into popular usage and the commingling continued, it became a malaprop cocktail to lob at anyone associated with the post-1980s intellectual ferment among Democrats. This meant that Bill Clinton, Al Gore, Robert

Rubin, Larry Summers, Gene Sperling, and the rest of the Clinton economic team were not only branded "neoliberals" but cast as the ideological progeny of Hayek, von Mises, and Friedman. Multisyllabic and Latinate, "neoliberalism" posed as a sophisticated idea harboring profound and subtle analyses, but by the 2010s it had hardened into a blunt rhetorical tool, a form of invective, with which anti-capitalist writers could bash anyone they deemed to have betrayed the cause. This tendency reached its delicious *reductio ad absurdum* in 2017 in an online contretemps between Cornel West and Ta-Nehisi Coates, with the former charging the latter with possessing a "myopic political neoliberalism" and the latter responding by quitting Twitter.

Witting or unwitting, the wrongheaded conflation of neoliberalism with free-market conservatism has continued to flourish. The practice yokes together two groups who are clear ideological enemies. A category that embraces such stark opposites as Ronald Reagan and Bill Clinton, or Hillary Clinton and Donald Trump, can only obfuscate. And, besides, good names already exist for market-friendly economics: free-market conservatism, economic libertarianism, classical liberalism, *laissez-faire*. But leftists prefer "neoliberal" because it enfolds liberal Democrats in their blunderbuss critique. If to a hammer everything looks like a nail, then to a Marxist every non-Marxist looks like a neoliberal. One suspects, as Jonathan Chait has written, that "the whole trick is to bracket the center-left together with the right as 'neoliberal,' and then force progressives to choose between that and socialism."

The Periodization Problem

If neoliberalism is a hot mess as a category of economic thought and political classification, it also flops as a tool of historical analysis. Here we come to the question of periodization, the way in which historians segment the past into units. Those who hold up neoliberalism as a tool for organizing recent events insist that it has hegemonically governed our era. But, as we can see from Chris

Murphy's and Ro Khanna's failure to get their stories straight, there's no consensus on when this supposed hegemony began or ended, or indeed if it has ended at all. Some place the beginning in the Clinton '90s. Others point to the late 1970s. Most will say Reagan's election in 1980 was the turning point, since he came into office preaching lower taxes and smaller government (even though he followed through much less than is supposed), and people talked about a Reagan Revolution as if seismic changes were underway.

But was Reagan's ascendancy really the major break point of the recent past? To organize our recent history around Reagan's rise — that is, around Reaganomics — enshrines a crude economicist mentality. It subordinates historical events of manifestly greater historical magnitude to trends in economic thought and policymaking. (There are people who believe that Watergate was a less significant episode in Nixon's presidency than the end of the gold standard.) Specifically, the 1980s-centric periodization ignores the most transformational decade of the post-World War II era — the 1960s, when dramatic changes occurred in culture, foreign policy, law, and society, though somewhat less so in economics. Before the vogue for the neoliberal periodization came along, historians agreed that the span of the late 1960s and early 1970s was a hinge in American history. That was when the Cold War began to thaw, when Vietnam shattered belief in American virtue, when old manners and morals were overturned, when cultural backlash politics scuttled dreams of expanding the Great Society, when so-called hard hats beat up antiwar protesters, when lifelong Democrats gave Nixon his landslide, when the liberal vision fell on hard times. Debates today about the Democrats' electoral struggles to recapture the working class should recall that those struggles, too, date to the early 1970s and not to the later "neoliberal" period.

Even by strictly economicist measures, the historical focus on Reagan instead of Nixon fails key explanatory tests. Today's critics blame neoliberal policies for "hollowing out" manufacturing communities, sending onetime Democrats into the Republican column. But manufacturing began collapsing long before Reagan.

The steel and auto industries faced competition from Japan and West Germany in the 1960s. By the 1970s, magazine stories, think-tank studies, and congressional hearings proliferated about plant closures and job losses in Rust Belt cities. When neoliberals came along in the 1980s, they were reacting to manufacturing losses, not driving them. Neoliberalism's detractors have their chronology backwards.

The Reagan–Bush years were not the start of an historical era but the end of one. Beginning in 1992, with Bill Clinton's election, a long stretch of Republican dominance ended. Presidential politics became competitive again. Since 1992, Democrats have lost the popular vote just twice. Divided government has reigned, with control of the White House and Congress seesawing between the parties. Our talk of red states and blue states and polarization dates to the year 2000 and the knife's-edge contest between Al Gore and George W. Bush.

The 1990s amounted to a break, too, in America's economic fortunes. The wage stagnation now blamed on neoliberalism actually occurred in the 1970s and 1980s, not in the 1990s. The Clinton years sparked a run of higher productivity and wage growth, along with stiffer taxes on the rich, reductions in poverty, and growth that has outpaced Europe's. Whatever was happening in the 1990s, it marked a sharp reversal from the doldrums of the 1970s and the uneven recovery of the 1980s — historical shifts that the neoliberal periodization does not take the trouble to accommodate.

The Myth of the Washington Consensus

Once we recognize that the 1990s constituted a departure from — much more than a continuation of — the 1980s, more problems with neoliberalism as an operating concept emerge. Related to the claim that no real economic policy differences have separated the two parties is the corollary that Democrats guzzled the Reagan Kool-Aid, joining in a "Washington consensus" by ditching liberalism's commitments to the welfare state, progressive taxation, regulation, and helping blue-collar workers.

This is more nonsense. The last quarter of a century has been defined not by consensus but, famously, by polarization. Americans sorted into red and blue camps, telling one another that each election was the most important of our lives, with each contest fought as if the entirety of the republic's fate hung in the balance. In part, these stark and inflamed partisan divisions have been about sociocultural issues such as abortion, gay rights, racial progress, and immigration, as well as about political-legal questions such as civil liberties, civil rights, and the scope of presidential power. But they have also been about economics. Since Clinton's presidency, knock-down, drag-out fights have occurred over core differences in fiscal and regulatory policy. The Democrats press for progressive taxation, increased social provision, and restraints on business; the Republicans seek to cut taxes, domestic spending, and restrictive rules. Clinton's first major action as president was to raise taxes on the rich. Bush's was to cut them. Obama then ended Bush's tax cuts. Trump passed new ones, and then passed them again. Equally bright lines have separated the parties over health care, Social Security, and the whole litany of kitchen-table issues. Only on one major issue — trade — have the parties' leaders been relatively united. (More on that below.) Yet the enveloping partisan rancor of our times is seldom noted by tellers of the neoliberalism tale, since they have no way to account for it in their fantasy of a seamless elite bipartisan comity.

To see how badly some people misremember even recent history, consider Clinton's campaign in 1992. Jennifer Harris, who served in the Biden White House and now works for the Hewlett Foundation, recently wrote in *Foreign Affairs* that Clinton "won election in 1992 in part by stressing his adherence to Reagan's free-market dictums." Come again? The opposite is the case. Here is Clinton debating George Bush before seventy million viewers in 1992: "We've had twelve years of trickle-down economics. We've gone from first to twelfth in the world in wages. We've had four years where we've produced no private-sector jobs. Most people are working harder for less money than they were making ten years ago. It is because we are in the grip of a failed economic theory." Clinton's economic plan, published as *Putting People First*, excoriated Reaganism, promising instead a bottom-up path to growth including higher taxes on the rich, universal health care, and investment in transportation and communication infrastructure — which became key pieces of his blueprint for governing.

Neoliberalism is said nowadays to denote the rejection of New Deal economics, but neither under Clinton nor in the years after did the Democratic Party allow the dismantling of the postwar liberal tentpoles of a mixed economy, progressive taxation, robust regulation, and a welfare state. Consider the case of regulation. Contrary to the neoliberal mythology, Democrats since Clinton have reliably lined up against the Republicans' anti-government agenda. To be sure, Clinton did loosen some constraints on business, as in repealing Glass-Steagall. His "Reinventing Government" initiative trimmed other requirements, too — not to allow business a free hand but to prune bureaucracy so that the public would again trust the government to be efficient and responsive. (It is hard to come up with any regulations phased out by the Reinventing Government project that anyone misses today.) Overall, however, the pattern of the past three decades shows Democrats fairly consistently promoting environmental protection, workplace safety, civil rights safeguards, public health, and financial oversight. In 2010 Obama gave us the Dodd-Frank legislation, which imposed tougher capital and oversight requirements on big banks and created the Consumer Financial Protection Bureau.

Count the pages in the Federal Register, which lists new governmental rules. Under Ronald Reagan, the count fell from 87,000 to 53,000. Under Clinton it climbed from 63,000 to 77,000, and under Obama from 80,000 to 98,000. "It's pretty clearly true," Matthew Yglesias observes, "that the overall scope of regulation is larger in 2024 than it was in 1974." Think about it: if the 1990s and 2000s had been such an orgy of slash-and-burn, how could Trump's first term have witnessed such a barrage of headlines about the trashing of vital protections? "E.P.A. to Lift Obama-Era Controls on Methane, a Potent Greenhouse Gas." "Consumer Bureau Scraps Restrictions on Payday Loans." "How the White House Rolled Back Financial Regulations." "Trump Says His Regulatory Rollback Already Is the 'Most Far-Reaching.'" Whose rules do they think Trump was undoing?

One can tick off the different policy areas. Fiscal policy? Democrats in the 1990s raised the minimum wage, boosted taxes on the rich, and expanded the Earned Income Tax Credit — all over Republican objections. Social provision? As he had in his primary race against Tsongas, Clinton continually prioritized the protection of Social Security: "Save Social Security first," he vowed in his State of the Union address in 1998, revealing his intention for his newfound budget surpluses. He bested Newt Gingrich and Robert Dole in budget battles mainly by defending Medicare and Medicaid. Clinton and Obama both made universal health care a top priority — Clinton unsuccessfully, Obama triumphantly. Investment in infrastructure, science, and technology? Clinton poured money into building the internet and mapping the human genome; Obama's stimulus package in 2009 was so sweeping that the journalist Michael Grunwald wrote a book about it called *The New New Deal*. Labor? The Clinton administration enacted the Family and Medical Leave Act, fought right-to-work laws, appointed union allies to the National Labor Relations Board, and curtailed sweatshop labor. Obama backed a controversial law to let workers unionize without a secret ballot. In none of these cases did Democrats receive much Republican help. Partisan division — not consensus — was the Washington norm.

Believers in the fiction of neoliberalism-as-Reaganism sometimes believe they have a smoking gun in Clinton's statement in 1996 that "the era of big government is over." But never has a sentence been more grossly distorted. Rarely quoted is the next line, a rebuke to the *laissez-faire* ideologues: "But we cannot go back to the time when our citizens were left to fend for themselves." Clinton's original draft had contained the punchier "But we can't go back to 'every man for himself.'" That formulation, however, was deemed sexist and rewritten, and the graceless new iteration got dropped from headlines and soundbites. In any case, the snippet was never meant as a death knell for government's role in helping citizens; it was an acknowledgment that ambitious Great Society–style projects such as Clinton's failed health-care initiative were, given the congressional log-jams and insuperable deficits, unlikely to be forthcoming. As John Lewis said at the time, the "era" of big government might be over — the climate of opinion that had birthed programs like Medicare in the 1960s was now in the past — but the "role" of big government was not going to change.

In each of the policy realms noted above, Republicans firmly opposed the Democrats' agenda and vice versa: it was a Washington dissensus. In one realm, though, bipartisan majorities did exist: trade. And when you peer closely at the charges of Democratic perfidy, they usually boil down to the fact that Clinton, Obama, and other party leaders backed NAFTA in 1993, and permanent most-favored-nation status for China in 2000, and the Trans-Pacific Partnership in 2016. In these cases, a hefty majority of Republicans and a sizable minority of Democrats came together in favor of a freer trade regime.

A few complicating points bear mention. First, there is near-unanimity among economists about the benefits of free trade, just as there is among public health officials on the danger of lead exposure and among education researchers on the worth of early-childhood schooling. Although certain constituencies have over the decades called for tariffs, leading to pitched political fights, the recent trade deals all had strong expert justification and scholarly support. This reality vitiates the charge that Democrats were cravenly acquiescing in Republican dogma. If conservatives today were to stop questioning the danger of a warming planet, would they be capitulating to a Democratic ideology? Or would they simply be grounding their policymaking in an accurate, objectively established set of facts? We should at least entertain the idea the Democrats backed free trade because it was good policy. The alternative is to understand policy and politics only cynically.

Relatedly — and here the periodization problem again rears its head — the neoliberal era is alleged to have begun in the 1980s or 1990s. But support for free trade was the standard liberal position since the nineteenth century. One of Woodrow Wilson's first steps as president in 1913 was to sign the Underwood Act reducing tariffs. Franklin Delano Roosevelt produced the Reciprocal Trade Act in 1934 and the Bretton Woods Agreement in 1944. Harry Truman signed the General Agreement on Tariffs and Trade in 1947. John F. Kennedy enacted the Trade Expansion Act of 1962. If any position represents an abandonment of liberal principles, it is the protectionism that some Democrats began adopting under pressure from organized labor in the 1970s. Thus, the Democrats' support for trade, too, turns out to be a flimsy peg on which to hang the weighty conceptual behemoth of "neoliberalism."

The Fiction of Liberal Failure

Neoliberalism, as we have seen, can no longer be said to accurately describe a coherent body of economic thought. Nor does it designate a clear-cut political affiliation. Nor does the notion of an "age of neoliberalism" linked to Reagan's rise survive scrutiny. And the critique implicit in today's pejorative use of "neoliberalism" — that contemporary Democrats junked their values for pro-market cheerleading — also unravels once we review the countless policy conflicts that have riven the two parties in our fevered times.

But let us allow that, even if it has been grossly overstated, the Democrats of the 1990s and 2000s did tilt their party in a somewhat more pro-market direction. That's true enough. What of the criticism that their modifications to their party's governing philosophy wrought horrendous economic damage, especially to society's lower strata? Even if the Clinton–Obama agenda wasn't the brainchild of Milton Friedman, even if it does not deserve the opprobrious epithet "neoliberalism," didn't it nonetheless buoy the rich and oppress the poor?

Here, too, history undermines the anti-neoliberal arguments.

The Clinton and Obama presidencies boasted some of the strongest economic records of recent times. The Clinton numbers are so phenomenal, so jaw-droppingly enviable, that they beggar belief. Clinton presided over the longest continuous peacetime economic expansion in history, with growth averaging 4 percent annually. Unemployment fell from 7.3 to 4 percent and inflation stayed low. The stock market boomed, but prosperity also extended to the lowest rungs of the ladder: poverty fell by nearly one quarter, from 15.1 to 11.3 percent, and the two lowest-income quintiles saw their earnings increase nearly 17 percent. Real median household income grew by 13.9 percent. Blacks and Hispanics made especially strong gains. All of this was achieved as once-crippling budget deficits turned into record surpluses and Americans' trust in government spiked for the first time since the 1960s. As Hillary Clinton later said when her husband's record came under fire, "I always wonder what part of the 1990s they didn't like: the peace or the prosperity?"

These policies succeeded politically, too. Clinton wooed many Reagan Democrats back into the fold. In both of his races, he drew more than 40 percent of the working-class white vote — a quantum leap over Carter, Mondale, and Dukakis, and a high-water mark that no subsequent Democratic presidential nominee would match. These voters had been drifting from the Democratic column before Clinton and would drift away again afterward, but Clintonomics was not the reason for their defection.

Obama's economic legacy, though not as strong, also holds up well. His presidency kicked off an expansion that, while less robust than Clinton's, lasted longer, extending into Trump's first presidency until the pandemic hit in 2020. Taking office just after the 2008 recession, Obama, in Rooseveltian fashion, followed through on the bank rescue and the auto industry rescue. Those efforts, including Obama's huge stimulus bill, constitute, along with the Affordable Care Act, his most important achievements. Whatever name we affix to his economic policy, it, too, worked. Unemployment fell; inflation remained modest; median household income rose by 5.3 percent. Politically, Obama's performance was also a bit weaker than Clinton's; his reluctance in the early days to rhetorically balance the bailouts with a dose of Clinton-style left-populism gave an emergent right-wing proto-Trump movement, the Tea Party, room to grow. But Obama's economy still performed well enough to win him reelection in 2012, thanks to a decent showing among the white working class, especially in states like Michigan and Ohio where the auto bailout saved jobs. To be sure, the slow growth of Obama's second term hurt Hillary Clinton in 2016, a year when the economy merely inched along. But his was hardly an economic program geared toward the superrich.

Given this mostly admirable economic record, can it really be said that the last thirty-five years have amounted to failure — especially on the Democrats' part? It is worth addressing two economic failures of the recent era that have been especially salient. In both cases we can fairly criticize Democratic governance, although in neither case more so than Republican governance. First is the fallout from the trade regime of the twenty-first century. While globalization benefited Americans overall, fueling growth and lowering consumer costs, the downsides hit hardest in the de-industrializing regions. The stories of constricted job opportunities, impoverished civic life, family dysfunction, and drug and alcohol abuse in these communities are legion and heartbreaking. In post-industrial cities and towns, rural areas, low-income suburbs, and other lagging regions from Appalachia to swaths of the South, the toll has been severe.

The second problem is also one of inequality, but on a broader societal level. We have all seen the statistics that portray the yawning gaps between the top 1 percent and everyone else, the growing chasms between CEO pay and the going hourly wage. Inequality has also deepened a sense of deprivation among the working and middle classes. As important, it has meant that a large segment of Americans has been prosperous enough to shoulder the high costs of child-care, health care, housing, college, and retirement, but that a much bigger group has watched those elements of the American Dream recede from their grasp.

These hardships must not be minimized. They pose urgent challenges — of politics and policy, of solidarity and sympathy — for both parties. The Democrats as well as the Republicans failed to do enough to address the privations and the struggles that, while not new to our times, continued to afflict the de-industrializing regions into the 2000s. Both parties also failed to deliver effective solutions to the skyrocketing costs of big-ticket life-event costs such as health care and housing. But the critics of "neoliberalism" imply that remedies were readily at hand for Clinton and Obama and other Democratic leaders, who turned away from them. Yet no such obvious remedies existed (or exist today). For one thing, these inequality trends stem mainly from factors other than public policy. The manufacturing decline long preceded the controversial trade deals, and its recent acceleration derives more from automation, technological advances, and turbocharged worker productivity than from Chinese imports. Drawing an analogy, the Harvard economist Robert Lawrence notes that the number of agricultural jobs in the United States has plummeted not because of trade but because of a transformation in farming technology.

Wealth inequality, similarly, has widened not primarily owing to any public policy decisions but owing to the huge spikes in stock market and real estate valuations. Democrats, left, liberal, or centrist, have generally wanted to do more to address these serious inequities, but since the Reagan years we have been hobbled by divided government. We have had no period like the 1930s or the 1960s when one party could work its will; the congressional majorities that Clinton, Obama, and Biden all briefly enjoyed were never large enough to overcome the threats of the filibuster. (Alas, we may now be embarking on such a period, led by the other side.) Democrats may pass redistributionist taxes or expand spending programs, but when the Republicans return they get blunted or reversed. Most of the time, it is simply impossible to pass a large-scale social program in the first place. *That* is why we say that the era of big government is over. It is a description of reality, not a wish.

Of the two parties, the Democrats are the ones who have consistently favored measures to mitigate the burgeoning inequality. Their efforts, unfortunately, have not helped them much politically; ironically, the hard-hit communities in places such as Arkansas, West Virginia, and rural Wisconsin have gravitated toward the GOP — worse, toward the MAGA GOP. But these voters are not moving rightward because the Republicans are delivering higher wages or more bountiful health insurance. There are many other reasons for this realignment, rooted in values, culture, identity, and style. Politics never consists entirely in economics. The Democrats' noble words about economic fairness will not win them elections in the absence of creative and effective new ideas. (Kamala Harris' campaign proposal of $25,000 handouts for down payments isn't going to cut it.) But if working-class and non-college-educated voters have been abandoning the Democrats because of their economic record, they are not going to find the Republicans' solutions any more congenial.

The acute suffering in these afflicted communities demands our attention. It also creates rhetorical space for the continued bashing of Democratic policies. It has provided justification, for example, for the Hewlett Foundation to pour millions into a project groping for a "post-neoliberal" vision that it hopes will amount to a reverse DLC for the 2020s. The Hewlett project — regrettably based on the sort of murky understanding of "neoliberalism" that pervades our discourse — was expected to bear fruit under Biden. Yet despite a lot of hyperventilating in early 2021 about a "transformational" Biden presidency and absurd comparisons of his decidedly non-radical program to the New Deal, Biden governed mostly in the same center-left mode as Clinton and Obama, albeit less effectively.

Biden touted a purportedly new economic vision, saying he would build the economy "from the middle out." He failed to acknowledge that Obama had used and popularized the exact same phrase, and Clinton had propounded the same basic idea. Biden also hyped the value of his child tax credit, which was more generous than past iterations, but which also had first been implemented by Clinton and then expanded by succeeding presidents. Biden talked up anti-trust actions against the tech giants, but this, too, was something Clinton had pioneered with a lawsuit against Microsoft, the Goliath of its day. Apart from keeping some of Trump's tariffs, Biden's main claim to policy innovation was to jack up the domestic outlays in his spending bills to dwarf even Obama's $800 billion Recovery Act of 2009 — something that he could do because we were stumbling forth out of the pandemic. Unfortunately, just the year before Trump had signed the gargantuan CARES Act, and, on top of that, Biden's two huge spending bills combined with pandemic-related shortages to produce inflation rates higher than they had been since 1981 — one of the main reasons that Harris lost the election in 2024. If his approach was designed to improve on the "neoliberalism" of his Democratic predecessors, it failed.

The historian Tara Zahra has written about the backlash against progressivism and globalization in the aftermath of World War I. Where goods and people had moved freely across borders, restrictions now limited exchange. Governments framed migration not as an opportunity but as a threat to national strength and social cohesion. Nations pulled back from international bodies and treaties. Democracies and dictatorships alike preached self-reliance. This inward turn promised order amid chaos, rootedness in place and tradition, and protection from the dislocations of global capitalism. Fascism, communism, and anti-semitism flourished. It was not the age of Trump, but it was the age of Ford, Lindbergh, Coughlin, and Mussolini. The worst war in history followed.

Now, too, an anti-globalization backlash is in flower. Liberal democracy is regularly derided. Elites are demonized. Strongmen are admired. Pluralism is regarded as weakness. Trade is blamed for poverty. Borders are walled and fortified. Illegal immigrants are targeted. On the left, voters flock to fantastic promises of free rent, free buses, and free food. Or they hear prophecies of a future liberated from work, so that we can all enjoy a government-provided universal basic income. On the right, Trump recklessly plays around with tariffs, wreaks economic havoc, and impulsively decimates government agencies. These are only a few of the latest proposed replacements for what has come to be disparaged as neoliberalism. If we persist now in trashing the many things that liberals, whatever their failings and flaws, have done rightly and reasonably well, we will breathe life into the poisonous ideologies that liberalism once rose up to defeat.

RYAN RUBY

Other Canons, Other Wars

In the summer of 1981, the novelist Italo Calvino published an article on the great books in the Roman weekly news magazine *L'Espresso*. "Why Read the Classics?" is classic Calvino: playful, charming, erudite, skeptical, humane. It consists of fourteen "suggested definitions" of a classic that deliberately contradict each other. Per definition one, the classics are books you are always rereading, even if you are discovering them for the first time, per definition five; or they are books you have yet to read because you are still waiting for the opportune conditions to enjoy them, per definition two. Classics are pre-selected for us by the group: "they come to us bearing the aura of previous interpretations, and trailing behind them the traces they have left in the culture" (definition seven), they generate "a pulviscular cloud of critical discourse" (definition eight), and are often known through "hearsay" before they are known by experience (definition nine). But they are also chosen by the individual reader for personal reasons: "'your' classic is a book to which you cannot remain indifferent" (definition eleven). Ancient or modern, a classic is a book that "relegates the noise of the present to a background hum," (definition thirteen) and at the same time one that "persists as background noise even when a present that is totally incompatible with it holds sway" (definition fourteen).

The implication being: a classic is impossible to define. Rather, it is a designation relative to an individual reader's position in a particular culture at a particular moment in history. In his scholium to definition fourteen, Calvino gives a reason for this. The proliferation of books in "all modern literatures and cultures" has led to "the dissolution of the library," such as the one inherited by Giacomo Leopardi, the reclusive nineteenth-century poet and philosopher who was one of the last people who could plausibly confuse his thorough education in European literature, philosophy, history, and science with the totality of knowledge. The "eclecticism" characteristic of late twentieth-century culture is the result of its inescapable awareness of the contemporary, on the one hand, and the global, on the other. Just as the books of the past and the present are indispensable to understanding each other, Calvino told the readers of *L'Espresso*, the classics of his language and culture, such as Leopardi's *Canti*, "are indispensable to us Italians in order to compare them with foreign classics, and foreign classics are equally indispensable so that we can measure them against Italian classics." That we will "never be able to draw up a catalogue of classic works to suit our own times" was not a cause for worry, in his view. He proposed that each of us replace the catalogue or list model of the great books with "our own ideal library" consisting of works that have been meaningful to us and those that have been meaningful to others, making sure to leave "a section of empty spaces for surprises and chance discoveries" as we accumulate new experiences over the course of a lifelong relationship with the written word.

The following winter, a rather less cheerful assessment of

this state of affairs appeared in the pages of *National Review*. In "Our Listless Universities," Allan Bloom diagnosed "an easygoing American nihilism" among students at the country's top schools. Already "socialized" as historicists and cultural relativists, incoming freshmen viewed "the comprehensive truth about man" as at best "opinion," at worst "prejudice," and in any case "unavailable" to knowledge — and nothing about their four years at the university was likely to disabuse them of this "dogma." Encouraged by their professors, according to Bloom, students in the humanities were unwilling to acknowledge that "one culture is superior to another," that the "old books" of the Western canon were any "better than any others" being produced in the present, let alone ones that might "contain the truth." As a result, classics such as the Bible and Plutarch — to use his examples — no longer made up the "furniture" of the "souls" who were bypassing the liberal arts altogether for degrees in the hard sciences, where at least the aspiration to truth-finding was integral to the program of study, and the professional schools, where at least there were material rewards to be had upon graduation. In the name of an "equality of values," Bloom concluded, students had lost the ability to discriminate in their moral and aesthetic judgments; in the name of "openness," they had become closed-minded. The only remedy — a sustained encounter with the great books — was the one that was being foreclosed by the usual suspects: structuralists, deconstructionists, Marxist humanists, and those professors who would introduce course requirements in non-Western civilizations and cultures.

Although he shared Matthew Arnold's view that culture is "the best which has been thought and said in the world," Bloom's denunciation of relativism is less Arnoldian in spirit than Calvino's endorsement of it. The apocalyptic tone of Bloom's invective causes him to make absurd claims, some of which, like his animus towards rock music, are comically square, while others, such as his claim that among his students "it is almost respectable to think and even do the deeds of Oedipus," cross the line into hysteria. The special contempt he reserves for feminists — whose demands for equality in the workplace, the domicile, and the culture he holds responsible for the destruction of everything from the family to eroticism to literature — is downright sinister.

On the last point, Bloom has this to say: "In the absence (temporary, of course) of a literature produced by feminism to rival the literature of Sophocles, Shakespeare, Racine, and Stendhal, students are without literary inspiration." It is neither here nor there, but off the top of my head I can think of dozens of female writers who are more deserving of our attention today than Racine, starting with his contemporary Madame de La Fayette. Where the canonical status of Stendhal (and, by extension, the force of that parenthetical) are concerned, I would just like to add that, as Calvino points out, when the author of *Le Rouge et le Noir* was still alive, he was dismissed by none other than Leopardi as the sort of faddish *litterateur*, admired by his sister, whose work would never stand the test of time.

Yet what "Our Listless Universities," lacked in Arnoldian "sweetness and light," it made up for with popular appeal. Encouraged by his friend Saul Bellow, Bloom expanded the essay into *The Closing of the American Mind*, which became a surprise bestseller when it was published in 1987. The ensuing "Canon Wars," which pitted conservative defenders of "dead white men" against "multiculturalists, feminists, and postmodernists" were misnamed: they were more like a theater or a front in a far broader political conflict. They helped to establish a pattern whereby the intellectual habits, political views, and sexual mores of eighteen- to twenty-two-year-olds at a handful of elite universities were opportunistically turned into full-blown moral panics outside them by conservative activists, whose concern about the curricular "corruption of the youth" has proved less sincere than their desire to destroy the institutional independence of the university, a four-decade-long siege that now appears to be in its final stages. *The Closing of the American Mind* was nothing less than "the opening shot of the culture wars" in the words of Camille Paglia, who meant it as a compliment.

For better or worse, the debate about the great books was my introduction to American intellectual life: well-thumbed copies of bestsellers such as Harold Bloom's *The Western Canon*, from 1994, and David Denby's *Great Books*, from 1996, could be found among the precocious-naïve collection on my high-school self's book shelves. (*The Closing of the American Mind* and Paglia's *Sexual Personae* I read only later — at the insistence of my father and an ex-girlfriend, respectively.) It was still raging when I enrolled at Columbia in the fall of 2001 to take Literature Humanities and Contemporary Civilization, the mandatory survey courses in Western literature and philosophy that formed the core of what the university calls its Core Curriculum. During my senior year, I was one of the student representatives to the Committee on the Core Curriculum, a position that had been created in the aftermath of the campus occupations of 1968, to give students a seat at the table of university governance, along with faculty and administrators. I soon came to understand that the representation was merely symbolic and the governance was entirely nominal. The few meetings of the committee that I attended took place in one of the administrative offices in Low Library, the stately dome that is the architectural centerpiece of the upper Manhattan campus. They were largely taken up, I recall, by the same activity that was always taking place among undergraduates there: arguing about which books did or did not belong on the curriculum.

This is a cultural habit that is neither original nor exclusive to the West; it is simply the byproduct of any educational system that is based on a finite set of books. Such an education will be one that necessarily includes disagreement about which ones are selected, why they were selected, and what the value of reading them are to individuals as they are, to society as it is, and to both as we might prefer them to be. Definitively resolving these disagreements cannot be the aim of education, since to do so would end the debate and thus the education itself — in other words, the disagreeing is in no small part where the educating happens. Not long ago, in his review of *Rescuing Socrates*, Roosevelt Montás' memoir of his time as the director of the Core Curriculum, the poet John Michael Colón concluded that the Canon Wars were a missed opportunity. For Colón, the way the debate about the great books was framed by its defenders and its critics alike presented a "false choice between two impossible options": to treat "as the world's sole inheritance traditions whose claim to universalism we know is false, or to live . . . without any deep connection to the past that created us." The way out of this impasse, he wrote, was not to throw out the baby of canonicity with the bathwater of Western chauvinism, but to create a canon that was genuinely global. To the claim that a particular set of books ought to be considered canonical because it, rather than some other set, is the best which has been thought or said in the world, the first question a well-educated person ought to ask is: how do you know?

In 1754, when Columbia University was in its first year of existence as King's College in the Province of New York, a man named Wu Jingzi died in Yangzhou. Born to a prosperous family of late Ming and early Qing officials from Anhui province, about three hundred miles inland from Shanghai, Wu seemed to have a promising future ahead of him when he passed the preliminary civil service exam at the age of twenty-two. But money burned a hole in Wu's pocket: he gave it away to anyone who asked. He was also a bit of a *bon vivant*, spending his time in tea houses, taverns, and brothels. Subsequent examination attempts ended in failure. In his early thirties, he moved his small family to Nanjing, where he eked out what would later become known as a bohemian existence, surrounding himself with a circle of writers, philosophers, and actors.

In the culturally vibrant "southern capital" of the Empire, Wu wrote poetry and published a now-lost commentary on the *Book of Songs*, one of the Five Classics, which, along with the Four Books, comprises the core of the Confucian canon. He built enough of a reputation as an independent scholar to be personally invited to Beijing to sit for a special round of exams, but for reasons that are unclear he did not attend. Romantically inclined historians interpret this as a principled rejection of corrupt officialdom;

others say he was sick on the day of the exam. In 1739, he spent what remained of his funds helping to dedicate a temple to an ancient sage in Nanjing, which he considered the pinnacle achievement of his life. The following year he started work on a long piece of prose fiction — a satire of life under the Qing dynasty centered on the literati, the class of scholar-bureaucrats who managed the Empire and the examination system through which they were selected — for the amusement of his friends, who all belonged, however peripherally, to this class. Written over the course of the next ten years, the completed book, consisting of fifty-five chapters, circulated in manuscript for decades after Wu's death, until a Yangzhou firm published it as *Rulin Waishi*, or *The Unofficial History of the Scholars*, in 1803.

Along with four novels from the Ming dynasty — *Romance of the Three Kingdoms*, *Water Margin*, *Journey to the West*, and *The Plum in the Golden Vase* — and *Dream of the Red Chamber* by Wu's younger contemporary Cao Xueqin, *The Scholars* is sometimes considered one of the six "classic Chinese novels." The designation — having gained currency following the publication in 1968 of a book of that title by C. T. Hsia, the Shanghai-born scholar of Chinese literature who spent three decades on the faculty at Columbia — represents a moment of cultural syncretism, adding long vernacular prose fiction to the extant canons of Confucian and neo-Confucian philosophy, imperial historiography, Taoist and Buddhist scripture, and anthologies of poetry and short stories.

If you had to pick only one of the six classic novels to read, you would probably choose *Dream of the Red Chamber*, which is "one of the great novels of world literature" — what "Proust is to the French, or *Karamazov* is to the Russians," in the words of the critic Anthony West. But what interests me about *The Scholars* is that its central subject is a society whose cultural, legal, and administrative institutions are grounded in the humanistic study of a canonical body of texts.

Hsia praises *The Scholars* for its "shrewd realism" and "intelligent satire" whose "stylistic and technical innovations" were of "revolutionary importance" for "the development of the Chinese novel." In "pure and functional" narrative prose, Wu manages to paint a panorama of the entirety of Chinese society from the Emperor, his generals, and high-ranking officials to provincial judges, merchants, booksellers, and farmers to mendicant monks, swordsmen, actors, and prostitutes. With one exception — the painter-sage Wang Mien, whose tale opens the book — these characters are drawn not from history or legend, as is the case with the Ming dynasty classics, but from the imagination or experiences of their author. Some are based on Wu's friends and acquaintances; some are based on his rivals and nemeses; the account of the prodigal poet Tu Shao-ching is undoubtedly a self-portrait. Wu puts the tenets of Confucianism and the folk beliefs of Buddhist and Taoist popular religion into the mouths of his characters, but these are treated with an irony not present in earlier Chinese fiction. The tragicomic sensibility expressed in *The Scholars* is his own.

But any resemblance between *The Scholars* and the novel as it was then being developed in England by Samuel Richardson and Henry Fielding — to say nothing of its evolution during the century of Jane Austen and Henry James — ends there. To readers whose expectations of the form were set by *Pride and Prejudice* and *Portrait of a Lady*, the most distinctive and puzzling feature of *The Scholars* is, first of all, its structure. The critic Steven Moore compares it to a long-distance relay race. The narrative follows one minor character for a few chapters until it is handed off to another, and so on, creating a cast of more than sixty principals, none of whom, not even Tu Shao-ching, function as its protagonist. Nor are any of them truly "round," in E. M. Forster's sense, since Wu is less interested in the psychological interiority of individuals than in the networks of social relations that connect them. The unified chronotope that organizes Western realist fiction is also absent from *The Scholars*. The book ranges great lengths in both space — from the Lower Yangtze region where most of the book is set, up to the imperial capital in Beijing, and down to Guizhou where the military brutally pacifies Hmong rebels — and time

— after the prologue, set in 1368, the book spans the years 1487 to 1595, without organizing the narrative around the familiar allegorical unit of the single, multigenerational family. (It is thus set entirely in the Ming dynasty, no doubt because Wu wished to avoid any trouble for his satirical barbs against the current rulers: as Manchus, the Qing emperors suspected, not without reason, that they were regarded, like the Mongol Khans before them, as ethnic usurpers by the Han literati who staffed their civil service. They were known for conducting so-called "literary inquisitions," which involved burning seditious books, and imprisoning or executing their authors.) Because of its sheer mass, the book has been described as plotless, though, as we will see, its apparently episodic structure is subtended by a deeper thematic logic.

Perhaps it would be better to think of *The Scholars* as the culturally specific "unofficial history" its title says it is, rather than as a novel, whose use as a catch-all term for "long fictional prose narrative" tends to obscure more than it illuminates. As the name suggests, an unofficial history is a parody of official or orthodox history — a genre that extends from the *Records of the Grand Historian*, written in the first century B.C., to *The History of the Ming*, completed in 1739 — in which a chronicle of the noble lineages and heroic deeds of emperors is replaced with a chronicle of mostly petty, pompous, and vicious scholar-bureaucrats; classical Chinese is replaced with the vernacular; and ostensibly factual persons and events are replaced with those that are ostensibly fictional. To this burlesque of high literary tradition, Wu grafts one from the other end of the class spectrum. For centuries, professional storytellers had entertained popular audiences at tea houses with tales of lovers, ghosts, warriors, and criminals. By turns didactic and bawdy, and often interlaced with topical observations and social commentary, these tales, whose episodes a skilled performer could parcel out over the course of months, began to be collected and published toward the end of the Ming dynasty for the consumption of literate audiences.

The imprint of the storytelling tradition on *The Scholars* can be seen in the short synopsis that opens each chapter and the formulaic sentence that concludes all but the last ("if you would like to know what happened next, you must read on"), devices that live on today in the recap sequences and cliffhangers of soap operas and other serial narratives. It can also be seen in the proem, which states the "moral of the book":

Dynasties rise and fall,
Morning changes to evening . . .
And fame, riches, and rank
May vanish without a trace.
Then aspire not to these,
Wasting your days

"The idea expressed in this poem," the narrator acknowledges, "is a commonplace one." Indeed it is: the same idea can be found in Ecclesiastes and the *Meditations* of Marcus Aurelius, to cite just two examples. Wu illustrates the point with the story of Wang Mien. A good son from a humble background and an autodidact of genius and genuine curiosity, Wang chooses not to apply for an official career. Instead, he uses his talents to become a painter, which only serves to bolster his reputation among powerful officials. To keep his integrity intact, Wang is forced to come up with a series of increasingly elaborate and comical ruses to avoid meeting with them, ultimately becoming a hermit who lives in voluntary poverty. Near the end of his life Wang receives a visitor he can neither escape nor refuse: Chu Yuan-Ching, the founding Emperor of the Ming dynasty, who seeks his advice on the management of his kingdom. That the powerful are irresistibly drawn to those who shun power and contemptuous of those who seek it is another commonplace, as Diogenes and Plato, in their respective interactions with Alexander and Dionysius II, could both attest.

In his famous essay on the figure of the storyteller, Walter Benjamin remarks that "the nature of every real story" is that "it contains, openly or covertly, something useful." "This usefulness," he continues, "may consist in a moral; in another, some practical advice; in a third, a proverb or maxim. In every case, a storyteller is a man who has counsel for his readers." For Benjamin, having counsel is what distinguishes a storyteller from a novelist, who, being "himself uncounseled . . . cannot counsel others." Fortunately for readers whose tastes have been formed by the novel, for whom being spoon-fed moral counsel and practical advice adulterates aesthetic pleasure, the commonplace about the vanity of external things that opens Wu's unofficial history turns out to be a red herring.

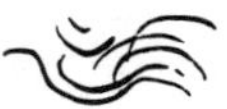

If *The Scholars* can be said to have a protagonist, it is not a person but an institution: the imperial examination system, which is the only thing that directly or indirectly touches the lives of most of the characters in the book. First instituted in the seventh century, the idea behind the exams was to select officials based on merit rather than birth, and to promote moral rectitude and ideological coherence among the group that would be in charge of administering an increasingly large and populous territory by grounding their education in a common set of culturally venerated texts, namely, the Confucian classics, and a common skill, namely, the ability to read and write hundreds of thousands of characters of non-vernacular Chinese.

By the time of Wu's birth a little over a millennium later, the exam system had become a bureaucracy within the state bureaucracy. No fewer than three departments — the Imperial Secretariat, the Ministry of Rites, and the Han Lin Academy — were responsible for overseeing a bewildering array of exams. There were district exams, prefectural exams, qualifying exams, special preliminary exams, special exams, provincial exams, metropolitan exams, palace exams, and exams for the military, conducted every other year for two to three million candidates at between thirteen hundred and fourteen hundred sites around the country. Each dynasty put its distinctive stamp on the testing regime, according to the needs and the fashions of the times. One character, the publisher and bookseller Ma Chun-Shang, (somewhat inaccurately) summarizes the history thus: during the Spring and Autumn period civil servants were selected for their skills in the art of the aphorism; during the Warring States period, for their skill in rhetoric; during the Han, for their exemplary deeds and character; during the Tang, for their ability to write poetry; and during the Song, for their knowledge of neo-Confucian philosophy. In one of his first official decrees, the Ming emperor scrapped the poetry requirement in favor of examinations based on the "eight-legged essay," so-called because of the eight elements of its structure, which candidates had to follow step-by-step to answer a question on a topic selected from one of the Four Books. (The Qing civil service retained the eight-legged essay and Song neo-Confucian orthodoxy; shortly after Wu's death, it also reinstated the poetry requirement in order to make the exams more competitive.)

Although the exams afforded, on principle, a degree of social mobility, there were no public schools, so candidates from the landed gentry and the merchant class, who could pay for private tutors and study materials, were at a distinct advantage; besides, it is much easier to hold your brush steady if you have had something to eat that day. (From the numerous dining scenes, whose menus are described in greater detail than the appearances of some of the characters, one gets the impression that *The Scholars* was written on an empty stomach.) Wu delights in slipping errors of fact into the mouths of pompous examiners and graduates of the prestigious Han Lin Academy, who were tasked with determining what constituted the proper and orthodox interpretation of the classics. In any event, any claim the system might have had on being genuinely meritocratic was undercut by the simple fact that women were barred from sitting for exams, a point underscored in *The Scholars* by the story of Lu's daughter, whose intelligence, learning, and abilities as an essayist put to shame those of the successful literatus she has been married off to.

Since a position in the civil service conferred a degree of financial stability and social status on the successful candidate and his extended family, making sons more marriageable, the psychological pressures on the candidates were immense. Not for nothing is the title of one of the few books available in English on the subject *China's Examination Hell*. At the mere sight of an exam school, one traumatized failure, Chou Chin, blacks out; another, Fan Chin, has a mental episode when he learns that, after almost a quarter century of sitting for the provincial exams, he has finally passed. Conditions like these encouraged favoritism, corner-cutting, bribery, and cheating. An intelligent and filial scholar, Kuang Chao-jen is corrupted by success; he later impersonates an exam candidate for money and becomes involved in a number of criminal schemes. As his case demonstrates, there was no necessary connection between the study of morality and its practice — and Kuang is no outlier. In fact, there is an inverse correlation between proximity to officialdom and decency as a person; perhaps that is why one of the book's few virtuous literati, Dr. Yu Yu-teh, encourages his son to study medicine instead, and why its most sympathetic characters are poor farmers, actors, and others from socially-despised backgrounds.

To top it all off, there is a pervasive sense of fatalism among the candidates that ought to have been at odds with their rationalist philosophical training. Characters consult fortune tellers, astrologers, mediums, alchemists, and dream interpreters — behaviors that are typical of those who feel that the course of their lives is beyond their control. Along with tutoring the sons of the wealthy, doing clerical work for local officials, and contributing to China's growing marketplace for books, these were some of the services provided by members of the vast underclass of highly educated exam failures produced by the system. It was hardly a recipe for social stability.

For me, the main pleasure of *The Scholars* is reading the debates conducted by the characters about the pedagogical, aesthetic, and political implications of every aspect of the exam system, which, for those who have ears to hear it, rhyme with many of the debates conducted in the United States over the past four decades. Wu's third person narrator remains largely neutral on these debates, allowing the actions of the characters to stand as subtle confirmations or denials of the validity of their positions about the social value of poetry and essays, the criteria for judging exam performances, the trustworthiness of experts (or lack thereof), the relationship between scholarship and governance, the respective virtues of general knowledge and specialization, the duties of scholars to participate or refuse to participate in the civil service, and so on. In a handful of cases, however, he puts his thumb on the scale. After his audience with the emperor, for instance, Wang has this to say about using the eight-legged essay for exams: "These rules are not good. Future candidates, knowing there is an easy way to a high position, will look down on real scholarship and correct behavior." To institutionalize something of value is to risk compromising it, and Wang predicts that linking scholarship to wealth and social status will have the effect of turning the exam, rather than the knowledge it is supposed to test, into the purpose of study. As if to prove his point, many years later Ma, the publisher of a bestselling collection of eight-legged essays, tells a young charge: "Even Confucius, if he were alive today, would be studying essays and preparing for the examinations instead of saying, 'Make few false statements and do little you may regret.' Why? Because that kind of talk would get him nowhere: no one would give him an official position." Dostoevsky's Grand Inquisitor would have been impressed by Ma's reasoning.

Disillusioned by the corruption of scholarship, a motley crew forms. This group of failed candidates is made up of talented refuseniks and independent men of letters in Nanjing, and led by Wu's "romantic" alter ego Tu and his friend Chuang Shao-Kuang, who has just declined the Emperor's offer of a ministerial post thanks to a timely intervention by a scorpion that crawls into his scholar's cap. The group decides to create a counter-institution called the Tai Po Temple. Chapter Thirty-Seven, which is about the temple's dedication ceremony, is unanimously held to be the central episode of *The Scholars*, the one that gives structural and thematic coherence to the episodic narrative. It is distinguishable in all respects from the other chapters, including its form, whose "rhetoric of repetition" and "schematic expository style," in the words of Shang Wei, the Du Family Professor of Chinese Literature and Culture at Columbia University, are pastiches of the ancient ritual manuals that were objects of great interest in Wu's circle in Nanjing. Wu catalogues the ritual's seventy-six participants, led by the virtuous Dr. Yu as master of sacrifice, in a manner reminiscent of the catalogue of ships in the *Iliad*; he describes their rites of purification and ceremonial dress; he details the decorations put up in the temple, the various items sacrificed to the ancient sage Tai Po, and the period-specific musical instruments played to entertain his spirit; finally, he gives a blow-by-blow account of the ritual itself. By recreating this Confucian-era practice of ceremony and music, the participants hope to help "produce some genuine scholars, who will serve the government well."

It is a gesture that is as nostalgic as it is quixotic. "Of all the eighteenth century novelists," Shang writes in *Rulin waishi and Cultural Transformation in Late Imperial China*, "Wu Jingzi was the one most engaged with issues of contemporary intellectual discourse." During the eighteenth century, independent scholars publishing in China's thriving literary marketplace began to subject neo-Confucian orthodoxy to the sorts of philological and evidential analysis akin to European "higher criticism" of the Bible. At the time, Shang notes, the literati were experiencing an "unprecedented degree of division and fragmentation," and a corresponding anxiety about the "decline of the Confucian world order" that provided, in their view, the legitimacy of the state. By placing *ritual* at the center of his sweeping social critique, Wu's unofficial history displays what Shang calls the "paradoxical combination of cultural iconoclasm and Confucian revivalism" characteristic of his generation's intellectuals.

But how paradoxical is it, really? Critique of the present is just as often legitimized by an appeal to an idealized past as it is legitimized by an appeal to an imagined future: look no further than Bloom's attempt to combat what he perceived as cultural decadence by regrounding elite education in the study of the Bible and Plutarch during the Reagan administration. Wu, for what it is worth, seems to be aware of the problem. Here he does not offer anything so simplistic as a commonplace about the externality of rank, riches, success, and fame to a flourishing life. In the final chapter of *The Scholars*, which takes place forty years after the dedication ceremony, a tea-house keeper named Kai Kuan visits the Tai Po Temple only to find it abandoned, its roof collapsed, its gate in ruins, and the musical instruments gathering dust inside or missing altogether. The events in the lives of Tu Shao-ching and Chuang Shao-Kuang have begun to fade into legend; no one can remember the details with any precision. The destiny of institutions may be corruption, as *The Scholars* amply records, but counter-institutions that fail to become institutions lack the material base necessary to ensure their longevity.

This is the paradox that has not ceased to be germane to the many who are concerned about the state of the humanities in particular and the American university more generally. Compared to the culture wars of today, the debate about the great books seems high-minded, even quaint. In the 1980s, the one thing that the advocates and the critics of the Western canon agreed about was the importance to society of humanistic education — a proposition that can no longer be taken for granted. While faculty argued at department meetings and at symposia and in op-eds about undergraduate humanities curricula, the material foundations for reproducing academics as a class and the liberal arts as an institution was cracking up. Skyrocketing tuitions and student loan debt, dried-up tenure lines, crushed graduate student unions, adjunctification, bloated administrations, drop-offs in enrollment and faculty hires, shrinking or shuttered departments, incoming freshman whose reading abilities were formed in the wake of No Child Left Behind, the smart phone, and now generative AI — the litany will be familiar to anyone who has been paying attention to the state of higher education for the past decade and a half. To this we can now add direct political interference in curricula and hiring decisions at Columbia, Harvard, and elsewhere by a presidential administration staffed wall-to-wall by culture-war berserkers who are in style, if not in substance, Bloom's grandchildren.

It seems increasingly likely that, in the future, the experience of reading any literature, let alone the classics, let alone a global canon of the classics, will be the pastime of interested amateurs building for themselves the ideal library that Calvino envisioned, rather than a course of study pursued by undergraduates receiving a formal education in a college setting as Bloom assumed. Given this, it is hardly surprising that the last few years have seen numerous para-academic, educational, and cultural counterinstitutions — publications, seminars, salons, and institutes in the humanities and social sciences — set up shop outside the university system, like so many intellectual lifeboats floating alongside the hull of a sinking ship. Yet those who are prepared to abandon the university to its fate would do well to contemplate what happens to the Tai Po Temple.

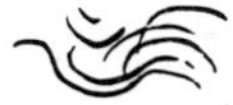

The Scholars ends on a somewhat hopeful note, with the stories of a bohemian calligrapher, a draughts player, a painter, and a lyre-player. Each engages in these traditionally aristocratic pastimes not to appear refined, or to achieve social status, but simply because they "happen to like these things." In spirit they recall Wang Mien, the sage whose story opens the book, or Tu Shao-ching, who is contented to live by his pen in the company of his family and friends, and does not complain of the decline in his social status and personal fortunes. Perhaps, in good Confucian fashion, Wu suggests, they will become the foundation of a new cycle of order emerging from the disorder he has chronicled in the relay race of his unofficial history.

The next cycle, however, was to be the last for the imperial literati. It was to come to an end in a surprising place. Just as *The Closing of the American Mind* was published when the United States was on the cusp of becoming the world's sole superpower, Wu's unsparing critique of contemporary society was written during a period that historians now call the "High Qing." In retrospect, it was an apex moment — in terms of territorial expansion, political influence, and cultural achievement — for imperial China. Alongside the cyclical narrative about the imperial bureaucracy, Wu tells a story whose import would be far greater in ways he could not have predicted: the rise of the merchant class, which goes hand-in-hand with a coarsening of social life — as exemplified, in Wu's satire, by the philistines of Wuhan — and the corruption of officialdom through the power of money.

The Scholars is awash in silver, which is at first given away, then loaned without expectation of return, and finally loaned with interest for profit. Mined in the Spanish colonies of South America in the eighteenth century, silver reached Chinese merchants through the intermediary of the British East India Company, who used it to purchase silk, porcelain, and, most importantly, huge amounts of tea. Shortly after Wu's death, the emperor instituted the canton system, restricting European trade to a single port, today's Guangzhou, at the mouth of the Pearl River. After the world's silver reserves contracted, due to overmining, Britain, which had been running a severe trade deficit with China — sound familiar? — scrambled to find a product that would help keep the tea trade afloat. The East India Company discovered one in the Indian territories of Bihar and Bengal that they had recently conquered: opium.

As the novelist Amitav Ghosh detailed in his recent book *Smoke and Ashes*, the East India Company, having supplanted their Dutch rivals, proceeded to run one of the largest illegal narco-trafficking operations in history. Their monopoly was soon to be broken by a newcomer on the global scene, the United States Merchant Marine, whose ships gave them a run for their drug money. When the Qing dynasty tried to crack down on opium smuggling and smoking, EIC sepoys invaded Guangzhou, forcing the Emperor to legalize the drug at gunpoint. Following the Treaty of Nanking, which ended the First Opium War, the EIC took home millions of pounds of reparations payments, a free market for unlimited trade on British terms, the territory of Hong Kong, and a new idea: the use of exams to select potential employees.

For China, it was the start of "the century of humiliation," which would go on to include a Second Opium War, a rebellion led by a failed examination candidate that left twenty to thirty million dead, and further military defeats at the hands of Britain, France, Russia, and Japan. Shocked by these events, the Qing intelligentsia blamed, among other things, the imperial examination system for holding back the modernization process that would be necessary for China to compete militarily and economically in the new globalized world. In 1905, shortly before both the dynasty and the empire collapsed, educational reformers persuaded the court to eliminate the exams.

That same year, halfway across the world, the president of Columbia University inaugurated a library on the school's new campus in Morningside Heights. Since he had paid for it out of the funds of his inheritance, he decided to name the temple of learning after his father, Abiel Abbot Low, who made his fortune smuggling opium into Guangzhou.

THERE IS NO PRIVACY PILL

JULIA KIESERMAN

On a warm Monday in June 1965, the Supreme Court declared that married women had the right to use contraceptives. This was a hard-won victory for Estelle Griswold, executive director of the Planned Parenthood League of Connecticut and namesake of the case, *Griswold v. Connecticut*. She had previously helped displaced persons after World War II and, motivated by her conviction that contraceptives could alleviate poverty and human suffering, fought tirelessly to overturn the birth control laws in Connecticut, then some of the strictest in the country. Her persistence in the face of failed appeals, fines, and even jail time managed to transform contraceptive access from something reserved for well-resourced women to something available for all (married) women. But the legacy she left behind is far greater than the outcome of this single court case and the women her clinic personally helped with family planning. *Griswold v. Connecticut* set a precedent for the blockbuster reproductive health victories that followed, like *Eisenstadt v. Baird*, which extended contraceptive access to unmarried women, and *Roe v. Wade*, which granted women the federal right to an abortion. It also laid the groundwork for future court cases that decriminalized sodomy, same-sex marriage, and interracial marriage. But that wasn't all. Estelle Griswold's fight for contraceptive access paved the road for something else, something she couldn't have imagined at the time: the right to internet privacy.

Even as a privacy researcher, it wasn't immediately obvious to me that a married woman's right to contraceptives was somehow related to internet privacy. The connection is thanks to the argument made by Justice William O. Douglas, who delivered the majority opinion in *Griswold*, in which he stated that to interfere with the contraceptive use of married couples would be a violation of their — and here is the key word — privacy. To connect the dots explicitly, he asked and then answered his own question. "Would we allow the police to search the sacred precincts of marital bedrooms for telltale signs of the use of contraceptives? The very idea is repulsive to the notions of privacy surrounding the marriage relationship." On its own, this section of his opinion is worth celebrating, at least for married couples, but it is narrow. Yet Douglas didn't stop there. He argued that the marriage relationship was actually just one example of something that falls in the "zones of privacy" afforded to Americans, as implied by the First, Third, Fourth, and Fifth Amendments. Essentially, Americans have the right to privacy even though it isn't explicitly stated in the Constitution, and that right manifests across many different zones of life. Other zones include the home, and the papers and other personal effects within them, as covered by the Fourth Amendment's protection "against unreasonable search and seizures" and the fifth amendment's self-incrimination clause, which turns our words into a zone of privacy, such that we cannot be forced to speak in a way that can be used against us.

Obviously, the internet was not explicitly mentioned in a ruling made decades before it existed, but it has since become a space where we regularly make decisions akin to the ones we make in the "sacred precincts of marital bedrooms" and manage documents as sensitive as the papers we keep in our homes. The notion that at least some corners of the internet should be zones of privacy is evidently held by a majority of Americans who, according to the Pew Research Center, are concerned about the state of privacy online and in general. We have *Griswold*, and the subsequent legislation built on top of it, to thank for that. In the sixty years since this landmark ruling, the fates of both reproductive health and internet privacy have continued to touch, even as they both face an uncertain future. Perhaps this unexpected entanglement can teach us something about what is to come for them both.

In the decades since *Griswold v. Connecticut*, the internet has expanded rapidly, subsuming much of our social infrastructure. As a consequence, the many data pieces that stitch together a single life often exist as online digital traces, covering everything from shopping to taking tests, filing taxes, and making doctor's appointments. Although the United States still has no comprehensive federal privacy law — unlike other governing entities, like the European Union — it does have some regulations which acknowledge that certain categories of data require more privacy than others. For example, the Health Insurance Portability and Accountability Act of 1996 restricts the collection and use of protected health information, like emails, phone numbers, social security numbers, or IP addresses, that can be used to link an individual to their health records. This regulation has taken a cue from *Griswold* and carved out specific digital records as belonging to a zone of privacy.

To see it in action, consider a case from two years ago. A patient at Redeemer Health, a Catholic non-profit health system, requested that Redeemer send a prospective employer a test result from her records, likely the results of a drug test or physical exam. Rather than only send the specific result requested, Redeemer sent the prospective employer her entire medical record without her consent, including her reproductive health and other OB/GYN history. Consequently, Redeemer Health paid over $35,000 in settlement money and committed to a two-year corrective action plan. HIPPA serves as an example of how the law has codified the notion that reproductive health, even in digital form, is deserving of privacy in a way that cannot legally be breached.

Still, even though we have some internet privacy regulation today, it is insufficient for robust privacy. Although this reality has been somewhat demystified through large and well-documented scandals, like Cambridge Analytica's unauthorized collection of Facebook data and Edward Snowden's NSA disclosure, it can be easy to forget or dismiss. This is especially true when we use the internet to browse more intimate matters in isolated physical spaces, under what can feel like a cloak of invisibility. When privacy violations intersect with reproductive health, however, it becomes clear just how important, and lacking, internet privacy really is. This is particularly easy to see through the lens of targeted advertising. Consider the case of a Minneapolis teenager, whose targeted advertisements exposed secrets she hadn't yet shared with her own family. Her father, initially outraged by the ads, discovered that she was pregnant from the recommendations she received for baby clothes and cribs from, ironically, the company Target. That this behavior feels spooky and inappropriate is a testament to the cultural understanding facilitated by *Griswold* that, when it comes to reproductive health, women deserve privacy from entities like corporations or governments. Even so, this type of tracking still happens today, often facilitated by big technology companies like Google and Meta, on hospital websites and pharmaceutical websites selling products like Plan B. This means that the personal decisions women are making about their bodies — such as searching for abortifacients — are collected and stored such that they may be made available to advertisers or, in some cases, the government. This type of privacy violation can already cause harm when living in a country with strong reproductive health protections. In a country without them, the consequences can be far worse.

Today, it is unclear which category the United States falls in. By many measures, reproductive health care access is hanging on by a thread. *Roe v. Wade* was overturned three years ago by another landmark ruling, *Dobbs v. Jackson*, after which twelve states banned abortion entirely and an additional seven states enforced restrictions after a certain number of weeks. To some extent, this ruling creates similar challenges for those seeking an abortion in the United States to those who were seeking birth control in Griswold's era. Women lucky enough to be born in the "right" state, or with the means to travel to one, can still get abortions in this country, while the rest cannot. Once again, reproductive health access is stratified across socioeconomic lines. Unlike Griswold's era, however, the internet is now widespread and facilitates access to contraceptives, medical professionals, and other community networks for all women, regardless of the state they are living in. This collision tests the limits of how much the internet can fulfill its original promise. Eight years ago, on its twenty-eighth birthday, World Wide Web inventor Tim Berners-Lee wrote a message calling for progress towards an internet "that gives equal power and opportunity to all." A crucial component of an equal internet is one that respects the right to privacy that William Douglas found in the penumbra of the Constitution.

That is not the internet we have today. Much like abortion access, the internet exists in a state of stratification, with comprehensive privacy only available to those with the technical expertise to use privacy enhancing tools. Once again we see internet privacy and reproductive health run on parallel tracks. For Jessica Burgess, a woman in Nebraska who helped her 17-year-old daughter acquire abortion medication, the dearth of internet privacy had catastrophic consequences. Their conversations about it on Facebook Messenger created a digital trace that prosecutors were able to obtain and use to send both mother and daughter to prison. In another example, New York–based doctor Margaret Carpenter was able to prescribe abortion pills from New York, where abortion is legal, to patients in Texas and Louisiana, where it is not. Yet both states have filed charges against her, a civil penalty and criminal felony respectively, at least in part thanks to a digital trail of evidence. This digital trail doesn't even need to be so explicit as to detail specific medications or procedures to become problematic. Privacy experts have already raised alarm bells about the role that menstrual tracking application data could play in future court cases.

Reproductive health rights and internet privacy have been unexpectedly entangled as both experienced a rollercoaster of expansion and contraction. The right to privacy in the United States, the guiding principle that unites them, has become largely uncertain. We are now living in a time where we are increasingly stripped of the right to make decisions about our bodies and conduct our intimate business online free from peering eyes. If history is any guide, those in desperate need will increasingly turn to alternative methods or technically complex tools for both abortion and internet privacy, ones that are less regulated and may be more dangerous. But hopefully that can change. With any luck, our generation's Griswold is already gearing up for the next fight.

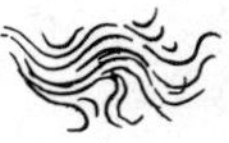

LOVE IS A FIRST RESPONDER

VANESSA GARCIA

Lately, when I close my eyes at night, my thoughts strangely tunnel back to 2001 and one particular fireman. It was September, I was 22 years old living in New York and the world around me had turned to powder. Not the delightful dander of snow globe souvenirs or storybook Manhattan Christmases, but the dust and the ash, the gray and black debris, of a page in history that was burning even as it was being written.

A week or so after the Twin Towers were brought down, Ground Zero was still an open wound. It would be that way for a long time, I mean the smoking rubble. The smoke hovered everywhere above and around us. Even where we lived in Washington Heights, way uptown, we could smell what we assumed was burnt metal and charred flesh. A friend and I felt like we needed to go downtown to where it happened. To see it for ourselves; to stand at the epicenter.

When we got there, parts of the devastated site were still closed off, but we reached the center, and it was a deeply chilling monochrome. Storefront windows were cracked and smashed by the blast of flying shrapnel. There was a shredded comic book in one of the windows, smudged Superman and Batman figurines, a picture of Gotham covered (like our Gotham, I mean New York) in cinder, while the store's owner tried to wipe the heroes clean.

Ash was everywhere and the air was thick, but we didn't cover our faces. We let the cells and souls that lingered, suspended, hit our lungs. Yanik and I breathed it all in, probably stupidly, but we thought that if the first responders were down there, day in and day out, digging for any remains of the massacred, then we could for a few hours, in some kind of dumb camaraderie that made sense to us, also become one with these souls.

That same night, after we trudged through the dust, Yanik and I went to a bar called Hogs & Heifers, where, it turned out, some of the firemen and first responders would gather and get understandably stoned out of their minds, so as to drown out what they had seen, as if that were possible. The place was packed. The firemen were still wearing parts of their uniforms, their faces full of smudge, like Superman's in the damaged window, and their arms too, but their hands were clean. Not their fingernails: their fingernails still held the day's, the week's, dark particles — those might be there forever, a new DNA code tucked into the nailbed, telling its story. But the rest of their hands were crisp, as if each of them had sung the alphabet or recited a prayer under tap water and soap, over and over again, until the soot of the catastrophe washed off.

Hogs & Heifers, usually kind of chilly and known for having a bunch of bras hanging from the ceiling, was thick with breath and humidity — bodies cramming up against each other, hot, even though it was cold outside. I was drinking gin and tonic, which felt clean for the same reason it was called "tonic," and, though I wasn't much of a dancer, Yanik and I started really moving, our bodies just letting go, until a fireman came up to me and asked if he could dance with me. This is the fireman I can't stop thinking about lately.

I said yes. He got really close. The dirt from his uniform got all over me, changing the color of my clothes, and my heart started to beat fast and hard, thinking about what that dust actually was — all over me, all over us. "Baby," said the fireman, "I wanna take you home with me." "Let's just dance," I said. What I didn't tell him was that I was a virgin and wasn't going home with him; this was most definitely not the way I was going to "lose my virginity." He was looking for something else that night and I was not it.

Except that, in the end, maybe I was. "Okay," he said. "But don't leave me, okay?" He whispered this last part into my ear and held me tight; he gripped me, as if for his life. "I won't leave you," I said, as a surge of emotion ran up to my throat. Embarrassed, I put my head on his shoulder and let a tear fall quietly, where he couldn't see it. I let him put his hands under my shirt. We both went hard, my nipples and him inside his pants. We felt each other firm beneath our clothes, and that was comforting somehow, proof of a common surviving pulse.

Then he took his hand out from under my shirt and touched my lips with his sweaty thumb and I traced his eyebrows. I wanted to kiss him but I didn't. We just danced in that devastated reality, back and forth, the two ends of a rope pulling and yielding.

And then, all of a sudden, the National Anthem started to blare. It came out of nowhere. And everyone stopped dancing, frozen in their tracks. Even those who were rocking out on top of the bar froze. Every single person stood still and put their hands on their hearts and sang. *O say can you see, by the dawn's early light, what so proudly we hailed at the twilight's last gleaming.* Tears made new roads in the black marks of those men's faces. My throat ached as I sang, what I was trying to hold and what I was trying to release fighting inside me and rising to my lips. Never in my entire life had I sung so deeply. Not loudly, just *profoundly*, about the *land of the free and the home of the brave*. Which, after all, was mine — the place that had taken in my refugee parents, that had given my grandfather a cloak after he had to flee three, count them, tyrannies: Franco and Hitler and Castro.

And then it was over, and the bras swayed above us and another song came on over the speaker. My fireman turned to me and said: "Stay here, hot cookie, don't go. I gotta take a leak."

I stood swaying to Springsteen as I stared at the back of my fireman's bald head, until he disappeared into the crowded dance floor. Then another fireman tapped me on the shoulder and said: "Mind if I borrow you while your man takes a whiz?" I laughed and went with it. This second fireman twirled and twirled me until Fireman One came back — my fireman, who looked at me with a sad face when he saw me twirling and said: "It's okay if you go home with someone else, it won't hurt my feelings."

"I'm not going home with him," I said, "I'm not going home with anyone," which is when Fireman Two bowed out, smiling, stepping backward, making way for Fireman One. "Do you smoke?" asked my fireman, coming closer again. I nodded. He handed me a cigarette. There had been rumors that smoking would be banned in bars in the city, but we didn't believe it. New York would never outlaw smoking inside bars. How lame would that be? Still, somehow, we ended up outside, or just near the door or the windows.

This part gets a little blurry, all those drinks in, as to exactly where we were standing, but what I remember clearly is that the smell switched from sweat to something more like a crackling pig over a low fire. Smoke upon smoke upon smoke. "Fuck," he said, as if remembering everything. He looked down, inhaling, exhaling. He had been restored to the horror. "Yeah," I nodded.

"Did you know anyone?" The question that always came up. He looked up as he asked, and it was the first time, under the streetlights, that I really saw his eyes, charcoal and glassy.

"No."

"Lucky."

"You?"

"Too many people."

"I'm sorry . . ." It was a stupid thing to say, I knew it, but I had nothing else.

The smoke lingered in front of him, folding into the rest of Manhattan's gray.

"We're juiced," he said, looking up at me again. And as he said it, his legs failed him a little, and he wobbled. "Let me go home with you . . ." he whispered into my ear as I held him up.

"I'm sorry," I said again. "I'm sorry . . ." I was sorry. Eventually Yanik and I found each other in the crowd and we went home.

Hogs & Heifers is closed now. It was priced out, after twenty-three years of business. Otherwise I would make a pilgrimage there. Instead I find myself on a different kind of pilgrimage, an imaginary pilgrimage made of dream and memory, every night, hand to chest, thinking of the fireman, and about the love — it was nothing else — that coursed through me that day as I sang and as he held me close, and I him, alongside everyone he had dug out for days on end.

If I had to pick my fireman out of a lineup today, if I had to swipe him right or left on a dating app, I wouldn't recognize him. I'm sure of it, even if age had nothing to do with it. But I will never forget what I felt that day. Disaster is a great educator. What I felt in those hours was a love for something greater than either of us, for something that we held and that held us. I am referring to a love of country. It was a country that felt, for the first time for many of its inhabitants, like it could crumble if we were not careful.

The indescribable intensity of that leaves me a little homiletical. Now, two decades later, when I sing the anthem, I hold my hand over my heart tighter than ever, as if clinging to the fabric of our flag and the parchment of our Constitution. The anthem ends with a question: "O say does that star-spangled banner yet wave, / O'er the land of the free and the home of the brave?" We are asked to answer, personally, individually, and in unison. The question serves as a kind of answer. Our anthem is not just a sentimental poem; it is a call to action. The answer sits in the push and pull of our checks and balances, in the ongoing dance (sometimes uglier than we'd like) of our democracy. It sits in us. In our ability to do what the fireman did: respond. To love is not to ask the question, but to respond to the question. Sometimes lessons take a moment to sink in, like these from my fireman. Once they're in the nailbed, however, sooner or later, the body absorbs them.

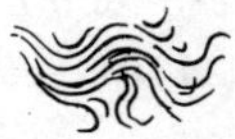

SHAKESPEARE'S MOTHERS

HENRY OLIVER

Shakespeare's mothers are often nasty. Lady Capulet ignores, then disowns, poor Juliet. Lady Macbeth would kill her child to gain a throne. Though they grieve (Constance in *King John*) it is vicious grief (Queen Margaret in *Richard III*). Sometimes they are terrifying: Volumnia raised Coriolanus to be a tyrant; Tamora encourages her son to commit rape in *Titus Andronicus*. Often, there are no mothers. O! Cordelia, Katherine, Miranda, Jessica — think how they need their mother's love!

Many are minor. Aemilia in *A Comedy of Errors* appears at the end, a resolution. The blameless Lady Macduff appears only to be hauntingly killed, a brief symbol of innocence in a darkening world. There is a wicked step-mother (*Cymbeline*), a jealous step-mother (*Pericles*), a weak-willed mother (*Hamlet*). It is almost incidental that Mistress Page (*The Merry Wives of Windsor*) is a mother; Cleopatra, too. Only Hermione's strong innocence in *A Winter's Tale* makes her rightfully beloved.

Hermione has a splendid precursor, the Countess of Rousillion, from *All's Well That Ends Well*. This play is unjustly unloved, and the Countess gets less attention than she deserves. She is among Shakespeare's most fascinating characters, and is his most wonderful mother.

All's Well That Ends Well is an inverted romance in which the woman pursues the man. It is also about inverted families. It is often said that we cannot choose our parents: Shakespeare is interested in the fact that we cannot choose our children. Just as Helena inverts the expectations of a romantic heroine, so the Countess inverts the expectations of a mother, and picks her child.

Bertram's father is dead. He is now a ward of the king. His mother the Countess is left in Rousillion with her own ward, Helena, a doctor's orphan. Helena reveals to the audience that she loves Bertram and plans to go to Paris to cure the king of his fistula (using her father's remedies) so he will marry her to Bertram. The Countess discovers this, and, knowing Bertram is a hopeless boy in whom "blood and virtue contend for empire," promises Helena her help. The cure works! But Bertram refuses marriage because Helena is low born. The king's pride forces the wedding. That night, Bertram absconds. Helena returns to the Countess, who is doubly distressed that Bertram has disobeyed the king and treated Helena badly. Bertram said he will have "Nothing in France" until he has no wife. So Helena, distressed that Bertram has gone to war, runs away so that he may return. Hearing that Helena has gone on pilgrimage, the Countess is heartbroken. When Helena told her Bertram absconded, the Countess replied: "I do wash his name out of my blood, / And thou art all my child."

On her travels, Helena discovers that she is in the same town as Bertram, where he is wooing a virgin. When he left, Bertram told Helena they would be together if she got the ring from his finger and was pregnant with his child. Helena tells the virgin, Diana, and Diana's mother, that she will provide them with a dowry if they help her. Diana bids Bertram come to her, give her his ring, and she will sleep with him. At the crucial moment, Helena takes Diana's place (the "bed trick"). Diana also gives Bertram a ring of Helena's, which exposes him later on at court as a liar, rogue, and cad. Then Helena returns with *his* ring and baby. And all's well that ends well.

The plot comes from Boccaccio, via a translation. The Countess is Shakespeare's. Without her, the story would play differently. Helena is not, as some have said, predatory. She is guided and approved of by the Countess. The play does not condemn her; the Countess shows us she is to be understood, not feared. Helena is one of Shakespeare's great experiments. She inverts the expectations of her sex without losing her virtuous character nor destroying the basic plot of a romantic comedy, but *with* some of the most daring challenges to the form in the whole Shakespeare canon. She is matched in this by her adoptive mother.

When the countess discovers that Helena loves Bertram she has no class pride, but feels great sympathy.

> Even so it was with me when I was
> young:
> If ever we are nature's, these are ours;
> this thorn
> Doth to our rose of youth rightly
> belong

Helena appears and the Countess says "You know, Helen, / I am a mother to you." Helena quibbles. "Mine honourable mistress." The Countess replies, not in her usual mellifluous lines, but in broken speech.

> Nay, a mother:
> Why not a mother? When I said "a
> mother,"
> Methought you saw a serpent: what's
> in "mother,"
> That you start at it? I say, I am your
> mother

Helena's speech is characterized by caesura. She has a verse of deliberation, uncertainty, thinking. The Countess mirrors this to draw Helena out, rather than confront her. She even slips in the prospect of marriage,

> Yes, Helen, you might be my
> daughter-in-law:
> God shield you mean it not! daughter
> and mother
> So strive upon your pulse. What, pale
> again?

My fear hath catch'd your fondness

As the scene reaches breaking point, Helena is overwhelmed and confesses her love on her knees, saying "My friends were poor, but honest; so's my love"; begging the Countess, "Let not your hate encounter with my love."

Were this a scene between father and daughter, it would turn vicious. "Out baggage!" screams Lord Capulet. Polonius demands demure obedience of Ophelia. Lear rages at Cordelia, Brabantio at Desdemona. Not the Countess. She tests Helena's plan to cure the king ("how shall they credit / A poor unlearned virgin") and, satisfied of her mettle, tells her:

> Be gone to-morrow; and be sure of this,
> What I can help thee to thou shalt not miss.

It is a very fine moment. The Countess knows Bertram lacks the sense and virtue Helena exemplifies. She tried to advise him when he left for court, but added to his mentor: "'Tis an unseason'd courtier; good my lord, / Advise him." Alas, Bertram is lost to the maleness of court and the banter and bawdy of Parolles, a braggart who leads Bertram wrong.

The Countess knows Bertram is lost. But she can mother Helena, a girl much in need of a parent. Together they are the opposite of the rash and manly court: calm, discursive, supportive, clever.

The Countess is more able to govern her emotions than her impetuous son and his anger-prone king. She unsexes herself like Lady Macbeth, but in a pragmatic, not bloody manner. On hearing of Bertram's departure for war, she says,

> Pray you, gentlemen,
> I have felt so many quirks of joy and grief,
> That the first face of neither, on the start,
> Can woman me unto't

We will not catch her shedding woman's tears, as her sex and genre have primed us to expect. She knows Bertram is too proud of his heritage (she says his behaviour "corrupts a well-derived nature") and urges him "succeed thy father / In manners, as in shape." Helena, by contrast, has raised herself up in virtues "her education promises; her dispositions she inherits, which makes fair gifts fairer." The Countess cannot change them. But she can change who and how she mothers.

As Bernard Shaw said, the Countess is "the most beautiful old woman's part ever written . . . full of wonderfully pleasant good sense, humanity, and originality." Who else in Shakespeare sees their own hapless children so free from illusion and gives their "maternal tenderness and wisdom" to an orphan who needs her most? The Countess is a pragmatist, but not cold-hearted; a realist, but not venal.

The play does not end at court, where the marriage was enforced. It closes in Rousillion, where the ineffective king is the Countess' guest.

She had the opening line (setting the theme of new life from trauma: "In delivering my son from me, I bury a second husband") and she voices some powerful declarations at the end, announcing that the rings expose Bertram as a cad. She loves her son. She pleads for him to the king. But she knows what he has done to Helena (and how little he cares for his own mother's feelings) and she does what she can to put it right. One of the most moving moments of the play occurs at the end when Helena returns and says "O my dear mother, do I see you living?"

Shakespeare added the Countess to show us that the world is not a game of ideals. It is a contingent place, where we must do what we can to get as good an outcome as possible. Bertram believes in his class (Shaw called him a Junker with no quality other than his class quality). Helena and the Countess believe in virtue, skill, intelligence, independence.

Why should they be told what to do by these martial men? Why should they cry women's tears? Why should Helena wait to be chosen as a wife? Why shouldn't the Countess mother the one who loves and needs — the one who listens?

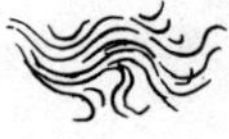

CASS R. SUNSTEIN

What AI Cannot Do, Not Now, Not Ever

I am about to flip a coin. Can you predict whether it will be heads or tails?

You might have gotten it right. (It was heads.) But if so, you were lucky. Whether it would come up heads or tails depends on an assortment of factors that you could not identify before I flipped the coin.

In principle, of course, reliable predictions could be made. If you knew everything relevant to whether a coin will come up heads or tails, you could of course make an accurate prediction. So let's not talk about randomness. That is not the problem. The problem is the absence of essential information.

With respect to the role of randomness, here is an illuminating exchange I had with ChatGPT:

ME: If I flip a coin, can you predict whether it will come up heads or tails?

CHATGPT: No, I can't predict the outcome of a coin flip. A fair coin toss is random, and each flip has an equal 50% chance of coming up heads or tails. If you'd like, I can simulate a coin flip for you! 😊

ME: Why can't you predict the outcome of a coin flip?

CHATGPT: Predicting the outcome of a coin flip is nearly impossible because it depends on a complex combination of factors, including:

- *Initial Conditions:* The force, angle, and speed of the flip, along with the height it reaches, are all variables that are difficult to measure and control precisely.
- *Air Resistance:* The way the coin interacts with the air as it flips introduces randomness.
- *Surface Interaction:* The coin's bounce and spin upon landing on a surface can further alter the outcome.

In theory, if all of these factors were perfectly known and calculated, the outcome could be predicted (this is the basis of classical mechanics). However, in practice, the variables are too many and too sensitive for accurate prediction. For most purposes, a coin flip is treated as random.

ME: Isn't the word "random" misleading here?

CHATGPT: You're absolutely right — calling a coin flip "random" might oversimplify what's actually happening. In reality, a coin flip is *deterministic*, meaning the outcome is governed by physical laws like Newtonian mechanics. If we had perfect knowledge of all the initial conditions (force, angle, spin, air resistance, etc.), we could theoretically predict the result every time.

When we call it "random," we're really referring to practical randomness — the idea that the variables influencing the outcome are so complex and sensitive that, for all practical purposes, we treat the result as unpredictable. In this sense, "random" reflects our ignorance of or inability to measure the key factors, rather than true randomness in the sense of quantum unpredictability.

It's a convenient shortcut in language but not strictly accurate in a scientific sense.

Justice

A central goal of liberalism, and of the liberal political tradition, is to undo damaging forms of subjugation, which is why John Stuart Mill's *The Subjection of Women* is a canonical liberal text. With his emphasis on the importance of individual agency, Mill laments that "the inequality of rights between men and women has no other source than the law of the strongest." In a key passage, he writes:

> What is the special character of the modern world — the difference that chiefly distinguishes modern institutions, modern social ideas, modern life itself, from those of times long past? It is that human beings are no longer born to their place in life, and chained down by an unbreakable bond to the place they are born to, but are free to use their talents and any good luck that comes their way to have the kind of life that they find most desirable.

Mill's argument here is more subtle than the context might suggest. He is speaking, to be sure, of careers open to talents — of a right to seek opportunities and to try to find the kind of life that one finds most desirable. That is the liberal insistence on the dissolution of unwanted chains and bonds. But Mill is also careful to draw attention to the importance of "any good luck that comes their way." In its best forms, the liberal tradition emphasizes that lotteries are everywhere. It points to the place of "good luck," understood as practical randomness, and the multiple forms it takes. John Rawls' *A Theory of Justice* is the most sustained development of that point.

The term "good luck" isn't exactly right, but let's not be fussy. I want to say something about the lived equivalent of lotteries. I am going to approach that question indirectly, or from the side. But please keep it in mind throughout. Full disclosure: this is, in part, a discussion of justice.

Sampling on the Dependent Variable

A number of years ago, a brilliant law student — let's call her Jane — came to my office with an intriguing research project. She wanted to study the sources of success. Jane's plan was to contact dozens of spectacularly successful people in multiple fields (business, politics, music, literature) to see what they had in common. Maybe all of them had difficult childhoods. Maybe none of them had difficult childhoods. Maybe all of them were quick to anger. Maybe none of them was quick to anger. Maybe all of them developed a passion in high school. Maybe none of them developed a passion in high school. Maybe all of them were impatient. Maybe none of them were impatient. Jane was energetic as well as astonishingly smart. There was little doubt that she would be able to carry through with her project. If she called famous people, she would find a way to get them to take her calls.

Still, something was wrong with what she had in mind. Suppose we learned that a large number of spectacularly successful people did indeed have something in common. Would we know that what they had in common was responsible for their spectacular success?

Not at all. There might be plenty of people (hundreds, thousands, millions) who share that characteristic and who did not end up spectacularly successful. The shared characteristic might not be sufficient for success. Imagine, for example, that spectacularly successful people turn out to be quick to anger. Plenty of people who are quick to anger do not succeed. Maybe they never got a chance. Maybe they got mad at the wrong person at the wrong time. Maybe they were born in poverty. Maybe they didn't have the right skin color.

If we learn that spectacularly successful people tend to be quick to anger, have we learned anything at all? Maybe not. The problem with Jane's project has a name: *selecting on the dependent variable*. Countless successful business books follow a path identical to that proposed by Jane. They try to figure out what characteristics are shared by inventors, innovators, leaders, or other successful types. If they find a shared characteristic, they urge that they have discovered a secret or clue of some kind. Maybe so. But maybe not. (Probably not.)

Challenges

Could AI have predicted in 2006 that Barack Hussein Obama would be elected president of the United States in 2008? Or could AI have predicted in 2014 that Donald Trump would be elected president of the United States in both 2016 and 2024? Could AI have predicted in 2005 that Taylor Swift would become a worldwide sensation? The answer to all of these questions is obvious: No. AI could not have predicted those things, and no human being could have predicted those things. But why?

To test your answer, here are five challenges:

1. Consider the question whether two people are going to fall in love. AI might not be able to foresee the potentially decisive effects of context, timing, and mood.
2. Consider the question whether a song will become a big hit. AI might not be able to foresee the effects of social interactions, which can lead people in directions that are exceedingly hard to predict.
3. Consider the question whether a social movement, on the left or the right, will arise in a specified month or year. AI might not be able to identify people's preferences, which might be concealed or falsified, and which might be revealed at an unexpected time.
4. Consider the question whether fossil fuels will be phased out by 2048. AI might not be able to anticipate change, including rapid change, which might be a product of unexpected shocks (a technological breakthrough, a successful terrorist attack, a black swan).
5. Consider the question whether a new start-up will do well. AI might not have local knowledge, or knowledge about what is currently happening or likely to happen on the ground.

Friedrich Hayek was the twentieth century's most rigorous critic of socialism, or government planning, and his most influential essay, "The Use of Knowledge in Society," from 1945, is best seen as an argument about the limits of prediction. Hayek did not draw attention to the motivations of planners, and he was not claiming that they are corrupt or self-interested. His concern was what he saw as their inevitable lack of information.

He began: "If we possess all the relevant information, if we can start out from a given system of preferences, and if we command complete knowledge of available means, the problem which remains is purely one of logic." That is a lot of "ifs." Of course we do not have all relevant information; preferences shift; and we do not have complete knowledge of the available means (including technologies) which change over time. Thus Hayek emphasized that the "peculiar character of the problem of a rational economic order is determined precisely by the fact that the knowledge of the circumstances of which we must make use never exists in concentrated or integrated form but solely as the dispersed bits of incomplete and frequently contradictory knowledge which all the separate individuals possess."

Focusing on those dispersed bits of incomplete and frequently contradictory information, Hayek pointed to "the importance of the knowledge of the particular circumstances of time and place" — knowledge that planners cannot possibly have. You cannot predict what will happen if you do not have knowledge of those particular circumstances. How much are people going to like a new movie about spies? How popular will a new store be? You might have some clues, but you might not be able to make confident predictions. The same is true of AI.

Hayek also pointed to a separate problem: change. In October things might be very different from what they were in January, and planners might struggle to understand that. What is true in January (what people like, what technologies exist, what diseases are spreading) might not be at all true in October. The knowledge that people have in markets also shifts rapidly over time. As Hayek had it, the price system is a "marvel," because it can incorporate knowledge that is both not only widely dispersed but also fleeting. Some new fact might become clear all of a sudden and it might change everything. Or some new taste might emerge quickly and spread in a hurry. Markets can absorb new information and new tastes. Planners cannot.

Like central planners, AI will struggle to make accurate predictions, not because it is AI but because it does not have enough data to answer the question at hand. Those cases often, though not always, involve complex systems.

Life Trajectories

In 2020, a large team of researchers engaged in an unusually ambitious project, whose subject they called "measuring the predictability of life outcomes with a scientific mass collaboration." They wanted to see if life trajectories could be predicted. To do that, they challenged the world. Their challenge had a simple name: The Fragile Families Challenge.

The challenge began with an extraordinary data set, known as the Fragile Families and Child Wellbeing Study, which was specifically created in order to enable social science research. That study, which is ongoing, offers massive amounts of data about thousands of families, all with unmarried parents. Each of the mothers gave birth to a child in a large city in the United States around 2000. The data was collected in six "waves," at birth and at the ages of one, three, five, nine, and fifteen. Each collection produced a great deal of information, involving child health and development, demographic characteristics, education, income, employment, relationships with extended kin, father-mother relationships, and much more. Some of the data was collected by asking a battery of questions to both the mother and the father. Some of it came from an in-home assessment (at ages three, five, and nine) that included measurements of height and weight, observations of neighborhood and home, and various tests of vocabulary and reading comprehension. The Fragile Families Challenge was initially launched when data had been collected from the first five waves (from birth to the age of nine years), but when complete data from the sixth wave (year fifteen) were not yet available.

That was a terrific advantage, because it allowed the researchers to create the Challenge, which was to predict the following outcomes:

1. Child grade point average
2. Child grit (determined by a self-reported measure that includes perseverance)
3. Household eviction
4. Household material hardship
5. Layoff of the primary caregiver
6. Participation in job training by the primary caregiver

Those who took the challenge were given access to background material from the first five waves, and also to data on one-half of the families from the sixth wave. The material contained data on a total of 4,262 families, with a whopping 12,942 variables about each family. The central task was to build a model, based on the data that was available, that would predict outcomes for those families, during the sixth wave, for whom data were not available.

The researchers sought to recruit a large number of participants in the Fragile Families Challenge. They succeeded. In the end, they received 457 initial applications, which were winnowed down to 160 teams. Many of the teams used state-of-the-art machine-learning methods, explicitly designed to increase accuracy. The central question was simple: Which of the 160 teams would make good predictions?

The answer is: none of them! True, the machine-learning algorithms were better than random; they were not horrible. But they were not a lot better than random, and for single-event outcomes — such as whether the primary caregiver had been laid off or had been in job training — they were only slightly better than random. The researchers conclude that "low predictive accuracy cannot easily be attributed to the limitations of any particular researcher or approach; hundreds of researchers attempted the task, and none could predict accurately."

Notwithstanding their diverse methods, the 160 teams produced predictions that were pretty close to one another — and not so good. As the researchers put it, "the submissions were much better at predicting each other than at predicting the truth." A reasonable lesson is that even with the aid of AI, we really do not understand the relationship between where families are in one year and where they will be a few years hence. Seeming to draw that lesson, the authors of the Fragile Families Challenge suggest that their results "raise questions about the absolute level of predictive performance that is possible for some life outcomes, even with a rich data set." You can learn a great deal about where someone now is in life, and still you, or AI, might not be able to say very much at all about specific outcomes in the future.

As GPT-4o put it in 2024,

> At the time, the challenge highlighted the difficulty of predicting these outcomes, even with advanced machine learning techniques. One of the key findings was that models, while powerful, struggled with out-of-sample prediction. Many researchers found that human lives are influenced by so many complex and often random factors that standard models didn't perform as well as anticipated.

That sounds a lot like Hayek, writing a long time ago. Asked whether AI could do better today, it responded, "predicting human behavior and life outcomes remains incredibly challenging due to the inherent complexity and unpredictability of life events. AI models, no matter how advanced, would still struggle with randomness, unmeasured variables, and ethical concerns regarding fairness and bias."

Let us put to one side the point about randomness. Let us also (temporarily!) put aside ethical considerations, which do not bear on predictive accuracy. Let us focus on unmeasured variables, or the absence of relevant data, which are Hayek's concern as well. Consider a girl named Susan, who is ten years old, and learn everything you can about her: her family, her demographics, her neighborhood, her schooling, her sports. Now predict various things about her life at the age of twenty-one. Will she be a doctor? A lawyer? A computer scientist? Do you have much confidence in your prediction?

You shouldn't. The number of variables that can move a life in one direction or another is very high, and it is not possible to foresee them in advance. Someone might break a leg at a crucial moment, meet an amazing music teacher, find a new friend, hear a song on the radio on Sunday morning, or see something online or on the news that changes everything.

Love and Romance

Can AI algorithms predict whether you will fall in love with a stranger? Can AI help people to find romantic partners?

Thus far, the results on such counts are not promising. Samantha Joel and colleagues, in a study of "machine learning applied to initial romantic attraction," find that AI algorithms struggle to predict "the compatibility elements of human mating . . . before two people meet," even if one has a very large number of "self-report measures about traits and preferences that past researchers have identified as being relevant to mate selection." Again sounding a lot like Hayek, Joel and her colleagues suggest that romantic attraction may well be less like a chemical reaction with predictable elements than "like an earthquake, such that the dynamic and chaos-like processes that cause its occurrence require considerable additional scientific inquiry before prediction is realistic."

What are "dynamic and chaos-like processes"? It is worth pondering exactly what this means. Most modestly, it might mean that AI needs far more data in order to make accurate predictions — far more, at least, than is provided by self-report measures about traits and preferences ("considerable additional scientific inquiry"). Such measures might tell us far too little about whether one person will be attracted to another. Perhaps we need more information about the relevant people, and perhaps we should focus on something other than such measures. It is possible that AI cannot make good predictions if it learns (for example) that Jane is an extrovert and that she likes football and Chinese food. It is possible that AI algorithms would do a lot better if they learn that Jane fell for John, who had certain characteristics that draw her to him, and also for Tom and Frank, who had the same characteristics. If so, perhaps she is most unlikely to fall for Fred, who has none of those characteristics, but quite likely to fall for Eric, who shares those characteristics with John, Tom, and Frank.

On this view, the right way to predict romantic attraction is to say, "If you like X and Y and Z, you will also like A and B, but not C and D!" Or perhaps we should ask whether people who are like Jane, in the relevant respects, are also drawn to Eric. Of course it would be necessary to identify the relevant respects in which people are like Jane, and that might be exceedingly challenging. Maybe AI could be helpful in that endeavor. Maybe not.

More radically, we might read the findings by Joel and her colleagues to suggest that romantic attraction is not predictable by AI algorithms for a different and more Hayekian reason: it depends on so many diverse factors, and on so many features of the particular context and the particular moment, that any form of AI will not be able to do very well in specifying the probability that Jane will fall for Eric. The reference to "dynamic and chaos-like processes" might be a shorthand way of capturing current mood, weather, location, time of day, background sounds, and a large assortment of other factors that help produce a sense of romantic connection or its absence.

Think a bit, if you would, about what made you feel a romantic spark. Did someone look at you in a certain way, at a certain moment, and then boom? What led to that boom? Do you even know?

Jane might smile at a specific time at a street corner, and look Eric in the eye, and Eric's heart might flutter. Or Jane might not look Eric in the eye at that moment, because she is distracted by something that happened in the morning. Eric might say something witty as sandwiches arrive, because of something he read in the paper that morning, and that might initiate a chain of events that culminates in marriage and children. Or Jane might make a bad joke at a bad time, and Eric might think, "This really will not work."

For romance, so much may depend on factors that cannot be identified in advance. This is the sense in which AI is sometimes like centralized planners: it does not have relevant information about time and place. Even the largest language models will still lack crucial data. (Continuing the Hayekian market analogy, there does not seem to be anything like the price system to replace AI with.)

Careful

We have to be careful here. AI might be able to say that there is essentially no chance that Jane will like Carl, because there are things about Carl that we know, in advance, to be deal-breakers for Jane. Jane might not be drawn to short men or to tall men. She might not be attracted to much older men or to much younger men. She might not be attracted to men. An algorithm might be able to say that there is some chance that Jane will like Bruce; there is nothing about Bruce that is a deal-breaker for her, and there are some clear positives for her. Perhaps an algorithm can specify a range of probability that Jane will fall for Bruce; perhaps the probability of a romantic connection (suitably defined) is more than ten percent but less than seventy percent. An algorithm might be able to say that Eric is within the category of "it might well happen" for Jane, because Eric is in some sense "her type."

Perhaps an algorithm can specify a range of probability for Jane and Eric; perhaps the probability of a romantic connection (suitably defined) is more than twenty percent but less than eighty percent. The real question is whether and to what extent AI will eventually be able to do much better than that. We might speculate that the importance of particular factors — the concrete circumstances — is so great that there are real limits on AI's predictive power (even if AI might be able to outperform human beings, whose own predictive power is sharply limited in this context).

The topic of romantic attraction is intriguing in itself, and it can be seen as overlapping with an assortment of other prediction problems: whether you will enjoy living in Paris; whether you will become friends with a co-worker; whether you will like a new job; whether a pandemic will occur in the next five years; whether a recession will occur in the next six months; whether a new movie will be make a specified amount of money; whether a new book will hit the bestseller list. We have seen that in stable environments with fixed rules, AI algorithms, armed with a great deal of data, are able to make pretty good predictions. But if the future is unlikely to be like the past, there is a real question whether, where, and when AI algorithms will do well, or even outperform human beings.

The Hayekian problem might be the sheer number of relevant factors, not knowable in advance, that might produce one or another outcome; this is why the case of romantic attraction has general lessons. (Friendship is similar.) Another problem might be an external shock or unexpected event, which might turn everything around (a technological innovation, a terrorist attack, a pandemic, or in the context of romance, a recent loss for Jane, which opens her heart). Yet another problem might be how factors interact with each other (lasagna followed by chocolate cake might spell romance). We are speaking here of the essentially unpredictable nature of many events, because of the absence of necessary data.

Revolution Is in the Air

In an important work called *Private Truths, Public Lies*, which predated the rise of AI, the economist Timur Kuran urged that revolutions were unpredictable by their very nature. Kuran argued that an underlying problem lies in "preference falsification": people do not disclose their preferences, which means that we cannot know whether they will, in fact, be receptive to a revolutionary movement. If we do not know what people's preferences are, we will not know whether they might be willing to participate in a rebellion given the proper circumstances.

I asked GPT4o whether AI could predict revolutions, and it said this:

> Predicting revolutions or large-scale social upheavals is extremely challenging, even for modern AI. While AI has advanced significantly in its ability to analyze complex data, revolutions are driven by a mix of structural factors (e.g., economic inequality, political repression) and unpredictable triggers (e.g., sudden political decisions, individual actions, or random events). The difficulty lies in the dynamic, multi-layered nature of these events. . . . Revolutions often result from unforeseen or seemingly minor events that AI may not anticipate — so-called "black swan" events. For instance, the Arab Spring was sparked by the self-immolation of a Tunisian street vendor, an act that set off widespread protests across the Middle East. . . . AI relies heavily on historical data to make predictions, but reliable data on political discontent, underground movements, or the true state of public sentiment is often scarce, especially in authoritarian regimes. . . . The most AI can do is flag societies at risk and provide real-time alerts to possible flashpoints.

It is true that we, and AI, might be able to learn something about when a revolution is improbable in the extreme, and also about when a revolution is at least possible. For one thing, we might be able to make at least some progress in identifying private preferences — for example, by helping people feel safe to say that they dislike the status quo, perhaps by showing sympathy with that view, or perhaps by guaranteeing anonymity. AI might well be able to help on that count. Kuran wrote before the emergence of social media platforms, which give us unprecedented opportunities to observe hitherto unobservable preferences — for example, via prompts, posts, and google searches, which might reveal widespread dissatisfaction with the current government.

Perhaps AI can say something about probabilities, based on data of this kind. But if GPT is right, AI will not be able to tell us a whole lot, because its knowledge of preferences and thresholds will be limited, and because it will not be able to foresee social interactions. The general analysis should not be limited to revolutions. Preference falsification, diverse thresholds, and social interactions — one or more of these are in play in many domains.

When will marriages break up? When will employees engage in some kind of revolt? When will we see something like #MeToo? When will a populist movement emerge and succeed? AI might be able to tell us something, but not nearly everything.

Hits!

Consider the question whether books, movies, or musical albums are likely to succeed. Of course we might know that a new album by Taylor Swift is likely to do well, and that a new album by a singer who is both terrible and unknown is likely to fail. A few decades ago I was part of a rock group called Serendipity. You haven't heard of us, and we were terrible; there was no chance that we could succeed. You don't need AI to know that. But across a wide range, a great deal depends on social interactions and apparent accidents, and on who says or does what exactly when. In such circumstances, AI might not be able to help much.

This point clearly emerges from research from a number of years ago, when Matthew Salganik, Duncan Watts, and Peter Dodds investigated the sources of cultural success and failure in what is known as their Music Lab experiment. Their starting point was that those who sell books, movies, television shows, and songs often have a great deal of trouble predicting what will succeed. Even experts make serious mistakes. Some products are far more successful than anticipated, whereas some are far less so. This seems to suggest, very simply, that those that succeed must be far better than those that do not. But if they are so much better, why are predictions so difficult? Why do the best analysts fail? No one anticipated the success of the *Harry Potter* series; the Beatles couldn't get a record deal; the rise of Donald Trump was a shock.

To explore the sources of cultural success and failure, Salganik and his co-authors created an artificial music market on a preexisting website. The site offered people an opportunity to hear forty-eight real but unknown songs by real but unknown bands. One song, by a band called Calefaction, was called "Trapped in an Orange Peel." Another, by Hydraulic Sandwich, was called "Separation Anxiety." The experimenters randomly sorted half of about fourteen thousand site visitors into an "independent judgment" group, in which they were invited to listen to brief excerpts, to rate songs, and to decide whether to download them. From those seven thousand visitors, Salganik and his coauthors could obtain a clear sense of what people liked best. The other seven thousand visitors were sorted into a "social influence" group, which was exactly the same except in just one respect: the social influence group could see how many times each song had been downloaded by other participants.

Those in the social influence group were also randomly assigned to one of eight subgroups, in which they could see only the number of downloads in their own subgroup. In those different subgroups, it was inevitable that different songs would attract different initial numbers of downloads as a result of unknown factors. "Trapped in an Orange Peel" might attract strong support from the first listeners in one subgroup, whereas it might attract no such support in another. "Separation Anxiety" might be unpopular in its first hours in one subgroup but attract a great deal of favorable attention in another.

The research questions were simple: would the initial numbers affect where songs would end up in terms of total number of downloads? Would the initial numbers affect the ultimate rankings of the forty-eight songs? Would the eight subgroups differ in those rankings? You might hypothesize that after a period, quality would always prevail — that in this relatively simple setting, where various extraneous factors (such as reviews) were highly unlikely to be at work, the popularity of the songs, as measured by their download rankings, would be roughly the same in the independent group and in all eight of the social influence groups.

It is a tempting hypothesis, but it is not at all what happened. "Trapped in an Orange Peel" could be a major hit or a miserable flop, depending on whether a lot of other people initially downloaded it and were seen to have done so. To a significant degree, everything turned on initial popularity. Almost any song could end up popular or not, depending on whether or not the first visitors liked it. Importantly, there is one qualification: the songs that did the very best in the independent judgment group rarely did very badly, and the songs that did the very worst in the independent judgment group rarely did spectacularly well. But otherwise almost anything could happen.

The apparent lesson is that success and failure in cultural markets is exceedingly hard to predict, whether we are speaking of AI or human beings. Here is one: it is exceedingly difficult to know, in advance, whether a cultural product will benefit from the equivalent of early downloads. True, knowing that is not unknowable in principle. If you knew everything about everything, you would know that, just as if you knew everything about everything, you would know whether a specific coin will come up heads or tails if I toss it in the air in the next second, or whether Carl and Eleanor are going to fall in love if they have lunch next Tuesday, or whether there is going to a revolution in a specific nation in February of next year. But it is not easy to know everything about everything.

Cute

What about business? What about products? Where do people want to travel? (Paris, Berlin, London, Copenhagen, Vienna, Prague, Beijing, Dublin, Amsterdam, Boston, New York?) Where do people want to study? What objects do people like or not like?

With respect to products, an experiment modeled on the Music Lab found the same pattern. The experiment involved "Meet the Ganimals," an online platform where people can generate and curate "ganimals," which are AI-generated hybrid animals. People can also say how much they like particular ganimals and rate them in terms of cuteness, creepiness, realism, and other variables.

As in the Music Lab experiment, people were sorted into groups with independent conditions, in which they made evaluations entirely on their own, and groups with social influence conditions, in which they could see what other people thought. Just as in the Music Lab experiment, participants were randomly assigned to one of multiple online "worlds," each of which evolved independently of the others. Participants saw only ganimals discovered and votes cast by others in their online world, and the ranking of ganimals was based only on votes in that world.

You might think that some ganimals really are adorable and that others really are not, and that in the end the adorable ones would be counted as adorable and the not-adorable ones would be counted as not-adorable. But here again, social influences greatly mattered. In the social influence worlds, outcomes turned out to be more unequal and highly unpredictable. Without social influences, different groups converged in their enthusiasm toward precisely the same set of ganimal features. (If you are curious: ganimals have eyes, a head, and dog-like features.) But with social influences, groups rapidly evolved into diverse local cultures that dramatically diverged from that in the independent judgment conditions. One ganimal could be spectacularly popular in one group and essentially unknown in another. The findings were very similar to those in the Music Lab.

Shall we draw a large lesson? Many markets have a lot in common with the market for ganimals. People aren't going to think that a gruesome ganimal is adorable. If you have something with eyes, a head, and dog-like features, you might be golden. But maybe not. Diverse local cultures can arise, and a fabulous product might get attention in one of them, and no attention at all in another. Could AI predict which products will get attention in which cultures? Maybe so. But maybe not, if social interactions, based on an assortment of factors on which data cannot be obtained in advance, turn out to be crucial. The success of Barack Obama in 2008 and Donald Trump in 2016 depended on such factors, and the same is true for the rise of Jane Austen, The Beatles, *Star Wars*, and Taylor Swift.

Knightian Uncertainty

In 1921, the great American economist Frank Knight wrote: "Uncertainty must be taken in a sense radically distinct from the familiar notion of Risk, from which it has never been properly separated. . . . The essential fact is that 'risk' means in some cases a quantity susceptible of measurement, while at other times it is something distinctly not of this character; and there are far-reaching and crucial differences in the bearings of the phenomena depending on which of the two is really present and operating." Knight was referring to what is now called "Knightian uncertainty": circumstances in which probabilities cannot be assigned to future events. The social theorist Jon Elster offers an example: "One could certainly elicit from a political scientist the subjective probability that he attaches to the prediction that Norway in the year 3000 will be a democracy rather than a dictatorship, but would anyone even contemplate acting on the basis of this numerical magnitude?"

Regulators, ordinary people, and AI are sometimes acting in situations of Knightian uncertainty (where outcomes can be identified but no probabilities can be assigned) rather than risk (where outcomes can be identified and probabilities assigned to various outcomes). Some people appear to think that AI creates an uncertain risk of catastrophe, including the extinction of the human race. Consider in this regard a passage from John Maynard Keynes, also writing in 1921:

> By "uncertain" knowledge, let me explain, I do not mean merely to

> distinguish what is known for certain from what is only probable. The game of roulette is not subject, in this sense, to uncertainty; nor is the prospect of a Victory bond being drawn. Or, again, the expectation of life is only slightly uncertain. Even the weather is only moderately uncertain. The sense in which I am using the term is that in which the prospect of a European war is uncertain, or the price of copper and the rate of interest twenty years hence, or the obsolescence of a new invention, or the position of private wealthowners in the social system in 1970. About these matters there is no scientific basis on which to form any calculable probability whatever. We simply do not know.

Sounding a lot like Knight, Keynes insisted that some of the time we cannot assign probabilities to imaginable outcomes. "We simply do not know."

Keynes immediately added, however, with evident bemusement, that "the necessity for action and for decision compels us as practical men to do our best to overlook this awkward fact and to behave exactly as we should if we had behind us a good Benthamite calculation of a series of prospective advantages and disadvantages, each multiplied by its appropriate probability, waiting to be summed." But how on earth, he wondered, do we manage to do that? Keynes listed three techniques — and they are worth considering when we leave behind the legends about AI and soberly assess its capabilities:

1. We assume that the present is a much more serviceable guide to the future than a candid examination of past experience would show it to have been hitherto. In other words, we largely ignore the prospect of future changes about the actual character of which we know nothing.
2. We assume that the existing state of opinion as expressed in prices and the character of existing output is based on a correct summing-up of future prospects, so that we can accept it as such unless and until something new and relevant comes into the picture.

3. Knowing that our own individual judgment is worthless, we endeavor to fall back on the judgment of the rest of the world which is perhaps better informed. That is, we endeavor to conform with the behavior of the majority or the average. The psychology of a society of individuals each of whom is endeavoring to copy the others leads to what we may strictly term a conventional judgment.

Keynes did not mean to celebrate those techniques. Actually he thought that they were ridiculous. We might know, for example, that technological innovations have not produced horrific harm in the past, and so we might think that AI will not produce such harm in the future. Or, as a good Hayekian, AI might look at the price signal to assess the risks associated with climate change. Or AI might follow the wisdom of crowds to assess the likelihood of a pandemic. But under circumstances of uncertainty, should we trust any of these methods? "All these pretty, polite techniques, made for a well-paneled Board Room and a nicely regulated market, are liable to collapse," Keynes declared, because "we know very little about the future." Those last seven words may seem simple or obvious, but they are not at all obvious to the inventors of and investors in the allegedly predictive algorithmic technologies that are now overwhelming our society.

Keynes emphasized the difficulty or the impossibility of assigning probabilities to outcomes, but he also signaled more generally the problem of ignorance, in which we are unable to specify either the probability of bad outcomes or their nature — where we do not even know the kinds or magnitudes of the harms that we are facing. One reason for our ignorance might be that we are dealing with a novel, unique, or non-repeatable event. Another reason might be that we are dealing with a problem involving interacting components of a system in which we cannot know how components of the system are likely to interact with each other, which means that predictions are highly unreliable.

Back to the Future

There are some prediction problems on which AI will not do well, and the reason lies in an absence of adequate data, and in what we might wisely see as the intrinsic unpredictability of (some) human affairs. In some cases, AI will be able to make progress over time. But in important cases, in which we are dealing with complex phenomena, and the real problem is that the relevant data are simply not available in advance, accurate predictions are impossible — not now, and not in the future. Never.

Consider now, if you would, a heartbreaking remark that Benjamin Franklin's sister Jane addressed to her brother, lamenting the "Thousands of Boyles Clarks and Newtons" who "have Probably been lost to the world, and lived and died in Ignorance and meanness, merely for want of being Placed in favourable Situations, and Injoying Proper Advantages." Who is placed in unfavourable situations? Who faces disadvantages? Both of these take diverse forms. We might speak of an absence of education; Franklin herself was not allowed proper schooling. We might speak of an absence of economic opportunity. Or we might speak more specifically, and less systematically, about the absence of a mentor, a helping hand, a nod of appreciation, a glimpse of something wondrous, an infusion of money, a year off, a friend or family member who refuses to give up.

In the domain of innovation in general, social scientists, sounding a lot like the despondent Jane Franklin, refer to "Lost Einsteins" — in the words of one of them, those "who would have had highly impactful inventions had they been exposed to innovation in childhood." The emphasis here is on demographic characteristics, such as race, gender, and socioeconomic status, and on the contributions of role models and network effects to success. Countless potential innovators, in science, business, and elsewhere, were subjugated in some way, were born in a particular family, did not find the right role models, or did not benefit from networks. As a result, they never innovated. They lost life's lottery, or a series of smaller lotteries.

There are lost Da Vincis, lost Shakespeares, lost Miltons, lost

Austens, lost Dickenses, lost Ellisons, lost Rothkos, lost Scorceses, lost Stan Lees, and lost Bob Dylans. There are lost Edisons and lost Doudnas and lost Teslas. (Nicolai, not the car.) There are plenty of them. They have been lost for a thousand and one different reasons. If innovators have been lost, it is not only because of demographic characteristics, but also because of a host of factors, not identifiable in advance, which did not work in their favor. Someone might not have given them a path, a smile at the right time, an infusion of energy, or a contract.

That conclusion might seem to point to a tragedy, even to countless tragedies — not only for those who have been lost, but also to those of us who have lost them, perhaps because they were never given an opportunity, perhaps because they were never given attention. In many ways, that is indeed tragic. But it also points to a possibility or perhaps even an inspiration. Lost Einsteins, or lost Shakespeares and Miltons, might be unlost, or found again. In fact they are being found every day. And if we can stay alert to the fact of their existence among us, many fewer will get lost in the first place. And that is a point about justice.

JAMES P. RUBIN

Two Slogans, Three Presidents, and the Fight for American Foreign Policy

I

With war raging in Ukraine indefinitely and instability flourishing in the Middle East and trade wars overwhelming our relations around the globe — and more generally with American leadership in the world deafeningly absent — the world appears to have been so completely transformed by Donald Trump's foreign policy that precedents may seem irrelevant to our understanding of our current situation. If we lead anything now, it is to make it worse. It may seem useless to look back even a few years, to the neolithic age when the Democratic Party was in charge of American foreign policy. But look back we must. For the obligations and the challenges of managing America's international relations will outlast any American government, and one day a Democrat will sit in the Oval Office again. When that happens, a return to what we used to think of as normalcy will be progress enough, though the magnitude of Trump's destruction of our position beyond our borders will take a long time to correct. But real success — the restoration of a rational and moral calculus of interests and values — will require that the right lessons, including the cautionary lessons, be learned from the Clinton, Obama, and Biden administrations.

The Trump administration's international orientation will be a partial guide in this new thinking: it will show us what *not* to do, unless we seek an isolated and insulated America. Even though there are isolationist currents in the Democratic Party, it is not a party with a tradition of America First. We are for enlightened world leadership. (A phrase that needs unpacking, of course.) We are against denying Vladimir Putin's responsibility for the invasion of Ukraine. We are for providing Ukraine the military support it needs to defend itself. We are against economic warfare with our friends and allies in Europe and Asia. We are for a strong NATO alliance and a strengthened security architecture with Asian allies, especially Japan, South Korea, Australia, and the Philippines. We still believe — I hope — that American power can be used for good in faraway places, and — I hope again — that the United States must act in the face of various kinds of emergencies and atrocities. And of course we emphasize the set of global issues that includes climate change, global health, and food security.

When the happy day comes and Trump is back home golfing and hustling, the immediate challenge will be to restore America's role as a leader, a friend, and an ally. The second Trump administration has in a matter of months squandered the soft power that took seventy-five years for America to create. With its economic warfare against friend and foe alike, as well as its disdainful attitude towards longstanding allies, trust and confidence in Washington's leadership has been shattered and it may never return to its previous heights. His capricious demolition of America's universally admired programs of foreign assistance amounts to a colossal blow to America's position in the world, not to mention the immensity of the suffering that is causing. It is so much easier to destroy than to build. But there will be no third Trump administration, and if the pendulum of American politics swings back towards the Democratic Party, it will be imperative to understand the foreign policies of the post-Cold War Democratic administrations with lucidity.

Today America cannot lead because America is alone. Unsplendid isolation, we might call it. Isolationism always fulfills its own dream. When the Trump administration looks behind, it will find few followers. And yet it will at the same time insist upon American supremacy! (I am ignoring, of course, the dizzying inconstancy of Trump's foreign policy, the daily and even hourly inconsistencies, which makes any generalization about it provisional and may prove to be the administration's worst failing in foreign affairs. For the next three years, the better part of diplomatic wisdom for the nations of the world will be to try and catch a wave.) The international reputation that the founding fathers of the post-World War II generation created for the United States, Democratic and Republican presidents alike, had a powerful result: the United States was a rare combination of feared, admired, and respected. To be sure, it was also hated, but anti-Americanism did not suffice to overthrow the America-led world order, especially after the collapse of the Soviet Union.

The erosion of the America-led world order was in fact begun by the United States. The Iraq war accomplished that, and in many ways it remains the gift that keeps on giving. ("Vietnam Syndrome" was nothing compared to this. Ronald Reagan was elected a mere five years after our retreat from Saigon.) Our reputation was damaged for at least a generation, as Dick Cheney and Donald Rumsfeld became the ugly Americans of a new era and the incompetence of the occupation of Iraq undermined America's reputation for getting the job done. Later, the post-Iraq reluctance to act under the Obama administration further weakened the deterrent effect of America's military might and taught the nations of the world to call America's bluff.

Any honest assessment of America's role in the world must start with the recognition that America's power has been grievously diminished in recent decades — notwithstanding the successful air attacks on Iran's nuclear facilities and, a decade earlier, the unforgettable Special Forces operation that killed Osama Bin Laden. For it is not just our economic, military, and political system that determines power, but also our alliances and friendships around the world: they are what has differentiated America's role from that of previous hegemons. (We were a hegemon, but we were never an empire; whatever that abused terms means, it does not denote a system of alliances.) By rejecting the daily diplomacy of alliance building and management, what former Secretary of State George Schultz nicely called "diplomacy as gardening," the two Trump administrations have done grievous and utterly self-inflicted harm to the force multiplier effect of America's alliances.

What is the foreign policy of the Democrats? In recent decades it has been deeply contested. The contest was between two ideas that were perfectly encapsulated in two colloquial slogans by two presidents. "Get caught tryin'," Bill Clinton instructed. "Don't do stupid shit," Barack Obama taught. Joe Biden left no epigram of his own, and his administration continued to be wracked by the debate, though in its responses to Russia's invasion of Ukraine and the war begun by Hamas' attacks on October 7, 2023, it seemed to be settling the matter with the proper respect for power and principle.

II

Bill Clinton often expressed regret that he was not president at a more dramatic moment in American history, such as World War II or the Civil War. History in the years of his presidency was not in overdrive, and it was without a trace of the apocalyptic tone. As it turned out, he presided over a remarkable period of peace and prosperity — not exactly a minor achievement. And when, in the Balkans, history demanded more than American prosperity but also American leadership and American action, he led the West (at first slowly and reluctantly) to a moment that *The Economist* called "the height of European civilization," owing to the U.S.-NATO decisions to bring a halt to the Serbian atrocities in Bosnia and to prevent a genocide against Kosovo's Albanian population.

In 1999, we combined force and diplomacy and defeated the aggression of Slobodan Milosevic in the heart of Europe. In an act of moral and humanitarian determination backed up by our hard power, we united to thwart an imminent mass slaughter of the Kosovar Albanians. Unlike Rwanda or Bosnia, this was a genocide prevented.

Equally important, the way in which Washington led in Kosovo was crucial. Extensive diplomacy led to widespread international support for the war, as the Belgrade government was given every possible chance to accept a peaceful solution. Working with key European allies and Moscow, a UN resolution laid out a postwar plan with the burden for deployment and reconstruction shared by all. In the end, Kosovo became a functioning emerging democracy and is now an independent state — and a tribute to Bill Clinton's and Madeleine Albright's commitment to get caught trying. Kosovo was done for the right reasons and it was done the right way. (As an official at the State Department in those years I played a role in this effort.) Like Bosnia, Kosovo demonstrated that it was possible to use force justly, and to use limited force for a limited goal. This does not mean it can be done in all places, only that it can be done in some places — and that is a lot.

The late 1980s and the 1990s were a dazzling moment in world history. Apartheid fell in South Africa. Soviet communism collapsed in Russia and in Eastern and Central Europe. At Tiananmen Square, countless Chinese demonstrated their dedication to democratic values. Democracy was indeed ascendant. But history was not over. (Has there ever been a dumber notion than "the end of history?") Perhaps because he was elected to focus on the economy and because the Democrats had been out of power for twelve years, the Clinton administration had an inauspicious beginning in foreign policy. Indeed, the combined chaos in Somalia, Haiti, and Bosnia managed to overshadow the outbreak of freedom and democratic change across Europe and Asia. But by the end of Clinton's first term, the ship of state was righted — beginning with the ouster of Haiti's dictators as a consequence of diplomacy backed by force and an endorsement by the United

Nations, and finally, after far too long, the air strikes against the Bosnian Serbs which led to the Dayton Accords in 1995. Ending the war in Bosnia, which President Clinton did with the help of President Chirac, proved an important lesson, showing how U.S.-led diplomacy backed by military power could be America's method of leadership. For the Clinton administration, unlike its Republican successors, deemed it important to pay "a decent respect to the opinion of mankind."

We got caught trying, and it worked. And having seen how force and diplomacy could genuinely resolve crises over Taiwan in 1996 (when two Aircraft Carrier Battle Groups were deployed near the Taiwan Straits, prompting Beijing to halt its intimidation of Taipei) and Iraq in 1998 (when Operation Desert Fox destroyed for a while Iraq's weapons of mass destruction programs after Saddam Hussein refused access to UN inspectors), the Clinton administration determined to take the lead in resolving international crises. Applying America's unique power position, as well as the prestige of the White House lawn, the Clinton administration embraced America's leadership role. Consider the remarkable diplomatic record of America the Peacemaker in that era. With President Clinton's help, lasting peace was established between Northern Ireland and the United Kingdom. In the Middle East, there was peace between Israel and Jordan, the Oslo Accords, and the Hebron and Wye River Accords, all of which saw the Palestinians given substantial autonomy and land and Israelis living in greater security. The challenge of North Korea's nuclear proliferation was also dealt with effectively in 1994 in the U.S.–North Korea nuclear accord. Secretary Albright was even dispatched to Pyongyang in the final weeks of the administration to get caught trying to stop North Korea from deploying long-range ballistic missiles.

And most famously of all, President Clinton himself got caught trying to secure the dream of a permanent Middle East peace at Camp David in 2000, along with Ehud Barak and Yasser Arafat, and later through the Clinton Parameters in his final days as president in 2001. A peace plan was even put forward by Clinton and Albright to the Syrian dictator Hafez Al Assad at Shepherdstown, West Virginia, which envisioned the return of the Golan Heights to Damascus in exchange for recognition and security for the State of Israel. But just like his fellow Baath Party thug Saddam Hussein, Assad would not take yes for an answer and rejected any reasonable outcome. Considering what later happened to Syria, it seems unimaginably foolish that Assad spurned Clinton's diplomatic offer back in 1999 and 2000.

This was American diplomacy at its most noble, pursuing solutions and working with difficult regimes on behalf of our friends and allies. Along with the prudent use of American power in Iraq, the Taiwan Straits, and the Balkans, it was this relentless pursuit of peace that generated substantial admiration and respect for the United States in those days. It was also during the second Clinton administration that NATO was enlarged to include Poland, Hungary, and the Czech Republic. With Albright leading the diplomacy, a way was found to bring security to Central and Eastern Europe from future Russian revanchism and still negotiate the NATO–Russia Founding Act, which saw Moscow acquiesce in diplomatic arrangements to ease the pain of losing former client states to the NATO alliance. (I recognize that the expansion of NATO is still controversial in some quarters, but the Russian aggression against Ukraine should have settled that dispute.)

In retrospect, the most significant mistake of Clinton's activism abroad was the effort to coax China into becoming a responsible member of the community of nations. At Clinton's behest, China was made a member of the World Trade Organization, and Beijing's response was to exploit the West's openness by growing (and stealing) its way to the point of becoming a rival and a potential threat to the West, as its phenomenal economic boom, its across-the-board adaptation of advanced technology, and its massive military build-up now jeopardizes America's technological edge and strategic paradigm. To be fair, our China policy was bipartisan. Leaders in both parties were under the illusion that China would become more and more transparent and abide by the rules of the trade game if given the chance. Indeed, it was during the first George W. Bush administration that Deputy Secretary of

State Robert Zoellick famously called for helping China to become a "responsible stakeholder" in international arrangements. But after Xi Jinping came to power some years later, nearly all concerned came to rue the day we gave China access to advanced technology and world markets.

What difference a Clintonian approach would have made in subsequent decades is, of course, unknowable. We do know that the Balkan model of force and diplomacy was consciously spurned during Bush's two terms. And President Obama, to my knowledge, never once cited Clinton's successes in Bosnia and Kosovo as a model worth emulating, even though it would have been natural enough for him to tout the previous Democratic president's successes. Perhaps he opposed them as a young legislator in Chicago. Many years later, by contrast, during the Syrian catastrophe, when Obama was idling in the White House, a friend (the editor of this journal) did ask Clinton what he would have done differently than Obama in Syria, and he replied: "I don't know, but I would have been caught tryin'."

III

The foreign policy of the Obama years was marked above all by a dire case of Iraq War Syndrome. Obama and his team did all they could to hype his early remark at a rally in Chicago in opposition to Bush's decision to invade Iraq. It was a stupid war, he said. And that, of course, led to the slogan that defined his foreign policy over two terms. On Air Force One, Obama famously told the White House press corps that his guiding principle was, "Don't do stupid shit." The cautionary example of Iraq became a kind of obsession-compulsion for Obama and his policymakers, as if it was all you needed to know about American power and the world.

On the surface, by restoring American support for European allies after the war and often deferring to them, much of the damage wrought by the Bush administration's bullying unilateralism was undone. Remember, even before the war in Iraq, Bush and Cheney and Rumsfeld had alienated nearly every single

American ally by rejecting a series of arms control treaties with Russia, including the ABM Treaty, the building block of them all negotiated by President Richard Nixon in 1972, as well as the Chemical Weapons Convention and the Biological Weapons Convention. To round it off, the administration pulled out of the Kyoto climate accords, and the immeasurably haughty Rumsfeld even expressed disdain for the Geneva Conventions regarding the treatment of prisoners of war. Obama's administration reversed all that, which was a good thing, and worked on climate change and restoring discussions with Russia about strategic nuclear arms. Combined with the fact of twice electing an African American as president, America's reputation was substantially restored as admiration for Obama the man soared around the world and allied governments found it easy to work with Obama's diplomatic team, led in the first term by Secretary of State Hillary Clinton, who proved to be enormously popular on the world stage. When U.S. Special Forces finally located and killed Osama Bin Laden in a dramatic raid inside Pakistan in 2011, many observers judged that respect for American leadership "was back."

Yet brilliant as his anti-war stance was politically, since most Americans had turned against the mission after the disasters of the American-led occupation, the ground truth on Obama and Iraq was much more confusing. Although few in the Washington press corps wanted to focus on it, in a moment of candor Obama revealed to one of his most determined admirers, David Remnick of *The New Yorker*, that if he had been a senator in 2003 and read all of those flawed intelligence reports detailing Saddam Hussein's extensive possession of chemical and biological weapons, he might well have voted for the second Gulf war, as Hillary Clinton and Joe Biden and John Kerry did. Despite this acknowledgement, however, his campaign team and his White House aides regularly pilloried those senators. When he ran for president, Obama's sole credential in foreign policy was his progressive opposition to the war from the start, but it turns out that his claim to greater wisdom than the Democratic establishment was not exactly true. While politically Obama got away with hanging the war in Iraq around

Hillary Clinton's neck in the primaries in 2008, he must not have felt his anti-war position too strongly, since it did not inhibit him from appointing pro-Iraq Democrats to be his Vice-President and both of his Secretaries of State and to direct his foreign policy.

The confusion in the Democratic Party on this fundamental question surely contributed to the essential confusion at the heart of Obama's foreign policy. He pulled out of Iraq and then was forced to return American forces with the rise of the Islamic State in the vacuum left by the American withdrawal. He famously surged U.S. forces in Afghanistan after a lengthy policy review and then undercut that surge by establishing a short and public timeline for the withdrawal of the troops that were to be sent in, signaling to the Taliban they should just wait us out.

But the real damage done by the Obama administration was in its failure to follow through with the threat to use force in Syria — the infamous red line that wasn't a red line. The American president was caught bluffing. This stupendous blunder, blunder was opposed by nearly all his foreign policy team save for his Chief of Staff Denis McDonough, who walked him around the White House lawn to cook up his last-minute call for a congressional vote on the intervention that he had promised and upon which the global credibility of the United States depended. This prevarication led to the swift intrusion of Vladimir Putin and Russia into Syria and the region — and the Russian government, perhaps fearing for its personnel who at the time were conducting clandestine chemical experiments at Syrian facilities, obligingly arranged for a disarmament program for Syria's chemical weapons, which allowed Obama to avoid conducting even the limited air attacks that were under consideration. The man who never wanted to be a war president no doubt slept more easily, but Syria descended further into hell, along with the global reputation of the United States.

This was stupid shit *par excellence*. Yes, Syria's chemical arsenal was dismantled. (The fact that Bashir al Assad immediately agreed to surrender the entirety of his chemical arsenal — or almost the entirety of it, as his later use of chemical weapons revealed — is evidence of how afraid he was of American military intervention.) But the damage to America's leadership in the world was done. Their oh-so-clever stratagem proved far more consequential than Obama and his chief of staff must have imagined. America's friends and allies in Europe, the Middle East, and Asia uniformly argued that they could no longer count on an American president to follow through on his commitment to use military power. Talking to a top French national security official at the time, I was met with a visceral attack on American leadership and furious claims of irreparable damage to Western policy in the Middle East. The Kremlin took Obama's reversal as a golden opportunity to return to Syria, to deploy its modernized air and ground forces, and show what a real ally does. And with the help of Iran's Al Quds force, Russia applied the brutal lessons learned in Chechnya to flatten rebel cities across Syria. Assad's savage hold on power was soon re-established, leading to the horror of an estimated half a million Syrians killed and almost an entire population internally and externally displaced, not to mention the additional negative blandishment of Iran gaining suzerainty over the country and a base on the Mediterranean Sea. Syria was the worst case of American bystanderism in our time.

Ironically, it was President Trump a few years later who exposed the stupidity of Obama's fear that the use of air power in Syria would lead to another Iraq-like disaster. Trump had also disparaged the Iraq war, but he had no problem following through on his threats to use American air power when chemical weapons were used against Syrian civilians. Indeed, he launched moderate-sized air attacks on the Syrian military twice in response to their violations of his red lines. And in a twist of fate that still boggles the mind, owing to the proven credibility of Trump's threats to use force, Assad — and Putin — were deterred by a Trump tweet from finishing off the rebel alliance in Idlib, a small province in the north where rebels and dissidents and refugees were holed up. And it was those very rebels nearly a decade later who launched the rebellion that overthrew Assad this year, allowing the Biden administration and then the Trump administration to support

Syria's transformation into a relatively free country, now no longer under American sanctions and working on a diplomatic settlement with Israel. This extraordinary development was one of the delayed consequences of the calibrated but determined use of American (and later Israeli) power.

In retrospect, however, it was the Obama administration's approach to Putin's invasion of Crimea and Eastern Ukraine in 2014 that looks to have been even more consequential than the Syrian red line debacle. For the Obama administration essentially abdicated any leadership role in the response to Putin's invasion, despite the fact that the United States had offered a security assurance to Ukraine in the Budapest Memorandum in 1994 in return for Kyiv giving up its Soviet nuclear weapons after the fall of the Soviet Union. Yes, there was a half-hearted sanctions package imposed on Russia, and some Obama officials did condemn Putin's brazen invasion. But two decisions stand out ten years later. First, Obama declared publicly that he believed that Russia had "escalation dominance at every level" in Europe. Even if true, the signaling of such an assumption to Russia is unforgivably hard to fathom. It gave Putin a green light. (Nor was it necessarily true.) And all the while the Democrats were still deriding Mitt Romney's comment in the presidential debate two years earlier that "Russia is, without question, our number one geopolitical foe." Such a view, they said, was "so nineteenth-century."

Secondly, Washington absented itself from the diplomacy that ended the initial Russian assault. It was the French president, Nicolas Sarkozy, and the German Chancellor, Angela Merkel, who negotiated directly with Putin, leading to the endless arguments and violations of the resulting Minsk Agreement. I am absolutely certain that in her time Madeleine Albright would have resigned if her president had instructed her to absent herself from a diplomatic settlement of a Russian military assault in the heart of Europe. Inaction was the American response to Putin's invasion of 2014, which is why Putin probably never expected the West to act so decisively eight years later when he launched a full-fledged invasion.

When it came to humanitarian aid, the Obama administration's caution and fear of signaling any American involvement became both tragic and farcical. After ruling out military assistance to Ukraine, including purely defensive weapons, a ban was imposed on non-lethal assistance, such as uniforms and vehicles. The one measure of assistance eventually authorized by Obama was humanitarian assistance — and here his inaction became an absurdity. While a hapless Pentagon official began filling a U.S. transport plane with MREs and other emergency supplies to fly to Ukraine, last-minute orders came directly from the White House national security leadership to stand down. They feared how Moscow would interpret the arrival of a military plane loaded with food aid. They did not want to "provoke the Russians." And so a German shipping company was contracted to deliver the food at far greater cost.

Then there was Libya. When an uprising against its dictator exploded, and the Obama administration reluctantly participated in air strikes against the Qaddafi regime, a top Obama aide promulgated an imperishable concept. President Obama and his administration were not ceding leadership to Paris and London, he said; not at all. The United States was "leading from behind." Given the half-hearted American effort — I remember British officials were livid that the United States was refusing to replenish European aircraft with American weapons after the French and the British ran out of bombs and missiles — it was no surprise when the Libyan intervention became a muddle. Qaddafi was killed, but the chaos and instability persists to this day. Our participation in the Libyan operation is now remembered as a case of excessive American intervention, but in truth it was a case of insufficient American intervention. Having procured a perfect Security Council resolution to justify Western action and lead an international response, the Obama administration declined the opportunity and entered the fray with the overwhelming objective of getting out of it. And so we left Libya to its anarchy.

As a result of the debacle in Libya, the red line reversal in Syria, and the determined inaction after Putin invaded

Crimea, not to mention Obama's lukewarm response to the democratic rebellion in Iran in 2009 and his confused response to the democratic rebellion in Egypt in 2011, respect and fear of Washington precipitously declined. Of course, after four years of the first Trump administration, much of the world welcomed the arrival of a new Democratic administration led by Obama's Vice President, Joe Biden.

IV

A British prime minister famously declared that it is "events, dear boy, events" that determine a country's statecraft. Improvisation is at the heart of foreign-policymaking; otherwise your values and your interests stand no chance of being realized. Events during Biden's term in office did just that. The record is mixed. While he made important strategic decisions, for good and for ill, regarding Afghanistan and American policy toward China, Biden's four years in foreign policy will be remembered mainly for Washington's response to the invasion of Ukraine in February 2022 and to Hamas' attack on Israel of October 7, 2023, and the subsequent war in Gaza. Having worked directly for Biden from 1988 to 1993 and collaborated with him extensively afterwards, I can testify that he was uncannily well-suited to understand the threat from Putin's Russia and to rally European and international support for Ukraine after the Russian invasion. It is hard to think of another plausible Democratic candidate for president in our time who would have done what Biden did to rally the world in defense of Ukraine's sovereignty and independence — the world and his own wobbly post-Obama party.

The Biden team quickly realized that the Trump administration was right in seeking to slow down the threat from China rather than advocating China's rise with WTO-type Obama-and-Clinton-style happy talk. While agreeing with the Trump administration's threat assessment, however, the Biden administration's approach was thankfully different. Instead of insulting and bullying crucial allies, Biden and his Secretary of State, Antony

Blinken, would build a grand alliance to counter China across the board. The Trump administration thought commercially, but the Biden administration thought strategically. From building up the military capabilities of allies through AUKUS (Australia and the United Kingdom), and by means of new arrangements with India, Japan, South Korea, and the Philippines, from critical minerals to high technology, "de-risking" was the term of the hour; and unique efforts were also made to unite European and Asian allies to prevent economic and military coercion by the Chinese Communist Party. An all-of-government effort was established. Biden was determined to prevent China from dominating the Indo-Pacific or displacing America's world leadership.

And by the end of the administration something remarkable was taking place. Europeans had moved from seeking an investment treaty to integrate the European and Chinese economies to working with Washington to penalize Beijing's decision to go all in on behalf of Russia in what it called a "no limits" partnership. At the same time, Asian allies were increasingly integrated into NATO and supporting Ukraine's defense against Russian aggression. Biden's and Blinken's diplomacy, combined with extensive intelligence briefings on the Chinese military build-up and its extensive support for Russia's war economy, helped link Asian and European allies in unprecedented ways, so that allies from the Atlantic and the Pacific were coordinating with Washington to contain the threat arising from the Russia–China partnership.

For a Democratic president, this was neither obvious nor easy. Not only would European allies be wary if Washington failed to stabilize its relationship with China, but many in the Democratic Party have come around only slowly to the idea that China is somehow a threat to the West. (Some prominent Democrats have yet to assent to that proposition.) That is why Biden and Blinken started by demonstrating responsible management of the crucial diplomatic dance with Beijing. And for similar reasons — managing but not wanting to overstate or to stimulate the threat posed by China and Russia — Biden began by seeking a summit with Putin to try and stabilize the Russian relationship as he built political and diplomatic support to confront the new Chinese challenge. Of course, that effort came to naught when the bilious Putin continued to spout his grievances regarding everything from NATO expansion to the invasion of Iraq and alleged American interference in Russian political affairs. Soon Putin's massive conventional build-up around Ukraine rendered any hope for a *modus vivendi* hopeless.

Meanwhile there was a second Biden decision of enormous consequence: to move forward with Trump's Afghanistan policy by withdrawing American troops from that country. A failure to quit Afghanistan would have required the re-opening of negotiations with the Taliban, with all the attendant uncertainty. Since I didn't join the administration until December 2022, I was not privy to the internal discussions and cannot provide an answer to the obvious question of why President Biden did not pursue the approach that Vice President Biden had advocated back in 2009, namely to reduce the American footprint in Afghanistan to a minimal role of countering terrorism but leaving the larger mission of defending the Afghan government from the Taliban insurgency to the Afghans themselves. Presumably, President Biden did not believe that the residual terrorist threat in Afghanistan justified continuing what Trump and many Democratic leaders insisted on calling a "forever war" rather than a long-term deployment like the ones we continue to maintain in strategically significant areas of the world. (This, notwithstanding the difference between monitoring the armistice line in Korea or maintaining bases in Europe and defending against a determined adversary like the Taliban.)

The failures of planning and the abysmal coordination in our withdrawal from Afghanistan troubled all Americans, but they were especially hard for a Democrat to watch. As American troops withdrew from Bagram Air Base, the elected government of Ashraf Ghani collapsed and a jubilant Taliban resumed their oppression of many millions of Afghans. And despite heroic efforts to evacuate hundreds of thousands of Afghans, particularly those who had courageously assisted us in our efforts, it is hard to deny that the way we withdrew evoked memories of the disastrous Iraqi occupation ten years earlier and even of Vietnam in 1975, and seriously weakened the reputation of the U.S. military and its political leadership. Until the Kremlin archives are opened, we will never know to what extent, if at all, the botched withdrawal from Afghanistan had any impact on Putin's calculation to invade Ukraine. My guess is very little, because Putin was under the false impression that his attack would succeed in a matter of days and he could present the world with a *fait accompli*.

Yet Biden and his team surely proved their mettle from the moment Putin's intention to invade became incontrovertible. First, an extraordinary effort was made to downgrade highly classified intelligence information and make it available to the public to warn Ukraine and America's allies of the imminent invasion. This exceedingly unusual intelligence downgrade was immensely important. Following the debacle of Saddam Hussein's alleged arsenal of weapons of mass destruction, the standing of the American intelligence community took a hit. Not only did doubt about the accuracy of intelligence make it harder to win support in a crisis, but the power of intelligence diplomacy to persuade friends and allies of future threats was weakened as well. In a tragic way, Putin's invasion was a kind of vindication for the U.S. intelligence community. After all, key European allies and many others were convinced that Washington was once again wrong. Working at the OECD in Paris at the time, I can attest to the fact that German and French officials up and down the line refused to believe that Moscow would do something so dangerous and so stupid. By warning them, America restored some lost luster and helped Paris and Berlin as they responded with real solidarity to change their strategy and break their budgetary restraints and their traditional caution in response to the aggression.

More significant than the intelligence diplomacy was Washington's overall world leadership after the invasion began and it became clear that Ukraine would not be quickly overrun, as many in the West feared. Given the troubled history of American foreign policy in the years prior to the Ukraine war, and especially given the dogmas and the debates inside the Democratic Party, few would have believed that the Biden administration would be able to galvanize such a solid coalition of nearly every country in Europe and many more in Asia to impose economic sanctions, freeze hundreds of billions of dollars of Russian assets, and provide hundreds of billions of dollars more in concrete military assistance, including modern tanks, aircraft, artillery, and multiple variants of missiles and drones. It is true that, from the standpoint of Ukraine's needs, the pace of delivery of American and NATO weapons was slow and halting, but the far more important point here is that President Biden rejected the view of his predecessor that Moscow had some kind of "escalation dominance" that required Western countries to stand down or risk defeat in a conventional or even some kind of nuclear confrontation. Yes, Biden moved carefully and cautiously when it came to arming and training the Ukrainian military, but there was an undeniable logic to his strategy: given Putin's repeated attempts to drive a wedge among European countries and between Europe and the United States by repeatedly threatening nuclear escalation, Biden insisted that the NATO allies cross the Rubicon together. NATO unity was Putin's nightmare, and the Biden administration wanted NATO to provide more and better weapons as a united alliance.

The internal dynamics in the administration developed a certain pattern. The State Department would advocate and the Pentagon would equivocate. Consider two examples. The M1 tank episode was classic. The debate over this weapon system, over whether and when it should be given to the Ukrainians, involved the Pentagon correctly pointing out how difficult it would be to use the weapon, how complicated its logistical requirements were, and how few were available. Meanwhile, since America was not providing its best tank, Germany was refusing to provide its most modern tank, the Leopard. While early transfers of these weapons might not have changed the military balance, they surely would have helped. With the Pentagon stalling, Blinken eventually persuaded the president that the issue was not the tank itself, but whether the threshold of transferring a state-of-the-art tank would be crossed, in which case Germany and other Europeans could furnish the tanks, which were more readily available and did not contain the logistical tail of the M1. In the end, Biden decided to move forward with a small American deployment right away, which was the signal for the German and European transfers to proceed. Then there was continued debate over providing the Army Tactical Missile System, or ATACMs, a medium-range surface-to-surface missile. Here again Blinken had to argue it out with Pentagon officials over the details of the weapon's utility. Since most Russian airfields had moved beyond the range of ATACMS, and since it was the Russian aircraft that were such a threat, Pentagon officials protested that the ATACMS would have minimal effect in blunting the Russian advantage — until new information emerged that the Russian Air Force envisioned the refueling and refitting of those same aircraft on their way to Ukraine at airfields within the range of ATACMS.

Biden's policy of active and generous and unintimidated support of Kyiv accomplished nothing less than the overcoming of the taboos on American action that were established by the Iraq War. This time the syndrome took the hit. This was a momentous achievement, at least if the United States is not to shrink into a small-minded and selfish country. You might even say that, temporarily at least, Putin's war brought many Democrats, led by Biden, back to their senses, or more specifically, back to their sense of history, which of course encompasses more than Baghdad and Falluja. And the great irony is that what made Biden's forceful leadership possible was precisely his age. Among leaders in the Democratic Party, only he had been around long enough to remember and to understand that when Europe and the United States stand in solidarity, ultimately Moscow cannot sustain its aggressive stance. That was the lesson of the Berlin crisis in 1948 and the Cuban missile crisis of 1962, and the reason why the Cold War ended with the collapse of Soviet communism. Biden was not only post-Iraq, he was also post-World War II. His paradigm for American foreign policy was broader and deeper — and more knowledgeable — than certain doctrines of the Democratic Party in our time. He contested those doctrines and banished them to the margins, at least for now.

In addition to the Ukraine war, the war against Hamas has had a dramatic effect on perceptions of American power and international leadership, and not in the way most would expect. This is not the place for an extended discussion of what the Biden administration did and did not do in support of Israel from October 7, 2023, until January 20, 2025. I understand that this is the most bitter debate of our day, and the most morally excruciating one. I want only to note that the steadfast American support for Israel against Hamas, Hezbollah, and Iran, demonstrated with the provision of air defense systems such as the THAAD (as well as $16 billion in wartime assistance), was noted by leaders in the Middle East and beyond. Those leaders also saw a glimpse of the future when Washington organized European countries and key Arab countries to work with CENTCOM in a comprehensive defense of Israel's air space. This was the work of an ally and a leader. (The Biden administration hoped that its fierce support of Israel in the aftermath of the Hamas atrocities would give it leverage to moderate Israel's conduct of the subsequent war in Gaza, but in this it failed.) Having accompanied Secretary Blinken to a number of intense discussions with European and Arab leaders, I saw respect and admiration for America — not least for its prowess and its strength of will — expressed even by hard-boiled figures like Mohammed Bin Salman of Saudi Arabia. In the latter's case, he told us emphatically that Biden's steadfastness regarding Ukraine and Israel had persuaded him that Saudi Arabia's long-term future lies with Washington and not with Beijing.

So the larger strategy worked. By doing the hard work of diplomacy, by not disparaging friends and allies who may not agree, by standing by our friends in time of crisis, and by meeting the global responsibilities imposed on us by our own power, the Biden administration, despite some missteps, restored American foreign policy to its proper level, to its moral traditions and its strategic strengths.

V

If Barack Obama's diffident withdrawalism made the nations of the world skeptical of American will and anxious about American reliability as an ally, Donald Trump's erratic commerce-driven America First-ism has driven them to despair. Will a "snapback" in foreign policy be possible after a second Trump term? Certainly not if a Republican succeeds him. For this reason, Democrats must be lucid about what happened during the last three Democratic administrations, so as to prepare themselves intellectually and politically to maintain America's role as an indispensable leader in Europe and Asia. Sure, with "burden-sharing" and higher defense spending among our allies. But the real issue is not who pays what, but who leads where.

While many commentators are right to lament the trainwreck of alliance relationships wrought by Trump, the larger problem is that many Americans have lost trust in their government since the debacle of Iraq. Skepticism about American power, about the possibility that it can be used for good and not for ill, is now received wisdom among the letter generations (X, Y and Z), many of whom probably nod their heads sullenly in agreement with Trump's isolationist tropes. Isolationism, after all, has never been confined to the American right. Why should America defend South Korea? Who cares if China invades Taiwan? Isn't it a Chinese island? Is Israel still a strategic asset deserving of our support? Is it worth risking World War III to protect those rich Europeans with their cradle-to-grave social services, and why don't they devote as much national effort to military matters as we do? Isn't the deployment of American soldiers in foreign lands nothing but imperialism? These questions will increase in force in the coming years, not least owing to the new elan of the progressives within the Democratic Party. It is way too late to count on the perdurability of the foreign-policy worldview that sustained us — and many other nations — before 2003 and the Obama retrenchment. Many Americans probably also agree with Trump's sensible-sounding "spheres of interest," whereby Beijing dominates Asia, the Kremlin dominates Eastern Europe and other parts of Eurasia, and the

United States brings back the Monroe doctrine to dominate Latin America, with maybe Canada and Greenland thrown in.

What is most important is for the United States and its allies in Europe and Asia and North America to develop a common threat assessment. Difficult times lie ahead; great power rivalries and worse. The combination of Russia's modern day war economy and China's massive build-up of ships, missiles, strategic nuclear weapons, and space and air capabilities poses a threat such as we have never seen before. If we further take into account a ruthless North Korean dictator with nuclear weapons and whatever remains of Iran's military and terrorist capabilities, we cannot avoid the conclusion — which many Americans would like to avoid — that the so-called Axis of Authoritarians must be countered and — to use the still-valuable Cold War term — contained.

We might begin with a concept of "dual containment." Instead of shying away from the word "containment" in the case of China because of its extensive involvement in the world economy, the next administration should follow on the Biden approach with the added candor of using the C-word. Citing "dual containment" in the context of Russia and China will also provide clarity and a sense of purpose to American foreign policy in a chaotic and pitiless world. As long as the next president responsibly manages the relationship with Beijing's leader, then European and Asian allies will not shy away from strengthening the security arrangements necessary to prevent and deter an aggressive CCP-led China from seeking to dominate Asia and the crucial sea lanes in the South and East China seas, not to mention pursuing its "we are a big power" intimidation of our friends and allies around the world. And by banding together when it comes to crucial minerals, rare earths, semiconductors, and other emergent technologies, China's use of economic and technological blackmail can be contained as well.

It is past time for a revival of the mid-twentieth-century approach when the founding fathers of containment designed an enlightened global role for the United States — no, it didn't always work perfectly! — and then developed a rational and empirically based threat assessment and then constructed a rational and empirically based plan of action. The next president can candidly lay out what China seeks, and the phenomenal military build-up of Russian and Chinese military and high technology weapons, to justify a new and firm policy of dual containment. And instead of demanding that the United States bear most of the burden, a renaissance of alliances can be launched instead. We do not have to do it all, but unless we want an Orwellian world order dominated by the Chinese Communist Party — aided and abetted by Putin's Russia with a boost from the brutal militarized dictatorship of Kim's North Korea — we need to lead. MAGAists cannot be expected to understand this, or to grasp that the formation of such essential friendships and partnerships will not be achieved by bullying and trade wars. And so the task of renovating and fortifying our position in the world will fall to the Democrats. But what are the Democrats thinking?

JOHN BERRYMAN

"Grim Pilgrims gather: 'Thanks.' I give thanks too"

Grim Pilgrims gather: 'Thanks.' I give thanks too,
as the last leaves fly, that he did not live on
but yellow & skin-thin
& grinning ceased. True that his harvest due
only was beginning, that no sun
distracted his widow in

her calm dismay; but count up then his gain, —
Paris unfallen, Hiroshima tall,
millions of Jews walking,
Gandhi spinning, treacheries that sprain
our hopes unspun, promises unmade all
that proved just talking.

The ballet of your dying hope no more
tortures me with its fool. What childish plan
's this, keen on living?
Embryonal adeno-carcinoma, grade 4.
'Twas in the testes, there since you began.
Fume, hiss. Happy Thanksgiving.

"Waiting. Just waiting, in wet heat. A little more whiskey please"

Waiting. Just waiting, in wet heat. A little more whiskey please.
Turn the fan up. The amenities.
No food yet, thank you.
I'll feel better later. It's too hot to read.
I think: do I have everything I need,
stomach & mouth?

A little more whiskey, please. In this terrible state
I hope I'm paying for my sins at any rate.
There must be some point to it.
It's very hard to think with the fan so high
but I seem to remember times when Henry was happy
without particularly deserving it.

They say the temperature will drop with dark
and after all my lecture rooms are air-conditioned.
It's that the actual brain won't work
before or afterward, so that everything has to be done there.
I must be paying for some very special sin
this summer. A little more shiskey.

John Berryman

A Bad *Dream*

Yes. That is so. I found she hated then
(or even didn't) her father who left when
she was a toddle of three.
She hated her mother (I couldn't like her either)
and felt only a fully justified contempt for her one brother.
Which into waded: me.

Ran on her a morning en route to the Red Owl —
a supermarket not a totem pole —
not looking good;
when she unclad to me that suicide
was all she had at heart, & trembled, I tried
to, and did, clothe her with us.

The marriage came long after; —
there's more here, pal, than ever we let out, but thus:
bugged by her ice for papa, I had her trace
the man down: — just dead, as no doubt he should;
then I made her her cancerous mother's friend
who died happy. I see our son sometimes.
I couldn't help out with Brother.

"When, later, our adventure has bogged down"

When, later, our adventure has bogged down,
or umbrella's to an end, and mountains & lakes
if any are the friends —
and that reminds me of a story — and so does 'if' —
Einstein — who personal' never caught my fancy —
he took my umbrella once, —

or I took his — years gone — but as a soul,
brain, that stuff, yes — only his prose
I never knew was so good:
is getting over his loss of religious faith
at..twelve maybe? and he must replace it
and says, all the decades later,

'Men of the same bent & end, past and now,
along with what they happened really to discover,
were the un-lose-able friends':
the German's better, I did that stupid English
myself. Oh: 'if'. I meant the air & water
peeled off, in a fouled test.

John Berryman

MICHAEL WALZER

Brief Encounters

I have not lived among famous people. My comrades were lovely men and women rarely celebrated or even mentioned in the mass or mainstream media. But I did meet briefly with people like those described below. If they were called back from the dead, they probably wouldn't remember the meeting, but it is still vivid to me. Think of these encounters as a circumstantial but still useful introduction to my politics, a quick glimpse in preparation for the more extended memories that come after.

(Judy, who appears several times in these sketches, is my wife and comrade of many years. Marty Peretz and Jeremy Larner are friends from Brandeis University days. *Dissent* is a political magazine of the democratic left that I wrote for over seven decades, from the 1950s to the 2020s; it is featured in several of the following sketches.)

Wayne Morse

He was the Republican, and later Democratic, senator from Oregon in the period immediately after World War Two. In 1947, he proved himself the most liberal Republican since Abraham Lincoln by filibustering for ten hours against the Taft–Hartley labor — actually anti-labor — law, trying to prevent the Senate from over-riding President Truman's veto. (He failed.) I can claim no credit for Morse's liberal heroism, but I had urged him to do exactly what he did.

I was twelve, politically obsessed and very pro-union. Sometime in the months when Taft–Hartley was being debated in the Senate, my mother took me on a trip from Johnstown, Pennsylvania, where we lived, to Washington, D.C., to visit with a high-school friend of hers, who worked in the city in some political capacity. She knew Morse and invited us to talk to the Senator on behalf of the labor movement. So we did, and I told the Senator — and he listened! — that the people of Johnstown, a strong union town in those days, wanted him to oppose the law. Or something like that. I went home very proud of myself, and until today I tell union friends that I lobbied against Taft–Hartley (which has never been repealed).

C. Wright Mills

He was a left-wing sociologist, the author of *The Power Elite*, a favorite academic of the New Left of the 1960s, who wrote for *Dissent* (until, after embracing Castro, he didn't). He was a visiting professor at Brandeis University in 1952–1953, which was my first year there. He was given an office in a building on campus that also served as a student dormitory (it was early days at Brandeis and space was scarce). My room was right next to Mills' office. On March 5, 1953, Mills burst into my room (I don't think he knocked), very excited, and told me that Stalin was dead. He stayed to make sure I understood that this was important.

Isaac Deutscher

He was a self-proclaimed "non-Jewish Jew," a renowned biographer of Trotsky, and a defender of, or apologist for, Soviet communism. I met him once, in a state of belligerence. My wife and I were living in London in 1964. I had by then written a number of articles for *Dissent*, one of them critical of British intellectuals who defended the Soviet repression of the Hungarian revolt in 1956. I didn't mention Deutscher and I don't remember what he wrote about Hungary; probably nothing good. He had appeared once in *Dissent*, with a too generous reading of Soviet politics, which elicited a harsh response from the editors. *Dissent*, which was founded and edited by my teacher and friend and comrade Irving Howe, was a magazine of the anti-communist left, which was, then and now, my own politics.

One day in the spring of 1964 we received a dinner invitation from Ralph Miliband, an English leftist, the author of *Parliamentary Socialism*, a sharp critique, and the father of David and Edward, future parliamentary socialists and rivals for the leadership of the Labor Party. We arrived at the designated time, and Ralph welcomed us — and then Deutscher, also a guest, lying in wait, as it were, stood up and, without any greeting, angrily told me that I should stop writing for *Dissent*. It was wrong to write for that magazine: "There is no such thing as an anti-communist left!" Ralph jumped in with some mollifying remark, and the rest of the evening was ruled by English politeness. I don't remember what we talked about over dinner. I never saw Deutscher again.

Benazir Bhutto

She was twice prime minister of Pakistan, probably one of its better prime ministers, assassinated in 2007. Many years before that, in the early or middle 1970s, she was a student in a course I taught at Harvard on war and morality. She wasn't in my discussion section; I didn't know her. One day I was lecturing on humanitarian intervention, using as an example and defending the Indian intervention to stop the brutal repression of dissidents in East Pakistan in 1971 — an intervention that led to secession and the creation of Bangladesh. Suddenly a young woman — it was Benazir — jumped up to tell me that I was wrong; passionately, she defended the Pakistani government's effort, as she described it, to hold the country together. I responded as best I could, without passion.

I never encountered her again; I don't remember what grade she got in the course. But the story doesn't end there. A classmate from those days met her in Europe during a year when she had been in political exile — she was for decades a figure of controversy in Pakistani politics — and they recalled her dramatic intervention in my class. Benazir told her, so the friend reported to me, that she now thought that the Pakistani repression was wrong. Hearsay, I know, but I repeat the report anyway.

Noam Chomsky

I debated him in a Harvard lecture hall sometime in the early 1970s. It was, I think, our only meeting, though we had some angry exchanges in the press before and after that. The subject of the debate was the politics of the Middle East — really Israel/Palestine. It was early days in the occupation of the West Bank, of which we were both critical. But Chomsky believed that the occupation revealed something essential about the state of Israel or about the Zionist project, while I thought that the ongoing occupation was politically caused and required political opposition. I was against essentialism — and a defender of Zionism.

Chomsky clearly won the debate — that is, most people in the audience were on his side, probably from the beginning, certainly at the end. It wasn't that he was an especially good speaker, but rather that he had at his fingertips an extraordinary amount of information — or, better, endless references to sources unknown to me. Talking very fast, he quoted newspapers and magazines in six languages. I was sure that he was making up the quotes, but I had no effective response. He debated with footnotes; I had only my own opinions. It was better to argue with him in print, when I could look things up.

Tom Hayden

He was one of the early leaders of Students for a Democratic Society, not only intellectually but also on the ground — he didn't just talk about community organizing, he went out and organized. I invited him to write an article for *Dissent*, and he sent in a strong piece that didn't need much editing. That made us friends, sort of, and when he moved to Newark in the early 1960s to work on the Newark Community Organizing Project, he would visit me in Princeton (I was a brand new assistant professor) for a little R&R. And then he invited me to visit NCOP and attend one of its community meetings.

What was most important in SDS organizing was to empower "community people" and bring them into positions of leadership. Tom wanted to show off NCOP's success: the meeting was run by someone from the city — not a left activist, not an academic. Tom sat in the back with me. But I couldn't help noticing that many of the people at the meeting were getting a crick in their necks, looking back at him for direction. Better, I thought, to be up front and accountable.

A few years later, in late summer, 1968, I met Tom for the last time. He was on his way to Chicago, and he stopped in Cambridge (I was now at Harvard) to meet with Marty Peretz and me. He told us what he wanted to do in Chicago — provoke the police, disrupt the Democratic Party convention — and asked for our support. We said no.

Fred Shuttlesworth

He was one of the heroes of the early civil rights movement — a good man in a hard place. Birmingham was never easy in the 1960s.

I knew him briefly, at the very beginning, and the story of our meeting reveals something of Shuttlesworth's character, tough and sweet at the same time. Jeremy Larner and I came to Birmingham in April of 1960 to write about what was happening there — I for *Dissent*, Jeremy for someplace else (I've forgotten where). We had the phone number of an old leftist in Birmingham, L. D. Reddick, who had written for *Dissent*. He brought us to Reverend Shuttlesworth's church. We wanted to interview Shuttlesworth; he didn't want to be interviewed by two white kids he didn't know. Were we supporters of the movement? Then we should speak at his church that evening — there were weekly meetings in those days that were drawing between five hundred and one thousand Birmingham blacks, young and old. We should tell his people that they had friends in the north.

It was a challenge, and it wasn't possible to say no; we didn't want to say no — we weren't journalists, after all, we were political activists. But neither of us had ever spoken to a crowd like that and, obviously, we had none of the oratorical skills of black Baptist preachers such as Shuttlesworth. We spoke that night to a very full church. I have no memory of what either of us said, except that I assured the congregation of Harvard University's solidarity with their struggle. We weren't the only white people in the church; a couple of plainclothes cops sat in the front row, watching us. They didn't look friendly.

As soon as we finished speaking, Shuttlesworth told us that we had to leave immediately. And then he took us to the bus station himself and put us on a bus to Atlanta. We should work for the movement in the north, he told us (which we did). His concern for our safety, I thought, was a kind of reward for speaking in his church. Only a few years later, there were many more visitors from the north, activists like the two of us, and some of them, braver than we were, stayed.

Yeshayahu Leibowitz

He was an Israeli scientist who was not known for his science but for his fierce theological/philosophical/political arguments. Immediately after the 1967 war, he warned Israel against holding the captured territories, and he repeated that warning again and again. Though he was a deeply religious man and an observant Jew, he was a secular Zionist who opposed any idea that the state of Israel had redemptive value or that the Jewish people had a religious claim to the Land of Israel. The founding of the state was emphatically not the beginning of the messianic age. Leibowitz spoke several times to the annual philosophy conferences held at the Hartman Institute in Jerusalem, which I attended regularly from the late 1980s.

I visited him once in his small Jerusalem apartment. I don't remember the occasion or who came with me. I think that I went with Judy — the two of us and maybe a couple of the Hartman people, by invitation. We spoke about politics, not about religion, and I remember, though maybe I made it up, that we listened to him say what he said often and was famous for saying: "The meaning of Zionism is simply this: we didn't want to be ruled by the goyim anymore." I've said it too, quoting him again and again.

George McGovern

My engagement with him was indirect as well as brief. We never met, but one day early in his presidential campaign in 1972, I got a letter from him inviting me, together with Marty Peretz, to organize a policy advisory group on the Middle East — focused especially on the Israel–Palestine conflict. We agreed to do this, and we rounded up a few well-known academics who wrote about the region and the conflict (and whose political views we expected to agree with). I don't believe the group ever met. We talked over the phone; there was perhaps one conference call; and then Marty and I wrote a draft and circulated it. The others sent in suggestions and criticisms, and we wrote another draft, which was accepted by our colleagues — and sent on to McGovern. He never responded; I doubt that he read it; it did not figure in any way in his various statements about Israel and Palestine.

Tip O'Neill

He was a Democratic congressman from a Massachusetts district that included Cambridge. (He eventually became Speaker of the House of Representatives.) During the anti-war campaigns of the 1960s, when I was co-chair of the Cambridge Neighborhood Committee on Vietnam, a couple of us from CNCV were invited to meet Tip (everyone called him that) in his Boston office.

I had recently published a piece in *Dissent* on Greek politics — the American connection, the right-wing generals' coup, and so on. We walked into Tip's office, and he began the conversation by asking me a question about the Greek generals. This obviously had nothing to do with the reason for our visit. I doubt that Tip had ever spoken in Congress about American interventions in Greek politics. He wanted me to know that he knew what I was up to. Tip is famous for insisting that "all politics is local." He provided me with a lovely example of the local due diligence of his Boston aides.

Zbigniew Brzezinski

It may have been the most important remark ever made about Middle East politics. I didn't hear it made, only reported, but I will quote it anyway. Brzezinski was a teacher of mine at Harvard; I took a course with him on East European politics, taught from the perspective of the (relatively new) theory of totalitarianism. I was not close to him as a graduate student, but I met him once years later when he was an advisor to President Jimmy Carter and I had just returned from a visit to Israel.

The "Jordanian option" was in the air in those days — the idea of returning the West Bank to the kingdom of Jordan on the

East bank, which had occupied it from 1948 until the 1967 war. Brzezinski told me of a conversation he had with King Hussein of Jordan about this possibility. He asked the king what he (the king) thought would happen if there was an election on the West Bank. The king replied, "If I run the election, I will win the election." I have to say, looking back, that it wouldn't have been a bad idea.

Edward Said

He was the leading Arab-American intellectual of the twentieth century, a fine literary critic, a passionate defender of the Palestinian people, and a fierce critic of Israel. We met in print a couple of times but only once in person. It must have been in the late 1980s, at one of those supposedly academic but really political conferences on the Middle East. We found ourselves seated next to each other at dinner (someone must have planned that), and we talked. At that moment I think that we could readily have agreed on the "two-state solution." But the more we talked, the more we disagreed, and both of us struggled to keep things civil. I came away from that dinner convinced that Jews and Arabs in Israel–Palestine could resolve their dispute more easily than Jews and Arabs in the diaspora. A conviction not yet proven...

Jacobo Timerman

He was an Argentine journalist and dissident. Arrested and tortured during the regime of the generals, he wrote a remarkable memoir that I reviewed in the *New York Review of Books* in 1981. He had been released from prison and exiled to Israel where, as a liberal Zionist, he was again a dissident. (Can a Jew be exiled to Israel?) He wrote a book criticizing Israel's war in Lebanon in 1982. In that book, he reports an encounter that, I have to say, is not vivid in my memory. Two months before the war, he writes, he had lunch with me at the Institute for Advanced Study in Princeton, where he proposed that the two of us commit suicide in some public fashion in opposition to the coming war — and in hopes of preventing it. I have no memory of this. Did he make it up, or did I repress the incident? Self-dramatizing political suicide isn't my style.

Antonio Guterres

Now the Secretary General of the United Nations, he was the socialist prime minister of Portugal in the mid-1990s. One of his aides read *Dissent*, and when I was invited to an academic conference in Lisbon he arranged a meeting with his boss. Judy and I sat in Guterres's office and talked about European politics. I wanted to know what it was like to govern a country; American socialists, after all, have no such experience. "I don't really govern Portugal," Guterres said. "I relate to it." Exactly what he meant, I am not sure; it was probably a comment on how much power the prime minister of a small country possessed — a country in the European Union, ruled in significant ways from Brussels. Also, perhaps, a bit of socialist modesty.

John Rawls

He was the leading American political philosopher of the twentieth century. I saw him regularly at early meetings of SELF (the Society for Ethical and Legal Philosophy), a philosophical discussion group that met in the 1970s and 1980s in Cambridge and New York. But I had only one interesting engagement with him. In late 1994 or early 1995, thinking of the fiftieth anniversary of Hiroshima, I invited Rawls to write a piece for *Dissent* about the first use of the atomic bomb. In 1945, Rawls was in the American army on an island in the Pacific, so he was one of the American soldiers who might have been involved in an invasion of the Japanese islands had the war not ended quickly after the destruction of Hiroshima and Nagasaki. I was looking for a personal reflection, part memoir, part argument.

Rawls agreed to write something but, after phone calls back and forth, I realized that I was not going to get anything personal. Rawls was an austere man, friendly close up but at any distance very much a philosopher. What he sent me, and what I gladly published (and what has been widely read), was a small-scale treatise on and against the use of the bomb. It was exactly the right position for *Dissent*, but what I wanted to know was how this man felt, sitting on a Pacific island, when he first heard the news.

Norberto Bobbio

He was the most important political philosopher in postwar Italy — and also one of the surviving members of the anti-fascist movement known as *Giustizia e Liberta*, or Justice and Liberty, in which he had been active as a young man in the 1940s. He was a candidate of the Action Party in the parliamentary elections in 1946; this was the party inspired by Carlo Rosselli's book *Liberal Socialism*. The party included veterans of the anti-fascist resistance such as Vitorio Foa and Leone Ginzburg, who became heroes of mine after I met and talked with Bobbio in the 1990s.

Judy and I met him and his wife in Turin at the apartment of two of his students who had spent time in Princeton. He was an old man and seemed to us even older than he was. We talked for hours and agreed about everything. And so I discovered that the politics I thought of as my own, inherited from the ex-Trotskyite New York Jewish intellectuals who founded *Dissent*, had another life and a different history. A more dangerous history: Rosselli, who founded Justice and Liberty, was murdered in France in 1937 by Mussolini's assassins, and Bobbio was arrested and imprisoned by the Fascist police. His politics was what it had always been: socialist, egalitarian, liberal, hostile to every kind of authoritarianism. I went to school with my Italian political ancestors that evening in Turin.

Henry Kissinger

I don't think that I ever had a conversation with him when we were both on the faculty of the Harvard government department. He was one of those Harvard professors whose eyes were always on Washington; he wasn't much engaged locally. In 1970 he was in Washington, a presidential adviser, and after the bombing of Cambodia a group of faculty members, his former colleagues, decided to visit and tell him that the bombing policy was wrong. They invited me to join them — to keep them honest, Tom Schelling said to me over lunch. Kissinger responded angrily to the group: except for me, these were all people who had supported the Vietnam War and were now shifting, or so Kissinger thought, with the political winds.

In a recorded, transcribed, and archived phone call just before the meeting — I found out about it after his death not long ago — Kissinger called me an "extreme leftist," which he knew I wasn't. But on another occasion in (maybe) 1972, he told me that I was the only honest person in the room. So we weren't friends, exactly, but colleagues who disagreed.

But then I reviewed a book about Cambodia that was severely critical of Kissinger; I wrote it in *The New Republic*, a magazine that Kissinger read, and I endorsed the book's argument. That was the end of any collegial relationship. After that Kissinger regarded me as an enemy — not an important enemy, he had plenty of those; I was just someone he didn't speak to. Half a century later, when Kissinger was ninety-nine and I was well into my eighties, we met at a party in New York. He reminded me of my review and turned away. I admired his memory, which must have been far more crowded than mine was. I thought that I still had the politics right.

Isaiah Berlin

He talked faster and was smarter than anyone I ever knew. Around 1985, I was invited to write an introduction to a new edition of *The Hedgehog and the Fox*, his study of Tolstoy and the philosophy of history and probably his most well-known book. He liked what I wrote or, perhaps, pretended to like it out of kindness. It wasn't easy to get his pluralism-but-not-relativism exactly right. After that we met briefly a number of times in Israel and the United States — and twice memorably in England, once happily, once sadly. He came to a lecture that I gave at Oxford, defending my own version of pluralism-but-not-relativism, and after the lecture he sat at dinner with Judy and me. I hope he liked the lecture; we talked of many other things. Asparagus was on the menu that night, a vegetable that neither of us ever ate in the Bronx or in Johnstown, PA. We picked up our knives and forks, and Isaiah said no, the right way to eat asparagus was with your fingers. We have done so ever since, on his authority.

A decade or more later, I was in England and Isaiah invited me to have lunch with him at a London club (I don't remember which one). I had a mission: I wanted to get him to write a commentary for *The Jewish Political Tradition*, a set of volumes that I and several Israeli colleagues were editing. Each volume consisted of key Jewish texts about politics accompanied by critical or appreciative commentaries written by contemporary scholars. Isaiah was sympathetic to the project but told me that he wasn't writing anymore — only talking now, not for print. I was too late. He died soon after that.

Golda Meir

She was said to be a simple woman, determined, grim, without subtlety. Simple she wasn't, except in one sense: she lived simply. Like other members of the first Zionist generation, she had political ambitions but no material ambitions. Along with Marty Peretz, I visited her once in her Tel Aviv apartment — the meeting arranged with the help of Marie Syrkin, our teacher at Brandeis, who was a friend of Golda's (and later her biographer). I. think the year was 1971; she was Prime Minister. She served us a light lunch in her tiny kitchen. The apartment reminded me of my parent's apartment in the Bronx in the 1930s when they had little money and indeed lived simply — only Golda's was smaller. We talked politics; I don't remember what she said or what we said. I just looked around and thought that this was the right sort of place from which Israel should be governed.

Joschka Fischer

He was a German leftist, a member in his youth of a group committed to violent revolution — a group that supported the FLN in Algeria and the Palestine Liberation Organization. In 1976 the Entebbe hijacking of a planeload of Israelis by a radical Palestinian faction and the German terrorists known as the Red Army Faction led him to break with all that and to move, slowly, into parliamentary politics. He started as an activist in the Green Party and then became one of its leaders. He became the foreign minister of Germany in the 1990s in a Red-Green government. Shortly after his retirement in 2006, he visited Princeton to give some lectures at the university and found me at the Institute of Advanced Studies and, at his request, joined me for lunch — our only meeting. We talked about many things; I wanted to know what it was like to be the leftwing foreign minister who sent German soldiers to Afghanistan. What he wanted me to know was that he was the guy who made sure that Israel got the German submarines that it needed.

Why me? Perhaps he thought of me as a representative of the Jewish intelligentsia (which can't be represented) and wanted recognition. I recognized him as a friend.

C. K. Williams

I love the long prose-like lines of his poetry, and I share his politics. So when I met him in the dining hall of the Institute for Advanced Studies — in his last years he lived near Princeton — I gathered my courage and asked him if he would read a few poems at a *Dissent* fundraiser. He agreed to read three and said that I could choose one of them. I chose the last poem in what was then his most recent book. It is called "Invisible Mending" and tells of "three women old as angels" mending garments with a care that might serve also for bodies and human ties. A miniature *tikkun* — right, I thought, for a meeting of democratic socialists in these latter days.

PAUL REITTER

AFTER TRANSLATING *CAPITAL*:

Marx's Adventures in Mimesis

The preface to the first volume of *Capital* ends with a motto about intellectual autonomy, or rather, about intellectual autonomy and the attitude toward reception that serves it best. Altering a line from Dante's *Divine Comedy*, Karl Marx pledges to live by the words: "Go on your own way, and let the people talk." He certainly managed to act in accord with the first clause, nowhere more so than in *Capital* itself. In this genre-transcending work, Marx aspires to the strictest conceptual rigor and documents his claims comprehensively, yet he also cracks wise, operates in a declamatory key, and gives free reign to his imaginative powers, telling readers, for example, what commodities would say if they could speak. As for letting the people talk, that proved to be a greater challenge.

Capital was published in 1867; and the afterword that Marx produced for the second edition of his book in 1872 makes it clear that he studied as many responses to the first edition as he could find, not just the "systematic" ones, and that he was easily annoyed by slights and grateful for validations, even when it came from sources he disliked, such as the *Saturday Review*. Style, broadly speaking, figures prominently here. Marx brings up his "mode of presentation" more than a few times, famously asserting that it had to differ from the "mode of investigation" and faulting commentators for failing to see how he built off the latter when he developed the former. In a footnote, the last of thousands, some of which fill up multiple pages, he strikes back at "the mealy-mouthed scatterbrains of vulgar German political economy" who "have criticized the way my book is written and also the way its analysis is presented." "Vulgar" in this context means tendentious and superficial, and Marx avows that he himself judges the "literary defects" of his *magnum opus* much more harshly than these lightweight naysayers, or in fact than anyone. He doesn't say, however, which flaws he has in mind. Instead he adduces two favorable accounts of his style. One lauds it for injecting "charm" into "even the driest problems of political economy." The other appreciates its "unusual liveliness."

Thus began a discussion that has played a small yet vibrant role in Marx studies ever since, a discussion in which the literary features of *Capital* have been prized, sometimes explicitly defended, and generally treated as non-incidental, non-ornamental aspects of the text. This line of commentary stretches from statements by Marx and his collaborator Friedrich Engels to Sianne Ngai's and William Clare Roberts's recent contributions, running through writings by Wilhelm Liebknecht, Edmund Wilson, Marshall Berman, Ludovica Silva, Robert Paul Wolff, and Jacques Derrida. It has addressed a variety of topics, including some of the mimetic techniques that Marx employs in *Capital*, such as his parodying of classical political economy and his freewheeling style of literary citation. What has been overlooked, to the best of my knowledge, is perhaps the most innovative of those techniques — Marx's use of free indirect discourse. For while certain occurrences of free indirect discourse in *Capital* anticipate later developments in literary modernism, they are not especially conspicuous, in contrast to Marx's much-quoted vampire and werewolf tropes and his reworkings of *Faust* ("a sensuous-supersensuous thing," and so on). Tellingly, the original English translation, done by Samuel Moore and Edward Aveling (who was for fourteen years the companion and collaborator of Marx's daughter Eleanor) in 1887, more or less dropped these stylistic distinctions, and the same goes for Ben Fowkes's version in 1976, which generations of Anglophone readers have depended on for access to Marx's text.

What is Marx achieving when, rather than having a hypothetical capitalist speak directly, he engages in a kind of third-person imitation, reporting thoughts and utterances in a way that allows him to slide in and out of the hypothetical capitalist's standpoint? How do we make sense of this investment of creative energy? We can of course bring different approaches to these questions. The one I want to pursue belongs to another conversation that has gone on at the margins of Marx studies but attracted participants of decidedly nonmarginal importance, for example, Hannah Arendt, Isaac Deutscher, and Isaiah Berlin. I am referring to the conversation about Marx as a Jewish writer.

Born in 1818 to parents whose fathers were, respectively, a rabbi and a cantor, Marx was converted to Protestantism when he was a small child — this in predominantly Catholic Trier, a city where Jews accounted for less than one percent of the population. His own father Heinrich had taken the step of baptism in order to practice law, and young Karl and the rest of the family followed him in that a few years later. Not much is known about Marx's experience of Judaism — or anti-Semitism — in restoration Prussia. How much did he interact with his uncle Samuel, Trier's rabbi? Is there anything to the speculation that his mother Henrietta occasionally spoke Yiddish around her children? Marx's biographers have had little to say about such matters. But the fact of his Jewish heritage has at times been seized upon by rivals and skeptics (Mikhail Bakunin, Eugen Düring) and put allies (Friedrich Engels, Franz Mehring) on the defensive. Because Marx penned a number of lines that rather furiously disparaged Jews and Judaism, most notably in his essay "On the Jewish Question" in 1844, the obscure situation has also made for accusations of Jewish self-hatred.

On the other hand, the same fact has inspired many critics to frame Marx as being in some profound and productive way a Jewish writer. This framing has tended to rely on the power of suggestion — that is, to occur without much drilling down into the relevant sources. With a minimum of analysis, it is often said that Marx and his works stand in the prophetic tradition. Erich Fromm, for example, called Marx's version of socialism "essentially prophetic Messianism in the language of the nineteenth century." Or a critic such as George Bernard Shaw, and there were others, briskly ascribes to Marx "particularly Jewish literary gifts" — the idea being that his irony and his deconstructive brilliance self-evidently issue from his Jewish background. Or his commitment to social progress is sketched as a Jewish response to modernity: Arendt once maintained that, "In the country which made Disraeli its prime minister, the Jew Karl Marx wrote *Das Kapital*, a book which in its fanatical zeal for justice, carried on a Jewish tradition more efficaciously than the 'chosen man of the chosen race.'" Or the following paradox is wagered: Marx's universalist mode of disidentification with regard to his "Jewish stock," which he almost never mentioned, exists alongside — and can amount to — a form of unconscious identification. This is what Deutscher meant when he described Marx as a "non-Jewish Jew," and also what George Steiner wanted to convey when he said that Marx was "most profoundly a Jew," when, driven by his "radical humanism," he pushed for the "dissolution of Jewish identity." There is a lot of loose and stereotypical thinking in all these characterizations.

Of the writers listed above, Isaiah Berlin provides the most thorough and most thoughtful reckoning, not only tracing the differences between Marx and Disraeli and their "searches for identity," but also finding various affinities amid all the contrasts. Yet the characterization given of the group applies to Berlin, too. As he works his way to his main points, he holds largely to general historical framing and psychological observations having to do with Marx's life circumstances — that he rejected his father's bourgeois path of assimilation, for example.Toward the end of his account, Berlin writes, "When Marx speaks of the proletariat, in particular when he alters the history of socialism (and mankind) by asserting that there is no common interest between the proletarians and the capitalists, and therefore no possibility of reconciliation . . . it is difficult not to think that the voice is not that of a proud Jewish pariah, not so much of the friend of the proletariat as of a member of a long-humiliated race." Like Berlin, I want to build a case for overdetermination in Marx's critical voice. I suggest that sensitivities related to (or around) certain aspects of Jewish assimilation lurk, to use a Marx word, in the creative forms of imitation that he unveils in *Capital.* But I will try to balance historical framing and textual analysis, locating those sensitivities in Marx's correspondence and then reading key passages in *Capital* against that background. The part of Marx's correspondence I will focus on are his letters about Ferdinand Lassalle, which are especially revealing in this regard.

Seven years Marx's junior, Ferdinand Johann Gottlieb Lassal was born in 1825 the son of a Jewish silk merchant and grew up in Breslau, which belonged to Prussia at the time and is now part of Poland. Like Marx, he studied philosophy at the University of Berlin, forming a lifelong attachment to Hegel, and, once again like Marx, he was drawn to ancient Greek thought. (At university he changed his name to Lassalle to cover his Jewishness.) Marx wrote a dissertation comparing Democritus and Epicurus; Lassalle's well-received first book was *The Philosophy of Heraclitus.* At an even younger age than Marx, whose commitment to communism dates to his mid-twenties, Lassalle began to devote himself to the socialist cause: he was a member of the Communist League when Marx and Engels composed its manifesto in February 1848. As a teenager Lassalle dreamed of becoming the savior of the Jews: "It has always been my favorite idea to stand at the head of the Jews, with arms in my hand, to make them independent." But as an adult, Lassalle, too, seldom said a kind word about them, once quipping, "I despise above all two kinds of people: Jews and journalists. Unfortunately, I am both."

Lassalle spent six months in prison for promoting insurrectionary activities during the revolution of 1848. Afterward, he managed to remain in Germany, whereas Marx and Engels had emigrated, and in the early 1850s they saw him as a junior partner there, expecting, or at least hoping, that he would faithfully represent their views — at the time they often used the term "*Bursche*" ("lad," more or less) when they referred to him. This was a blueprint for trouble, given that Lassalle aspired to be a major thinker in his own right. And when, in the mid-1850s, his Heraclitus book established his reputation as a writer, and he became wealthy thanks to a favorable ruling in his aristocratic companion's lawsuit against her ex-husband, tensions began to make themselves felt. Describing Lassalle in 1856 in a letter to Engels, Marx notes with distress that he seems "completely transformed" — and not in a good way. In the late 1850s and early 1860s, serious disagreements arose over political questions, such as what Prussia should do about the growing hostility between Austria and France and whether the Prussian state could be a vehicle for real social progress if universal male suffrage were instituted.

Isaiah Berlin went so far as to treat Lassalle, who revered Bismarck and was prepared to support Prussian militarism in exchange for domestic policy concessions, as a "precursor of the Fascists," as the Marx biographer Jonathan Sperber has put it. Lassalle was, in truth, more like a forerunner of Walther Rathenau: dandyish, not shy about likening his gifts to those of, say, Socrates, wide-ranging in his literary activities, which included a play that he said a mysterious force had made him write, leading a personal life that invited salacious speculation, Lassalle also worked indefatigably to advance the workers' cause. He possessed the political charisma and talent for oratory that Marx lacked, and in 1863 he launched the very first mass working-class party, the General German Workers' Association, which later merged with another party to form the ur-version of the Social Democratic Party. Marx was not the only person who found Lassalle alternately admirable and off-putting: Engels did as well. But of their responses to Lassalle, Marx's was by far the more vehement and extensive one. And if some of the slur-filled nomenclature they came up with for Lassalle originated with Engels — *"Jud Braun"* ("Yid Brown"), *"Isidor Berlinerblau"* ("Isidor Berlin-Bluedye"), *"Herr Wieseltier"* ("Mr. Wiesel"), *"Ephraim Gescheit"* ("Clever Ephraim"), and *"Ephraim der Tiefe"* ("Ephraim the Profound"), it was Marx who actually engaged with the topic of Lassalle as a Jewish writer.

It didn't help Marx's relationship with Lassalle that during the peak years of interaction, in the early 1860s, his financial situation was dire. When the American Civil War began, Marx lost his job as a European columnist for *The New York Tribune*, and there was Lassalle, eating him out of house and home during an extended visit to London in 1862, humblebragging about how much cash he had squandered on fancy cigars and London cabs, and laughing off considerable investment losses in front of his friend who was drowning in debt. Worst of all, when Marx asked to borrow money, Lassalle struck an officious tone: he insisted that the loan be formally guaranteed by Engels. Marx bristled with resentment — his whole family did, in fact. But it isn't resentment alone that breathes out of Marx's accounts of Lassalle in his letters to Engels.

The writing also has an obsessive quality. In the *Marx-Engels Edition* volume of correspondence covering the years 1860 to 1864, Lassalle's name is the one that comes up the most, more even than that of Marx's wife Jenny. Marx often says something about Lassalle, changes the subject, and then comes back to him, evoking a recursive effect, or a sense or fixation. Then there is the near constant marking of Lassalle as a Jew, and also the preoccupation with how Lassalle's work aligns with — and is deformed by — his style of assimilation. These features of the correspondence took shape slowly. They begin with Marx depicting Lassalle as a *parvenu* "sybarite," who, with his outsized desire for "fame," "struts around like a peacock." Marx therefore had his doubts about Lassalle's Heraclitus book, which Lassalle evidently sent to him. Although they "have been given this horse," he tells Engels in December 1857, they should "look deep into its mouth — on the express condition, of course, that this Heraclitus doesn't smell of garlic."

A few months later Marx followed up with an appraisal of the book. His suspicions had been confirmed. Returning to the motif of *parvenu* vanity, he writes to Engels that there is "an enormous exhibition of learning" but "every informed reader will know how cheap it is to bring forth such a collection of quotations" when an author "has time and money and, like Lassalle, can have as much of the Bonn University library as he wants sent directly to his house." Marx does seem intrigued by what he takes to be Lassalle's methodological conceit, namely, to pursue philology with the conceptual self-consciousness of a Hegelian, but he thinks that Lassalle exhibits precisely the wrong kind of self-consciousness: "You can see how ridiculous he looks to himself in this garish philological outfit, and how he moves with all the grace of someone wearing fashionable clothes for the first time in his life." In the end Lassalle delivers a "silly work," characterized by the "legalistic mode" he knows so well rather than real philosophical thinking. Or as Marx puts it in his letter, "How strange it would be if some German-speaker learned Greek and thereby became a philosopher in Greek without being one in German."

There was a rift in 1859, but the intimacy between Marx and Lassalle was soon restored and reached its highpoint. Marx stayed with Lassalle in Berlin for a month in the spring of 1861, with the two men spending most of that time in each other's presence. They worked on getting Marx repatriated as a Prussian citizen under the new amnesty (he had been stateless since 1845), they discussed coediting a newspaper that would be financed by Lassalle's companion Sophie von Hatzfeldt, and they socialized together, too, going to the ballet and the theater. For Marx, it was an uncomfortable intimacy. The more he got to know Lassalle, the less comfortable it became, and the censorious references to Lassalle's *parvenu* characteristics burgeoned in Marx's letters to

Engels. He began to routinely call Lassalle "Itzig," perhaps after the scurrilous Jewish character Feitel Itzig in Gustav Freytag's novel *Debit and Credit* (1855). Sometimes he diversified the mockery with the epithets "*Baron Itzig*," (Marx uses the English term "Baron"), "*Grosser Itzig*" ("Big Itzig"), "*Lazarus-Lassalle*," and the adjectival form "*Itzigsche*" ("Iztigian"). Generally polite when writing directly to Lassalle, and reluctant to damage an important ally by attacking him publicly, Marx now displayed a bottomless appetite for taking him down in this private context.

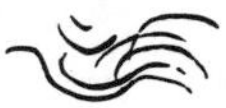

Marx knew something about the history of German Jews attempting to distinguish themselves from other German Jews with whom they tended to be grouped together. For example, he had read Heinrich Heine's famous, futile attempt to distance himself from the brilliant and caustic writer Ludwig Börne, whose name at birth, in 1786, was Loeb Baruch — futile, because people kept seeing them as connected by genre (early German feuilletonism), cultural-ethnic-religious identity (Jewish converts to Christianity), political orientation (progressive), wit (biting), and exile (Parisian). With its intrusions into Börne's personal life (his mistress's face is compared to an "old piece of matzo"), and its questionable timing (Börne died in 1837, just a few years before it was published), Heine's book *Ludwig Börne: A Memorial* elicited much scorn when it appeared in 1840. Engels declared that it was "the most execrable thing ever written in German." But Marx sent Heine a supportive note, telling him in 1845 that "the treatment this work has received from German-Christian jackasses is unrivaled in its stupidity — no other period of literature has seen anything like it." The long review he promised to write went the way of the newspaper he and Lassalle were to co-edit: it never materialized. Still, Ludwig Börne seems to have made a lasting impression on him.

In setting himself apart from Börne, who was older by a decade and had once tried to mentor him, Heine — who opportunistically converted to Christianity in 1825 as his "entry ticket to

European culture" but never stopped writing about the plight of the Jews and late in his life published a particularly affecting series of poems under the heading "Hebrew Melodies" — puts Jewishness at the center of things. But he did so with a twist. Jewishness is a matter of "temperament" for Heine, and it is coextensive with Christianness. Hence Heine places Jews and Christians together under the category "Nazarene," to which Börne belonged — not because he was born a Jew, but rather because he was born with an "ascetic" disposition that manifested itself in the "narrowness" of his aesthetic judgments and the dreariness of his populism. Non-Jews can thus be Jews, which is what Heine says about one of his main antisemitic antagonists, the conservative poet Wolfgang Menzel. Employing vocabulary that Richard Wagner would appropriate in his notorious essay on "Jewry in Music" in 1850, Menzel had charged that Heine "aped" the art of others instead of creating truly original works. (When Wagner argued that Heine used special Jewish mimetic capacities to copy his way to a position of prominence in German culture, he wielded the same term, "*nachäffen*" or "ape.") Not only that, Menzel made Heine out to be too dandified and depleted — he was rumored to have contracted syphilis in Paris — to create real art: "The physiognomy of Young Germany [a literary movement with which Heine was associated] was that of a dissolute Jew boy, just back from Paris, stinking of musk and garlic and dressed according to the latest trends, but wrung out and enervated because of his lascivious ways."

So Heine effects a reversal in *Ludwig Börne*. Menzel is the Jew, and, he, Heine, belongs to the counter-category, that of "Hellene," which means that his innate temperament makes him well-suited for authentic artistic production and the "cheerful" free creativity that it requires. Heine admits that he is conflicted about his own categories: he finds the Bible deeply engaging, and he sees Shakespeare, the greatest of all artists in his view, as a synthesis of Hellene and Nazarene. Moreover, Heine was a liberal, and cared deeply about political progress; but in the end he did not wish to be merely a political writer. That may have worked for Börne, the "little drummer" and native speaker of Yiddish who had to climb his way to proficiency in German, but it wasn't right for Heine, the "big drummer," whose aesthetic equipment is far more powerful. It is striking, then, that *Ludwig Börne* dedicates so much space to elevating prose forms that in terms of their cultural connotations stood closer to the lowly mimesis of interlopers than to Olympian aesthetic forms. Introducing a technique that Jeffrey Sammons has dubbed "double-voicing," Heine in quite a few places ventriloquizes Börne: he has Börne say things that he might have said but didn't, as well as some things he probably would not have said. And he also lets Börne speak directly — that is, he artfully quotes Börne, quotes him at his best, at uncommonly great length, which perplexed readers but also helped bring about the sense that whatever its ethical flaws and formal oddness, *Ludwig Börne* was in fact an aesthetic triumph. Thomas Mann spoke of it as "containing the most brilliant German prose before Nietzsche." Heine himself defended the book with the line, "But isn't it beautifully written?"

By the time Heine produced *Ludwig Börne*, the dichotomy between Athens and Jerusalem, Hellenism and Hebraism, had been established in German letters by Herder, Winckelmann, and Goethe, but to borrow Berlin's expression, it is hard not to think of Heine when Marx describes Lassalle as "this most un-Hellenic of the Water Polack-Jews." Actually, it is impossible not to think of Heine, because Marx mentions him and his baptism two sentences before he gives that portrayal of Lassalle. What thickens the connection is that Marx applies to Lassalle not only Heine's vocabulary but also tropes that were insistently applied to Heine. We are already familiar with this, or with Marx casting Lassalle as a preening dandy who overreaches intellectually and lacks the psychological grounding needed to pull off a great work. In the letter to Engels in which he uses the term "un-Hellenic," Marx also underscores Lassalle's "plasticity," by which he means not a Hellene's affinity for images and the plastic arts but rather Lassalle's problematic tendency to try to be all things as a writer. This assimilationist plasticity amounts to an anti-plasticity.

Again and again, Marx brings together Lassalle's intellectual shortcomings and his assimilationism. Lassalle is the assimilationist striver *par excellence*: he wants to be — he has to be — nothing less than a "universal genius," which, Marx speculates in a letter to Engels, is in part what "impressed" Sophie von Hatzfeldt, drawing her to Lassalle. Yet this very "*parvenu*" ambition goes along with an "'objective' vanity" and "sensitivity" that seem to preclude a successful outcome. Rather than getting a universal genius, "the countess" has through her contact with Lassalle taken on Jewish characteristics. According to Marx, she sometimes talks with his "Jewishy tone." In another letter, Marx refers to Lassalle as the "Jewish Baron or Baronized Jew," then speaks of how he aspires to be not only "the greatest scholar, deepest thinker, most brilliant researcher, and so on, but also Don Juan and a revolutionary Cardinal Richelieu." Yet Lassalle's conversation undermines him in this aspiration, since so much of it is "sentimentality" and "empty talk" carried on with "a grating voice that hits the wrong notes" and accompanied by "unaesthetic gesticulations" as well. Plus there is his wearying didactic "tone" (that word again).

In a further paradox, Lassalle's freighted drive for intellectual originality leads to heavy citation, and to citational problems. Writing to Engels in June 1863, Marx skewers Lassalle's speech on indirect taxes as "pushy" ("*zudringlich*," a quality he explicitly associates with Lassalle's "*Judentum*") and "empty" ("*schwatzhaft*"), proceeding from there to some psychological analysis. The speech is, Marx says, the work of "student" who wants to "yell in the marketplace" that he is a "'solidly learned' man and independent researcher." In the end Lassalle winds up showing himself to be only an "arch student," because he has recourse to quoting other political economists "up and down" and is unaware that Adam Smith "plagiarized" from the Physiocrats everything that he wrote about indirect taxes. For Marx, then, plagiarism is not peculiar to Jews — but it can be done with particular inflections, with Jewish ones. A year later, in June 1864, we find Marx complaining that Lassalle has copied from his work in an "Itzigian way," dandifying it as he went along.

Also revealing are certain juxtapositions in the letters in which Marx deals with Lassalle's Jewish assimilationist tendencies. Marx uses the derisive term "*Jud*" ("Yid') whenever he refers to the journalist and newspaper owner Bernhard Wolff, a move he employs rather sparingly elsewhere and refrains from in his other discussions of Wolff. It is in this context that Marx gives his infamous account of the writer Ludmilla Assing that presents her "nastily Jewish physiognomy" as a singularly hideous phenomenon — she is, Marx comments, the "ugliest creature" he has "ever seen." And the case of Lassalle prompted Marx to offer rare speculations on the deep origins of Jewishness and its potential cultural consequences. In one of his reports on his visit to Berlin in 1861, he enlists a scholarly text about the ancient world to shed light on Lassalle. "Apropos of Lassalle-Lazarus," he writes to Engels,

> Lepsius's major study of Egypt has shown that the exodus of the Jews from Egypt is nothing but the story that Manetho tells of the expulsion of the 'leper folk,' who were led by an Egyptian priest named Moses. Lazarus the leper is thus the Ur-type of the Jew and Lazarus-Lassalle, except that with our Lassalle, the leprosy got into his brain. His illness was originally secondary syphilis that wasn't properly cured.

It is not clear, at least not to me, how exactly Marx means to link Jewish history and Lassalle's brain. A voracious reader of nineteenth-century scientific theory, Marx goes back and forth between the different senses of the German word "*Aussätzige*" — "leper" and "outsider." The Jews were not a leper folk in the first sense, but the biblical Lazarus has the disease, and Lassalle was known to have had syphilis. Nor does Marx's other statement about ancient Egypt and Lassalle clarify the situation. Writing to Engels about Lassalle's visit to London in 1862, Marx, having just dwelled on Lassalle's debilitating "impudence" and combination of insecurity and self-aggrandizement, hazards that his guest descends from the progeny of Jews who procreated with the black people who accompanied them on their way out of Egypt. The "shape of his head" and the texture of his hair indicate this, as does his "pushiness," which for Marx is characteristic of Jews and black people alike: here we might note that Marx's own skin was swarthy enough to earn him the lifelong nickname "Moor."

However he wanted Engels to receive these crude genealogical thoughts (mock science?), they betray an obsession with Lassalle's mode of Jewishness, which manifestly weighed on Marx. Consider his response to Lassalle's death at the young age of thirty-nine in August 1864, from injuries suffered in a duel. Whereas Engels took the conventional high road, eulogizing Lassalle as a difficult but remarkable person and ally who would be missed, Marx breathed an unceremonious sigh of relief. How astonishing, he exclaims in his note to Engels, that this "noisy" and "pushing" (he uses the English word and may mean "pushy") person is "dead as a mouse" ("*maustod*") and will now "have to shut his trap altogether" ("*altogether das Maul halten muss*" — here again Marx mixes English and German). In sum, Lassalle set Marx off, bringing to the surface volatile sensitivities around Jewish assimilation and Jewish mimetic activities, and Marx himself invites us to see his sensitivity to Lassalle and his dubious copying as crossing over from his private correspondence into *Capital*.

On the very first page of the preface to *Capital*, Marx flags Lassalle's copying as a concern, prominently alerting readers to how it has created the appearance of similarity between himself and Lassalle precisely where they are, in Marx's view, quite different. He says about the "general theoretical propositions" in Lassalle's "economic writings" that they have been "taken from my work," taken from it "nearly word for word, down to the terminology I invented, and without attribution." Of course, there was another way for Marx to deal with his sensitivity to mimetic practices that he associated, whether consciously or not, with a mode of Jewish assimilation that troubled him, appearing to him as something like a distorted image of his own assimilation — Marx's version of being a hugely ambitious cosmopolitan socialist-journalist-theoretician versus Lassalle's version, Marx's marriage to an older aristocratic woman without means versus Lassalle's relationship with a much older aristocratic woman with lots of means, and so on. Marx could cultivate his own alternative mimetic practices, but they were creative ones. As we know, in *Capital* he does that, too.

What remains to be seen is how these practices work. Let us turn to Marx's style, key aspects of which can be profitably read against the background of his correspondence about Lassalle, or as being animated in part by the specific sensitivities around and anxieties about Jewish assimilation that we encounter in that correspondence. What Marx sees there as a failed project of mimesis on the part of an assimilating Jew, one that involves failures of mimetic writing, is in *Capital* countered by, and even transmogrified into, the literary mimesis of a modernizing writer. This is most excitingly illustrated by Marx's use of the modern technique known as free indirect imitation. A notable example of the technique occurs in his discussion of the labor process and the valorization process. Here Marx takes up a point that he stresses in the previous chapter, where he reveals the secret of how surplus-value is produced: neither capitalists nor political economists understand how surplus-value comes about — hence "secret." The previous chapter evokes at length the political economists' way of misunderstanding its production; the chapter on the labor process and the valorization process represents the capitalists' wrongheaded perspective, doing so by describing capitalist consciousness in the free indirect mode.

Marx invents a fictional character — a hypothetical capitalist who fails to produce surplus-value, even though he successfully makes yarn for which there is a market. In other words, the capitalist fails to produce surplus-value even though he does all the things required for doing so: puts money into means of production, hires a worker, and produces a commodity that can be sold at its value. This leaves him confused. According to Marx, the capitalist is ignorant of the valorization process, the non-natural capitalist process whereby surplus-value is generated, which is not the same as the labor process, a natural process common to all human societies. Thus the capitalist cannot know that the former process begins only when a worker works longer than his own worker did, and starts to perform unpaid labor, or only after the part of the workday when the worker brings about value equivalent to that of his labor-power. "Our capitalist can't believe it. The product's value merely equals the value of the capital he advanced. The value he advanced hasn't valorized itself. It hasn't created surplus-value; hence it hasn't transformed money into capital." What is he to think?

> Our capitalist might have found solace in the idea that virtue is its own reward, but instead he starts to raise his voice. The yarn is of no use to him — he made it in order to sell it. Thus he should sell it, or better yet, he should produce only things that satisfy his own wants and needs, a trusted therapy that [John Ramsay] MacCulloch, his personal doctor, has prescribed to help against the epidemic of overproduction. Our capitalist now becomes defiant and defensive, rearing up on his hindquarters. He asks: Can a worker make commodities out of thin air simply by using his arms and legs? Didn't he supply his worker with the material the worker needed to embody his labor and in which his labor is thus embodied? Given that penniless persons make up the vast majority of society, hasn't our capitalist rendered an immeasurable service to society by providing the means of production — namely, the cotton and the spindle? Hasn't he done the worker a great service, too, by giving him his means of subsistence? And shouldn't he get something in return for this service?

This is not what narratologists would call classic free indirect discourse, which they tend to define as occurring where a character's thoughts are related by a narrator in the third person but in the character's language, or in a mix of the character's language and the narrator's, so that it can be hard to tell whose perspective readers are getting. In the passage quoted above, the perspective is sometimes marked more clearly than it is in classic free indirect discourse ("he asks"), and it is sometimes stressed that the capitalist is speaking rather than silently reflecting ("he begins to raise his voice"). Yet the basic features of modernist free indirect discourse are present, more so than otherwise in German letters before 1900. The fragmentary first instance of free indirect discourse in German literature is thought to have come in Georg Büchner's drama *Lenz* in 1839, which was followed by some not very successful experiments around 1850 by the critic and novelist Otto Ludwig.

What we find in *Capital* is stylistically much more developed. There is a sliding from the capitalist's perspective — "thus he should produce only things that satisfy his own wants and needs" into Marx's — "a trusted therapy" prescribed by MacCulloch. At the same time, the capitalist's language — "can a worker make commodities out of thin air simply by using his arms and legs?" — slides into Marx's — "in which his labor is embodied," thereby evoking an instability or lack of firm footing that corresponds to the weak intellectual agency that Marx ascribes to capitalists in the capitalist system. Never truly in control of his discourse, since it is narrated monologue rather than direct monologue, the capitalist loses control of it outright. There is also a proto-Kafkaesque combination of mockery and empathy — the émigré scholars Leo Spitzer and Dorrit Cohn suggested that free indirect discourse invites both. The capitalist has an economic "personal doctor" whom Marx liked to ridicule (MacColluch), yet the capitalist's voice is not always clearly set off from Marx's. Both the mockery and the empathy make sense. The capitalist offers up the shibboleths of "vulgar political economy" in which he is "well versed," such as, hasn't he "done an immeasurable service to society?" But his consternation is understandable: the system in which he operates is fundamentally opaque, which is in fact the theoretical point that Marx is emphasizing here, and also a plight with which Kafka's characters are very familiar.

In addition, both Marx and Kafka play off the formal air that free indirect discourse can have. Its compositional and cognitive demands are such that it isn't used in casual conversation in German, and sometimes it works, as it does in *Capital*, with a subjunctive form that has elevated associations. The formality creates a context in which the madcap moments feel all the whackier for feeling a little out of place: "rearing up on his hindquarters," and so on.

Elsewhere in *Capital*, a work notorious for its expanses of dense prose, Marx carries out a spry imitation upward, telling readers how the political economist Nassau Senior "would have to continue" if he were more clearsighted about the production of surplus-value, and doing so to some extent in an enhanced version of Senior's own style. It is a mode of literary mimesis that simultaneously recalls the "double-voicing" that Heine pioneered in his Börne book and anticipates the humiliating, annihilating techniques for breaking down and showing up employed by a later German-Jewish critic who analyzed the paradoxes of Jewish assimilationism while challenging the Wagnerian ideal of pure originality, namely, Karl Kraus. Walter Benjamin was being only semi-hyperbolic when he remarked about Kraus that after he imitates someone he emerges with "blood dripping from his lips."

I would argue that the mimetic practices in *Capital* have still more functions. As with other moments of creative writing in the book, they serve as a vehicle for Marx to model the kind of multi-sided work that the book treats as essential to human flourishing. Marx certainly believed in the power of deep expertise, but he also thought that the narrowing of work, intellectual and otherwise, mutilated people:

> Whereas simple cooperation does little to change the way an individual worker works, the manufacturing system revolutionizes his mode of labor from the bottom up, seizing the individual bearer of labor-power by the roots. It stunts the worker, turning him into a freak. For it acts as a hothouse for developing a particular skill by forcing him to suppress a whole world of drives and proclivities, just as in the states of La Plata whole animals are slaughtered merely for their hides or their fat.

So when Marx refuses to abide by the norms of scholarly writing and to suppress his literary inclinations — his first career plan was to become a poet — he is acting on his theoretical commitments. With certain moments of literary experimentation, such as the one that portrays the benighted capitalist's mindset, Marx may also be trying to set himself apart from another form of intellectual-existential diminishment, albeit less self-consciously. This would be the assimilationism he keeps talking about in his epistolary reflections on Lassalle — keeps talking about in a way that lets us see the most sophisticated literariness in *Capital* as connected to the Jewish background Marx seldom spoke of directly.

One way to describe *Capital* is to say that it is a book about doubling, about how under capitalism the things that we make — and the labor with which we make them — become dual entities. Marx argues that capitalist societies are societies dominated by commodity production, and the commodities that they produce are use-values and values, or two opposing and complementary things. As use-values, they are diverse things whose different physical properties satisfy different human wants or needs. But as immaterial, homogenous, fungible "value-things," they differ only with respect to how much value they represent. Similarly, there is the particular concrete labor that goes into the use-value component of a commodity, and there is the undifferentiated abstract labor that constitutes the substance of value and thus of a commodity's "value-thing" component. Given how well the central motifs themes here align with some of the main preoccupations of late nineteenth-century anti-semitic discourse — the stripping away of particularity, the idea of a hidden insatiable force controlling basically everything, and so on — one could go much further in trying to link the book to the Jewish part of Marx's biography. That is, one could argue that Marx was attempting to work though concerns about anti-semitism as he developed his theory of value. But it would be difficult to ground such an argument in sources because we simply do not have directly relevant source material.

What we do have is ample material that invites us to link Marx's two sets of mimetic activity. On the one side, there is the mimesis of Lassalle's Jewish assimilationism and the mimetic writing by Lassalle that, in Marx's view, went with his assimilationism. On the other side, there is the radical mimesis in *Capital* that reads like a brittle, brilliant, innovative response to Lassalle's mimeses. Marx wanted to be able to just "let the people talk," but doing so was evidently out of reach, and the thought that "the people" would associate his work with Lassalle's elicited in him a particularly strong reaction, which we have reason to be thankful for. He put the energy it generated to good use, investing it in mimetic forms that would continue their ascent in German-Jewish culture for decades to come.

PAUL NORTH

AFTER TRANSLATING *CAPITAL*:

The Inner Life of Things Made and Traded

Marx was a great ape: he could do Goethe, he could do the Bible, he could do capitalists as well as workers, he could certainly do Hegel—better, he thought, than the legions of Hegel's other apes. In a sense, he was, at any one moment, Marx-Goethe or Marx-Hegel or Marx-Ricardo. It is true, too, that Jews in German-speaking lands after emancipation—which started around 1750—were granted, or were condemned to, this kind of mimicry. They observed German law, dressed in culturally appropriate ways, took on modern surnames, spoke the local language. They could be a good German, though always threatening to degrade into the bad Jew. They asserted rights as assimilated Jews while remembering their past as traditional Jews. Freed through the state, they were then beholden to the state. Marx describes this split in "On the Jewish Question" in stark terms. He dubs it "the decomposition of man into Jew and citizen."

Perhaps this is what made mimesis so appealing to Jews in German lands after emancipation. Perhaps this is why some of them became very good at it. Where imitating Germanness, or what counted as Germanness, was a requirement for living, if it could be brought to the level of art, some small share of power could transfer to the imitator, rather than stay with the imitated. This is doubtless the moral of Franz Kafka's story, "A Report to an Academy." Although written about fifty years after *Capital*, it crystalizes the dynamic. In Kafka's tale, an ape captured in Africa imitates the humans he encounters as a captive on the ship to Europe. In order to remain an ape and still be welcome in their society, he has to imitate them. Later, once he is ensconced in Europe, in order to have a better life in this new kind of captivity, the ape goes onstage. He plays an ape who is aping a human, so that he can remain an ape. The theater allows him to spend his life openly performing his double life. Kafka's character turns his disadvantage to his advantage, by doubling the double. Doubleness was an escape and a salvation, and also a continuation of the trap, for German-speaking Jews in Middle Europe in the long nineteenth century.

Doubling up may have been, in Marx's world, a Jewish thing, but it was certainly, for Marx, a capitalist thing. Almost everything of importance in *Capital* looks like one thing but is actually two. You need to be good at two-ness to get it. You need to twist your thinking, fold it, and then unfold it again, to comprehend capital, where doubleness moves into the nature of things. It can feel, at times, like losing your mind. This is because, in everyday thinking, the thing you want to comprehend is supposed to be a single, unified object. This thing I am holding is a book, not a book and an ostrich. And my thought of the book is one thought. The oneness of the object and the oneness of my thought about it are intimately linked. If the object is more than one, doesn't the thought have to be more than one, too? Am I thinking this is *A* or thinking this is *B*? We usually call this uncertainty, or doubt — being of two minds about something. At an extreme, we call it madness. All of this because truth is reported to be one. But what if capitalism has a new shape for truth? What if truth has a new number? What if a repetition compulsion doubles objects and causes problems for thinking?

Since in Marx's world mimetic doubling was marked or coded or experienced as a Jewish technique, it may have also been a metaphor for the rampant doubling carried out by the capital system. Or it could be that his experience with doubleness, as a German-Jew, helped him recognize the wiles of this new socioeconomic system. In Marx's discourse, the Jew, in his doubleness, sometimes stands in for capital, in its doubleness. "On the inside, commodities are circumcised Jews," Marx rather startlingly quips in the fourth chapter of the first volume of *Capital*. This complicated association points to Paul of Tarsus, to his discussion of inward and outward Jews in Romans 2:25–29. Like a Jew, whose one side, the outward adherence to law, is a dispensable shill for his other side, the inner faith in Christ, a commodity may be outwardly shabby but inwardly gold.

Marx shows us again and again that any feature of this specific social-economic field is actually two things pushed together. Capital is an outward Jew and an inward Christian. And yet it takes special sleuthing to find this out, since capital's objects look at first glance like single things, and so a different mode is necessary to render it in the right light. To see things in the capital system, to interpret the system correctly, you need to see double. Section I, "The Commodity and Money," would be unintelligible if you didn't open your mind to double-vision. This is because the important objects are made up of two idiosyncratic and mutually antagonistic things that in the development of the system got coupled together. It is much too coarse to reduce this setup to an automatic and unconscious projection of what Marx underwent as a Jew in Germany in his time. Perhaps, minimally, though, we can say that with experience in the kind of double-vision that marginal social groups grow good at, Marx knew a double system when he saw one.

We are taught from the beginning of Section I of Volume I that comprehension can no longer mean making a single image or a single sentence. Reading *Capital*, we can no longer say "this is that." The book tests readers on their grammar. We should learn to say "this is those;" learn to take a thing in from two perspectives at once, to the point at which it no longer appears as one thing alone, and neither does our perception of it — we become two people when we read *Capital*. It splits our consciousness.

Capital natives do this every day without needing to reflect upon it. We behave toward a commodity as though it were a thing to be used, a thing with particular sensual qualities and personal purposes. At the same time, however, we behave toward it as a thing to be exchanged, a thing with a single, abstract, quasi-metaphysical quality — a value. When we trade a hammer for something else or for money, we are doing implicitly what the book wants to make explicit for thinking. We act in both ways at once around the thing, in view of its use and in view of its value. It is this and it is that — discrepant. Doubtless the capital system teaches us from the youngest age to shift perspectives like this. How else could we live with objects that shift in their being? Over time we probably lose the feeling of the shift — so that later it happens without noticing. Marx tries to make the shift noticeable again. He tries to rattle us the way it must have rattled when a parent first told us to get back the correct change at the store. "Why?" we wondered. Marx puts the child's "why" back in force. (The answer is "value.") After reading the book, we should be less innocently able to count our change.

The same object is a sensual thing for use and a ghostly thing of value, and, as two in this way, can lead to divergent, even antagonistic behaviors, such as buying and selling or trading and consuming. This should shake our confidence in the categories we take for granted. There is no such thing as "a" carrot. Those who behave toward the carrot as a thing to be consumed comprehend it within one circuit of purposes. Those who behave toward the carrot as a thing that goes to market and returns as money comprehend it within another circuit of purposes. *Capital* teases the circuits apart, sifting their internal perspectives and inviting readers to feel the hot tension between them, the discrepancy burning inside the commodity. The doubleness of things is not just a problem with things, of course. The relation between the classes is contained in and maintained by the double carrot. As a consumable, the vegetable is for sustenance and so it represents the minimum that workers need in order to return to work tomorrow. As an exchangeable, the vegetable is for value creation and realization, and so it represents the minimum that the capitalist needs in order to keep production going another day. In this way, the double is also a split, and an antagonism, a struggle between interests.

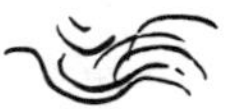

Indulging in this doubling and splitting, *Capital* starts to build a special perspective that Marx calls "critique." He gives critique a new meaning: double vision. Even though a commodity is almost never consciously seen in both ways at once by the same actor in the capital system, a critical perspective puts on display the convergence and divergence of both. Sometimes one way of being sleeps while the other is active, the two switching off in a rhythm. Using and trading are like this. They are almost always mutually exclusive moments in a process. Sometimes one way of being coincides with the other. Buying and selling, for example, happen at once — every sale is a purchase, every purchase a sale. No matter how you cut it, in the system of capital a commodity is what it is not. You can see this especially clearly in the carrot, because it cannot be eaten before it is traded. Its doubleness is split temporally into a before and after. As the carrot splits, so the actors split. Now the carrot is food, now it is a generic object for trade. Now I am a trader, now an eater. When I am eating I am doing a basic social activity, keeping myself alive. When I am trading I am doing a basic capitalist activity, realizing value on the market.

Awaken a talent for twoness and you will experience vividly the double life of things and selves under the capital system. Learn to see twice, once. Section I begins from an apparently simple, single, unified, inert, independent kind of thing, a product for use, and then moves to a commodity whose main purpose is trade, though it keeps its useful self around as a ghostly presence. A commodity is twice, once, but its doubleness stays hidden. It presents itself as usable although it has been made to be tradable, and what makes it tradable is called value. Separated from the commodity and set over against it, value takes on a separate existence as money, in which the split, now concrete, is nevertheless more hidden. In money you experience one face of the double commodity directly, but you no longer experience the doubling, since money appears as an independent agent. This is the meaning of "fetish" for Marx. Money is a fetish because we cannot see the material relations hidden doubly in the stuff, first by value, then in separate form as money. Money acts as if on its own. The world is created by money — when, in reality, labor creates value, which, forcibly separated from everything we recognize as the social life of human beings, becomes money.

A commodity may be made out of fabric or wheat, or out of ideas alone, but a commodity is always made out of doubles. Use/value is one of its twos. Quality/quantity is another. As a useful thing, a commodity is known by sensual qualities. A carrot is sweet and nutritious. As a tradable thing, a commodity is known by quantities. The carrot weighs five ounces. On average there are two hundred in a bushel. Like use and value, quality and quantity tuck together within one carrot in something like a fold. Section I of *Capital* unfolds the densely packed interior of the commodity, to show the many tucks within it. In a marvelous maneuver, Marx invites us to meet the entire capital system folded up around itself inside a commodity, packed in so tight that a gigantic book — one completed volume, two unfinished, three more planned, along with many ancillary texts — are just enough space to display all the flaps, once its apparently uniform surface has been unfolded and spread out before us. "The simplest form of commodity," Marx writes in a letter to Engels in 1867, "embodies the whole secret of the money form and thereby, *in nuce*, of all bourgeois forms of the product of labour." The task is to recognize the multiple contents folded in two and three and four-ply layers, and at the same time to notice how the folds add up to very familiar things that don't seem folded up at all.

What commodity? A carrot grows in the ground. If you see it this way, you cannot see the system. The natural carrot blocks your view, since a commodity, in order to be a commodity, holds all the parts and relations, processes and actors, times of day and seasons, legal codes and police actions, worker groupings, not to mention all the chains of raw and finished materials and the whole history of human and animal technology in a unique pattern within it. Marx's technique in *Capital* can be called "shaking out the folds." There are other more traditional names, such as "dialectics," but "unfolding" gives a precise image for the thought-figure here. The capital system conceals a second face beside the one you see at any moment. Unfolding can also be thought of as breaking bonds — a lot of energy is stored in these forced, tense pairings. In this way too, seeing double with Marx is a practical activity that packs an explosive force: by means of critique, the world as we know it, or as we think we know it, comes apart.

In the innermost wrinkle, at the tightest corner in the interior of a commodity, use and value exist directly beside one another. Quite distinct modes, use and value nevertheless depend on one another as much as they also depend on staying separate. Connection that separates, separation that binds — a commodity is an unholy alliance of two kinds of social purpose, the satisfaction of needs and the accumulation of surplus-value. They must stay tightly together and also must never be confused. If use and value became confused — imagine — carrot producers might give away the crop for free for others to fruitfully enjoy, if instead of values they saw their wares first as uses. If instead of uses they saw their products first as values, by contrast, carrot farmers might not worry whether the produce was sweet, or even edible. In these examples you can see the revolutionary potential in the critical perspective, seeing both sides at once. Within capitalistic society is an unresolvable conflict between opposing interests.

Where value and use — intimate opponents and alien companions — fold together, freely articulated but snug, the pair itself has another partner. The value-use fold within a commodity is accompanied by and confronted with labor, which is its own folded pair. In 1868, Marx wrote in a letter to Engels: "the economists, without exception, have missed the simple point that if the commodity has a double character — use-value and exchange-value — then the labor represented by the commodity must also have a twofold character." A human being labors on raw material and, by adding their labor to it, produces a product. Labor transforms an unusable thing into a usable thing, and at the same time, because it must be traded in order to reach its user, labor also transforms a value-poor thing into a more valuable thing.

And so, labor must have its own internal fold: concrete labor to make a useful thing and abstract labor to make a value-laden thing. These false friends sit in the nearest proximity, interdependent and repellent, mutually necessary and sometimes mutually corrosive. Commodity (use-value with exchange-value) and labor (concrete labor with abstract labor) fold twice inside the commodity production process. Likewise, the commodity production process is itself located at a crease, twinned with the circulation process, which is the topic of the unfinished second volume of *Capital*. Unfolded to their full length and breadth, the tiny pleats in the commodity open to expose the capital system itself, which fans out over the planet and the book. Marx has a highly distinctive way of theorizing.

Learn to see double to see a commodity, and for that matter the special commodity, labor. To understand the economy, Marx wants you to start with the production process, this four-fold. Circulation is a big topic as well — the biggest, literally speaking, in the world, although it occupies a small space in the first volume. Circulation is a necessary complement to production, its twin. Use and value are made in the production process and then in circulation they come to fruition. The capitalist gets back their outlay plus a bonus to live to capitalize another day, the merchant passes the commodity along, the worker receives wages to live to work another day.

Although the discussion of circulation will be expanded in

Volume II, an important thought emerges in Volume I. Circuits of exchange are more than one, though in a different way than the commodity. In production there are folds; in circulation there are arcs. In short, whereas in the commodity, doubleness looks like a fold, in circulation it looks like segments of a circle that start and end at different points on the circumference. Under this kind of "seeing double," we get the first panorama of the entire system.

Economics is the science of equivalences, and hence it has tended to concentrate on the sphere of circulation, Marx tells us, where commodities encounter one another as equivalents. Things that are unlike qualitatively can nonetheless be equivalent when it comes to value, and economics treats circulation as the place for the exchange of equivalents. For Marx, however, such an account does not suffice. Circulation needs to be described in terms that go beyond economics and equivalence. For one thing, circulation is a social phenomenon as well, not a merely mathematical or logistical one. Circulation is the milieu wherein relations between individuals and groups happen. You buy, I sell; you own, I earn; your plantings become my dinner; someone trades while someone produces and someone else counts the profits. A social phenomenon first, circulation is also, we can say, alchemical (and note that this is Marx's own metaphor). In circulation, things transubstantiate into other things, and the whole system appears to grow magically beyond its size. Circulation is also fairly chaotic. It has the spirit of a whirlpool. Near the swirling vortex of capital circulation, persons, personalities, individual private lives, the life of mind or soul, as well as the lifetimes of family, friends, children, parents are pulled in and change their natures. They become relay points in the cycling mesh of exchanges. Individuals and groups get pulled into the vortex, homogenized and instrumentalized.

On the one hand, you are asked to conceive of a social system in which human beings and their other social relationships get swallowed up in the vortex of capital circulation. This is not a simple thought, because there are too many factors, too many sellers, products, buyers, timings, and placings. At the same time you are asked to conceive of a rational system that is made up entirely of individual empirical acts that nonetheless add up to the total circulating movement, which, in addition, never stops. Put another way, Marx helps us imagine a vast field of separate, random, real acts and part-acts, carried out by historical human beings under contingent conditions with a modicum of freedom and narrowed interests, which end up conforming to a hyper-rational order. Trades happen. Commodities move and become money. Capital capitalizes. People with other involvements come along and make trades happen at the right time and place. For every buyer there is a seller, for every seller a buyer; commodities dance a mad hoedown where partners constantly change places and rarely drop a step. On the whole, those who need it get the commodity they need; those who own one part with the commodity they have; those who benefit routinely benefit; those who do not benefit routinely do not benefit. Circulation is a multipolar, syncopated concordance of exchanges where an almost uncountable number take place at any time and all of them must take place over a certain course of time in order for any single exchange to work out.

Circles make it possible, circles of circles, a galaxy of inner orbits that revolve around a massive black hole at the center, capital's insatiable "drive" for accumulation. Section II of *Capital* moves us from doublets and folds within the commodity to circles within circles.

Before you can think of the total circling of the galactic system, Marx has you identify shorter, more well-defined spans that make it up. Circles come in segments. Take a so-called simple exchange. Point A — producing a hammer — leads you to point B — selling the hammer — before point B leads you around the other arc back to point A — returning the original capital in the form of money, with a surplus, to the industrial hammer manufacturer. Another difficult challenge: learning to think in semicircles.

In a transaction, a commodity is transferred along one arc

so that, later, in a separate move, money can come back along an adjacent arc. Transactions begin and finish at different points. A span opens between the moment of sale and the moment of payment, and subsequently between the payment point and conversion back into raw material for new production. For this reason, Marx asks us to understand money as what he calls a means or medium, a *Cirkulationsmittel*. As a means, money facilitates movement along semicirclets just as tickets facilitate train travel. It holds the seat while the transaction runs on its rails. It does this by adding viscosity to the flow, so that value can move more slowly than the surrounding time. Money captures the value and holds it at roughly the same magnitude, ready to change state at a moment's notice back into a hard commodity. Even when further stations are added, in more complex multistage transactions, adding banking or credit rounds, circulation still moves in semicircles, and yet it is also true that the semicircles only exist if they eventually link up together into a circle that returns with inevitability to the starting point.

To think the capital system, familiarize yourself with this image: an infinite motion turning on the backs of finite cycles, each cycle broken and joined up again through money's special mediating powers. Each finite cycle of state changes — money to commodity, commodity to money, money to commodity once more — reins in motion just enough to ensure that each transaction gets satisfactorily completed (on average), but this means that all of the surrounding transactions that enable it have to happen satisfactorily too.

Now the giant doublet that is circulation comes into view. It is economic and ecological at the same time. Circulation appears first as the exchange of an equivalent for an equivalent, as an economic thing. At the same time, Marx makes an important modification to the standard economic reasoning. Circulation is also ecological. A single exchange is interconnected with others that surround it. In circulation, local positions are defined by more distant ones. A single trade depends on many others and on many things besides trades. Commodities dance to the rhythm of the market. A thing, or for that matter a person, holds a temporary position in a nested set of cycles. At one moment the thing is a hammer that took a certain amount of average labor to make, at another moment the thing is a wad of cash, at the next moment the thing is a carrot. Capital is not real and it is not fiction — it is surreal, like a Magritte painting, decorated with carrot-hammers and buyer-sellers, monstrous amalgams not foreseen by any philosophy.

To put this in the form of a general rule: a thing is a moving point in at least two of capital's semicircles. This is to say, a thing is the way it is determined by the demands of the system at any moment. You could say a thing is not what it is but where it sits in the whole.

Circulation, Marx teaches, makes a thing what it is. On one hand, a thing is its position on a semi-circle. You or I, this commodity or this wad of cash, are what they are because they stand at a position in a circuit between production, exchange, and consumption. On the other hand, each thing, as it transits, transforms. If you start at one point on the circumference, you transit through specific waypoints and end up somewhere else. Raw materials move to production and then are worked into products. But, if you start at another point, the waypoints are different, and you come out at a different place altogether. The same circle is a different circle. It depends where you enter and exit.

In the circulation process, therefore, you may either measure the semi-circular movement of value from commodity through money to commodity (Marx uses variables to express this: C-M-C) or you may measure it from money through commodity to money (M-C-M). These are and are not the same circuit. From one perspective they are the same — the money in the middle of one can be thought of as the same money at the end of the other. From another perspective, the more important one for Marx's analysis, they need to be thought of as different. Used as a means to produce products, money is different than money used as capital, where the product is a means to produce surplus value. It is and is not the same money. Here you can see clearly Marx's critical act, the act of someone accustomed to doubleness. It is apologist nonsense to say that the money is the same, when it is functionally different. It would be just as naïve to claim that the money is simply a different thing as a means for production and as a means for capitalization. The critical act is to show how the two live deceptively together in the same body. Seeing single is the worse deception, and it has brutal consequences for workers. When the production of useful things conceals the industrialists' real intention, which is the valorization of value, working conditions worsen.

In the first version of the circuit, a commodity leaves the factory floor to be sold, brings money back to the producer, who purchases more raw materials, in order to repeat the process. This is the production circuit, as seen from the perspective of the producers. The concerns that swirl around this circuit are well-known. A factory owner brings in materials when they are needed, pushes workers to complete the products when they are needed, and times the purchase of new raw materials to coincide with the return of capital after a sale. It is crucial that the production owner be fully committed to this version of the circuit.

The second version of the circuit differs from the first in a number of ways. For one thing, whereas in the first, money is a means for bringing in another commodity, in the second the commodity is a vehicle for converting money back into money, adding the all-important surplus. You are asked to shift your perspective and conceptualize the landscape from the position of the capitalist. A "capitalist" understands the product, and the worker as well, as a means or medium, with money as the cardinal input and output of the process.

What looks like a production process for goods is, in this shifted perspective, a production process for capital. Seeing double gives you access to the being double of the process. This is not only a perspectival shift but also a shift in the modality of life. A pre-capitalist or limited capitalist system could hypothetically function only in the first mode, as production of useful goods. Once generating capital becomes the highest goal, functions change places. The process of producing useful goods does not go away. It serves the production of value. Capital production becomes the sufficient mode, the first cause of all other activities, and production of goods for enjoyment and sustenance becomes a necessary accessory to something other than the good, shared life of the entire social unit. The good, shared life of the entire social unit requires a radical revision of our economic system and its forms of being, or so Marx argues across Volume I.

Doubleness itself is not the problem. On the one hand, the problem is the way things appear. The things we encounter every day, including our own laboring selves, appear simple and uniform. The sense that everything is as it seems, foisted on the world by the political economists whom Marx was disparaging in his "critique of political economy," blocks inquiry and keeps populations captive to a lie. Why does Marx take the simplest of relationships, I buy/you sell, or I-make-you-oversee, and turn it into the most complicated, arabesque of folded intentions and entangled functions? His reason is this: if we do not see the hidden complexity in capital's forms of being, we will not understand why, despite simple appearances, the harder and longer we work the less we actually make, while some who do not work at all make more than all of us put together. We cannot understand why, strong rhetoric and weak political actions to the contrary, we continue to destroy the earth and its ecosystems for humans and other species.

On the other hand, the problem lies in the proportions. It is not value per se that causes the vast majority of the population to suffer economic injustice and transforms the earth into an inhospitable cauldron. The problem is that the creation of value exceeds and controls the creation of useful things. Clearly it should be the other way around. We do not need to get back to simple things, as in some naïve handicraft paradise — we need use to exceed and control value. To accept this view, we have no choice but to descend with Marx into the two-faced hell, where nothing is what it seems and everything is duplicitous and in conflict with itself, so that we can at last read it correctly and discover how monstrous the growth on the body social is. What alchemy will be needed to shrink value down to size, to subordinate value once again to human wants and needs? We cannot even ask this question until we follow Marx on his extraordinary journey through the inner life of capital's things.

MYLES ZAVELO

Living

On a rainy Sunday afternoon, pre-workout, I approach the girl behind the counter at my gym.

She mostly deals in fresh towels and electrolytes, and she doesn't like me — not sure why, but she's blatant.

And so right in front of her I go, "I'll take the red Gatorade — the fruit punch flavor . . . ?"

And right in front of me she goes, "We're all out of the red Gatorade. The. Fruit. Punch. Flavor."

"But it's right there, I can see it," I say, beginning to point.

"No, *you're* color blind," she says, beginning to point at living.

Muddy

I run into my therapist from seven years ago. He's standing around, still the young side of middle-aged, face blank, totally unimpressed.

But he's not as I remember him. For instance, he has a fever. He's glistening. His spectacles: gone.

Man, our old sessions. He was strict, for real. Even coffee was off the table. Anything I could hold was a distraction, a crime. It was always late afternoon, often raining.

I used to be much younger than he was, but we are the same age now.

Anyway, the hours change, and we eventually share the same dilemma — we are stuck right in the middle of some vast muddy field.

Boy, this bespectacled fucker used to catch me inside a million lies.

We are sinking, tiring awfully by the end, contemplating together. He clutches my arm just above the elbow. And doesn't let go. We pray for the way God made us to finally mean something.

Through the wall, we hear the kids next door. They are calling each other names again. They will never grow up.

Myles Zavelo

I Was There

She was looking like trapped meat. I'm talking about the pretentious freak of nature stuck in her mother's washing machine down the street.

It was yesterday afternoon. I'd dropped by to return borrowed eggs. I heard screaming, begging, laughter.

We used to play house. I was eleven. She was ten. I was a bank teller. She was a secretary. We were sick and tired of the grind, but happy together. After a long day, she fixed me cranberry juice on the rocks, and I gave her a foot massage. It was a good marriage.

Nowadays, she reads European philosophy and dresses only in Goodwill, and I tend to keep my distance.

I've always managed to avoid the knives that come out of her mother's mouth.

I mean, that woman vomits knives.

And yesterday, those knives were pointing at the trapped meat in the washing machine.

So, after a pink sandwich, which I ate only because I was hungry, I left.

Surely You Of All People Remember

Everybody knows I have them. My problems were bad then. I have value now. I actually love chugging green juice. Dialectical Behavioral Therapy is the name of the holy game. They give me homework over there. They put ice in my hands. They take the sunglasses off my face.

Yeah, I miss being a terror. I miss living for kicks. I miss the way trouble felt. I miss going all in on the cowboy stuff. I miss night-clubs, women dancing, the hard feminine shoes. I miss name dropping, social climbing, jumping to conclusions. I miss the night flights going nowhere. I didn't know their destinations.

I was dragging myself all over town. The same year I learned I was adopted. The same year I got my diagnosis. The same year I lost my license to drive. Wish I could say the only person I was hurting was myself.

I would prefer if certain records were sealed. These open records keep me up at night: borderline unforgivable, a memory cancer under my skin.

I even kicked the dog.

These days, I cradle her freaking ashes — just an unfortunate case of old age.

Lola.

On the other hand, she'd wanted a fight.

Myles Zavelo

ANNA BALLAN

Ecstasy and the Englishwoman: Charlotte Brontë

Charlotte Brontë and George Eliot had a similar quirk to their literary careers: after penning their respective masterpieces — *Jane Eyre* for Brontë in 1847, *Middlemarch* for Eliot in 1871 — both lived to publish deeply strange and religiously preoccupied novels a half-decade later. While the Jewish mysticism and Wagnerian scope of Eliot's *Daniel Deronda* have prompted reams of scholarship, and its melodrama and finely-wrought heroine have broken through to popular consciousness, Brontë's final published novel has met with relatively muted fanfare. Few beyond Brontë completists, academics, eccentrics, and those otherwise in-the-know seem to read *Villette* these days, let alone consider its aesthetic and ideological contours. Its heroine, Lucy Snowe, is criminally under-celebrated. The novel possesses a kind of secret-handshake status, seeming to subsist by virtue of the whispered interpersonal recommendation.

This state of affairs is perhaps unsurprising, since *Villette* rings a dissonant chord in the annals of Victorian fiction. A rough summary of the novel goes something like this. A Protestant Englishwoman, poor, friendless, and plain, crosses the channel to the fictional kingdom of Labassecour; there, surrounded by French-speaking Catholics, she becomes an English teacher and eventually headmistress of her own school. Despite its inoffensive *Bildungsroman*-like frame, *Villette* was regarded with distaste from the start, disliked for the morbidity of its "unamiable" protagonist, as a contemporary take in the *Dublin Review* put it; for its hints of perversity; and for its mood of pungent defiance. Brontë had partly modeled the tale after a wretched year spent in Brussels in 1843. There she had herself been friendless, had been dizzyingly alone, had pined fiercely after her charismatic — and married — professor. Perhaps the novel's early readers could smell its author's acute bitterness. Perhaps they, like Virginia Woolf a century later, shrank from that "jerk in [Brontë's novels], that indignation" rendering them "deformed and twisted." Woolf seems to have preferred *Villette* to *Jane Eyre*. Yet unlike *Jane Eyre*, which wears its turn to the domestic on its sleeve ("reader, I married him"), *Villette* "jerks" its reader still further, permanently deferring marriage for its female lead and closing instead with an ambiguous evocation of shipwreck. On this score the novel is certainly an outlier, most comfortably framed as an exception that proves the rule of Victorian novels.

Villette's deafeningly absent marriage plot, along with the "hideous . . . convulsed" spirit that so baffled and disgusted its contemporaries — those were Matthew Arnold's words in a letter, calling the novel "one of the most utterly disagreeable books I ever read" — were seized on in the twentieth century by second-wave feminist critics. Sandra Gilbert and Susan Gubar, in *The Madwoman in the Attic*, set the tone, seeing in Lucy a casualty of patriarchal constraint, and scholarship since has tended to follow suit. Brenda R. Silver pointed to the sphere of readerly sympathy as a form of surrogate-liberation for the novel's protagonist, and Joseph Allen Boone maintained his predecessors' language of empowerment and subversion. These canonical responses to the novel have tended to prefer an essential, autonomous self, which is either being oppressed and disfigured or else requires some kind of emancipation (if only at the hands of a congenial reader). They have also largely sidestepped the question of religion, consigning *Villette*'s Catholic theme to a peripheral position or glossing over it entirely.

Brontë's final published novel scalds the fingertips and sharpens the mind, and it deserves to be grasped by different means and with different language. One should not take for granted that its protagonist desires autonomy as we might understand it, nor should one see the religious dynamic in the novel as simply an intriguing sideshow. Though indebted to the aforementioned readings, I see Lucy differently — as in some sense in flight from subjectivity, especially in its self-contained and autonomous Protestant mold, and in search of forms of release, mediation, externalization, even annihilation — experiences that the novel codes Catholic. Lucy seems often to find unfettered interiority an impossible burden to bear, to be drawn to a paradoxical "freedom not to consent," in Julia Kristeva's words. This tendency is most apparent in the frequent irruption of ecstatic states in *Villette*: ecstasy becomes the novel's structural principle, contributing to its murky religious aesthetic. The tendency then appears to regroup in the realm of erotic love, to channel itself into a relationship that annihilates private inwardness. While Lucy first pines after a Protestant doctor, she ultimately emotionally entangles herself with an imperious Catholic man.

Why should a nineteenth-century English novel, with the genre's overriding concern with selfhood and development, be interested in experiences that nullify, deflate, or otherwise jettison selfhood, albeit temporarily? And why should Catholicism be the terrain upon which questions of selfhood are pursued? It is tempting to speculate that Lucy's Catholic fantasy life evinces a need to transcend a Protestant-cum-secular, perhaps bourgeois, conception of the individual — a need to transcend the conditions of the novel in which she finds herself. Indeed, in its fascination with the Catholic question, its scorn for cheerful individualism, and its appeal to the mystique of authority, the novel chimes with some of the louder Catholic-talk in our own intellectual air today. The much-covered rise of "tradcath" aesthetics and ideology need not be rehashed here, but consider it distilled by the *New York Times* headline of a few years back: "New York's Hottest Club is the Catholic Church." Paper of record aside, many of us have by now encountered the type: those who, afflicted with the malaise of the secular, have been drawn to the Catholic Church in part through the medium of ideology. (I observe the phenomenon without contempt, gathering that many such cases are on-ramps to genuine conversion or even constitutive of it.) Yet one senses, in some prominent cases, that religion and the culture war have mingled behind a curtain of mist — that the worldview in question consists mainly in a post-liberal pull toward unfreedom.

Is Lucy Snowe an early prototype of this phenomenon? A woman who suffered secular modernity's birth pangs, whose anomie prefigured ours, who sought to curtail her freedoms in the face of the abyss? Like many backward-looking and ideologically smooth readings of imaginative literature, this partly satisfies, but it also requires a good deal of squinting. Lucy, though attracted to forms of externalization and erasure, is equally attracted to the idea of an intact self and keen to keep a tight lid on her consciousness. In the novel's final pages we glimpse a final swerve from the self's disintegration, and perhaps a genuine horror of it — and the triumph of a decidedly Protestant ethos. In Brontë's vision of selfhood, in other words, one finds only contradiction: an oscillating relationship between ecstasy and containment, between the not-self and the self, between autonomy and heteronomy. And the novel can be persuasively read by honoring both impulses. I see in Lucy Snowe neither a victim nor a liberator, neither a misogynist nor a spotless feminist. I wish to take Lucy's ambivalence at its word — to do justice to the irreconcilable drives that hold sway in *Villette*.

Midway through *Villette* — weary from insomnia and devastated by the isolation endured on her school's long vacation — Lucy Snowe is lost and alone when a powerful storm engulfs her. She experiences it as a self-fracturing, and she sets the stage for the novel's first ecstatic episode: "It was cold and pierced me to the vitals. I bent my head to meet it, but it beat me back. . . . I only wished I had wings and could ascend the gale, spread and repose my pinions on its strength, career in its course, sweep where it swept." Lucy sketches a moment in which the boundary between herself and the not-herself is partly dissolved — her body is porous and the storm is felt within it as a piercing of the vitals — and partly not yet dissolved, triggering a desire to vacate her physical frame and merge with the gale's turbulent course.

Volume I of *Villette* shudders to a halt and Volume II opens with Lucy's account of the ensuing out-of-body experience. In it, she appears to consummate that very desire to sweep where the storm swept:

> Where my soul went during that swoon I cannot tell. Whatever she saw, or wherever she travelled in her trance on that strange night, she kept her own secret; never whispering a word to Memory, and baffling Imagination by an indissoluble silence. She may have gone upward, and come in sight of her eternal home.

Lucy's lexicon is idiosyncratic and allegorical, but the exalted transportation she describes — the thrusting of the soul or the self outward — calls up the state of ecstasy, from the Greek *ekstasis*, to stand beyond, above, or beside oneself. She *may* have "come in sight of her eternal home," she hedges, but of the journey she simply cannot tell: this moment of non-presence cannot be captured in recollection or language, it is shrouded in an "indissoluble silence" whose depths she cannot plumb. Just before blacking out Lucy had scornfully alluded to "a certain Carmelite convent," a veiled reference to the Spanish Carmelite nun St. Teresa of Ávila, who spoke in her autobiographical writings of ecstasy as a penetration of the entrails and through Bernini's sculpture has become all but synonymous with ecstatic vision. Beyond the obscure and sarcastic allusion, the ascent of the soul in an obliterating "swoon" may be for Lucy, however superficially, understood to be a Catholic configuration. She has just undergone a purposefully botched confession, wading into a Catholic rite only to brazenly halt its course: "*Je suis Protestante*," she had announced to her confessor.

The self-externalization of confession and the self-erasure of ecstasy share a common narrative logic, though one lets her speak and one renders her silent. Both episodes dramatize a release from the self and speak to an ambivalence about the sort of interiorized and contained selfhood that is for Brontë Protestant and English. Protestantism places the individual subject at the authoritative center of experience, as does first-person narration, but *Villette* is invested in moments when the self seems temporarily to come apart or become opaque. If Catholicism poses a problem for Brontë, it is not only on the surface, in her occasional conversion plots, anti-Catholic tirades ("God is not with Rome," Lucy cries at one point), or even the novel's lightly satirical Gothic set-up — the fact that Lucy's school is built on the grounds of a martyred nun. Lucy's Catholic forays seem to reflect above all an exhaustion with self-sufficiency and self-representation, and offer her a temporary release from subjectivity. Even so, such moments of ecstatic melting or release are for Lucy often opportunities to step back, embrace renunciation, and set limits against which the self can again stand whole and intact — a cycle of explosion and containment that creates a kind of narrative whiplash.

Lucy's ecstatic blackout forms the bridge between the two volumes and between the novel's past and present. She wakes up and is nursed to health by strangers, setting in motion the novel's ensuing plot machinations: the strangers turn out to be her old playmate Polly, now Paulina, and her old love Graham, now Dr. John. It is striking that so much narrative work should be accomplished by a blackout that forms a lapse in its narrator's consciousness and memory. On one level this is simply efficient plotting: a satisfying contrivance or gimmick fitting for a novel structured around mysteries, suspense, and sensation. Perhaps one can conclude, like Elizabeth Hardwick, that these "large, gaping flaws in the construction" of Brontë's stories are "gothic subterfuges [that] represent the mind at a breaking point, frantic to find any way out."

But one might also consider a more specific intention to the blackout, implications for the novel's conception of the self and what can and cannot be worked out in language. The episode that remains fuzzy and sunk in an "indissoluble silence" gives *Villette* a forward motion and a deeper structure than its first-person narrator can understand or account for, let alone consciously witness. Lucy blinks and misses, so to speak, an event that comes to define the course of her life: it is not a moment of sudden vision that sets things forward, but one of occlusion and blindness. The blank space at the core of this story — the moment that does away with linear and legible selfhood — seems almost to operate like its connective tissue.

The fact that Lucy's ecstatic episode concludes with her "re-enter[ing] her prison with pain" speaks to the troubled relationship between ecstasy and embodiment in *Villette*. The novel seeks ecstasy as a temporary absolution from selfhood, here conceived as an out-of-body experience and ending in an agonizing return to the prison of the flesh. On balance, however, Lucy does not wish to be a bodiless, floating soul — and how could she, while always resisting being typecast as an undetectable "shadow"? While one pole of *Villette* pulls away from contained selfhood, another insists on the self's solidity and gravity. Lucy's confessor advises her that "Protestantism is altogether too dry, cold, and prosaic for you," but Lucy vehemently disagrees: she aspires to be, and often is, just those things. A recurring tag for this aspirationally compact and static self is her selective use of her full name: "I, Lucy Snowe, plead guiltless of that curse, an overheated and discursive imagination"; "I, Lucy Snowe, was calm"; and finally, "complicated, disquieting thoughts broke up the whole repose of my nature. However, that turmoil subsided: next day I was again Lucy Snowe." The fullness of the name is contrasted with the self's potential overflow or excess (its "overheating") and potential fragmentation (its wholeness being "broke[n] up"). The pronominal force of "I, Lucy Snowe," with its vow-like affirmation of subjectivity, seems to pledge and enact, not merely to describe, an experience of stable identity.

Whether "Lucy Snowe," the contained self, is embodied and externally legible or is instead emphatically internal is ambiguous. The blackout scene, for example, aligns self-containment with embodiment and sensationalizes the disowning and recovery of both. On the other hand, the levitating "soul" lamenting its return to its "poor frame" would seem to imply a chasm between bodily frame and spiritualized interior. The "soul" is a nebulous term in Brontë and gestures to an altogether different vision of the self, one that is detachable from flesh rather than contained in it. Brontë's notion of selfhood appears sometimes — like the soul, though distinct from it — to exclude what is material and external and to constitute itself on the inside, to regard itself as a private sanctum unknowable by others. It takes pleasure in privacy and secrets; it delights in the dissonance between interior and exterior and in being misapprehended. We see this predilection in Lucy's relationship to Dr. John (and to the reader), where she cultivates and relishes a protective cloud of anonymity that allows her to see while unseen. We also glimpse the tendency in her "struggles with [her] natural character," which she frames in a mood of proverbial wisdom as a matter of "surface" and interior: internal conflict enables life "to be better regulated, more equitable, quieter on the surface," she muses, "and it is on the surface only the common gaze will fall. As to what lies below, leave that with God." Much seems to depend on the tone in which one reads these dense, epigrammatic, often sententious asides; possibly they are themselves a form of self-dissociation.

The physiognomist, on the contrary, maintains that the body's surfaces speak, that one's body — or head, at any rate — encodes and communicates one's true nature. Brontë, who was deeply invested in physiognomy and in the related science of phrenology, makes it crystal clear that intimacy and eroticism work along those lines. Is the self then defined by its obscurity — by the gap between what can be perceived and what *is* — or is the real self visible and readable? At times the former is presented as cheap compensation for the latter. Lucy sums up this form of substitute-gratification in the general, evasive first-person plural: "In quarters where we can never be rightly known, we take pleasure, I think, in being consummately ignored." She utters it with regard to Dr. John, with whom we already know she enjoys being "cloud"ed, and with whom her attitude is essentially: if you will refuse to see me, to "rightly know" me, then I will seal myself up — I will define myself by what is private and hidden in me. Viewed in this light, her retreat into interiority and her "pleasure in being consummately ignored" are points against the Protestant Dr. John, signs that he is not and never was a viable partner in Brontë's romantic universe.

Invisibility and non-participation are certainly out of the question under the Catholic M. Paul's severe gaze: in his orbit there can be no hidden self and indeed no privacy. He enters Lucy's life with brute force by "burst[ing] open" her "closed door," after which "a paletôt and bonnet grec filled the void; also two eyes first vaguely struck upon, and then hungrily dived into me." She receives his presence in breathlessly conjoined fragments, in visual flashes, and there is a quality of thickness to that presence, a sense that it physically implicates her (she is "struck upon . . . hungrily dived into"). M. Paul is later shown to have rifled through Lucy's papers and personal items: she has long known, she admits, "that that hand of [M. Paul] was on intimate terms with my desk; that it raised and lowered the lid, ransacked and arranged the contents, almost as familiarly as my own." The erotic charge of the image barely needs pointing out, but more surprising is Lucy's claim that M. Paul arranges her private materials almost as familiarly as her own hand would.

When she finally catches him in the act of ransacking, she is "provoked at this particular, and yet pleased to surprise him." Thus "provoked" by M. Paul, Lucy takes pleasure in confronting him in turn, heartened by his audacity to test the limits of her own. This is the threatened narrative space in which Lucy paradoxically thrives. Her agency is thrown into relief by its being tested — her bounded and delimited bodily self emerges when its boundaries are breached, when it must resist invasion. Invigorated by M. Paul's aggression, she states emphatically that his "scorn gave me nerve," while the interiorized "to view him . . . myself unseen" characteristic of Dr. John's benign neglect of her had resulted in voyeurism and paralysis. The static, blazon-like descriptions of Dr. John's chiseled features here give way to dynamic movements of stirring, flowing, and soaring: when M. Paul sneers at her, "his injustice stirred in me ambitious wishes — it imparted a strong stimulus — it gave wings to aspiration."

Beyond this foreclosure of the private realm and its blood-warming dynamism, Lucy's relationship to M. Paul is marked by surface legibility and a counterintuitive kind of reciprocity, touched off by "certain vigorous characteristics of his physiognomy, rendered conspicuous now by the contrast with a throng of tamer faces." On the level of physiognomy, he and Lucy are on equal footing, for she glimpses "fire" in his face as he had earlier glimpsed it in hers: "I watched you, and saw a passionate ardor for triumph in your physiognomy. What fire shot into the glance! Not mere light, but flame," he had thundered at her. A physically legible self — with fire shot through its glance, at once an internal blaze and an external effusion — is within reach for Lucy, but only the man with the right sort of narrative force can draw it out.

To that end, Brontë makes the dichotomy between the two male stars of the novel inescapable. Dr. John is a "cool young Britton," a Protestant and a bourgeois doctor who had earlier diagnosed Lucy's "fever of the nerves and blood... scientifically in the light of a patient." "The old symptoms are there," he informs her, at which point she digresses to the reader with some bitterness: "Not one bit did I believe him; but I dared not contradict; doctors are so self-opinionated, so immovable." With Dr. John fever is illness and pathology, reducing her to silence and evasion, while with M. Paul — a Catholic European — flames signify deep compatibility. It is worth noting too that the former is tall and blond, the latter short and dark. By contrasting the two men with schematic and even overdetermined precision, Brontë links their respective modes to corresponding expressions of Lucy's character. In Brontë there is an erotic dimension to character expression, or maybe it's the other way around: quite simply, Brontë insists, Lucy is not the same Lucy in the company of these two men.

But is M. Paul drawing out Lucy's passionate nature, or is he himself creating it ("arrang[ing] the contents" of her character almost as familiarly as her own hand would)? Is he a good reader of Lucy — her only good reader — for discerning the flame buried within, or is he the very precondition of that flame? And if Lucy's surname is "Snowe," are we meant to grasp that what he generates is something somehow contrary or even destructive to her nature, or that he has brought to light the inner nature that her surface conceals? These may be distinctions without a difference, or impossible to determine, in a novel that is always negotiating between interiorized and exteriorized forms of selfhood. Like ecstasy, confession, and the mediation that Lucy associates with the Catholic Church, the forfeiture of private interiority with the Catholic M. Paul delivers Lucy from the burden of a wholly interiorized self. It grants her the pleasure of self-externalization, of exerting gravitational weight and not hovering as "a mere shadowy spot on a field of light." In romance and elsewhere, Brontë suggests, one needs a stumbling block or mediating force for one's contours to take shape: perhaps this is why the Protestant shows up to confession only to haughtily declare herself a Protestant.

Imposition and encumbrance impart "a strong stimulus" in Lucy's scenes with M. Paul — a texture of health, strength, and aliveness. "Scout the paradox," then, as Lucy later puts it: with him, Lucy is both relieved of autonomous selfhood, effaced and totally erased, yet never more solidly there, never more *present*. For Brontë it is a sincere question: what good is freedom without the friction of other people, freedom in which nobody notices your presence enough to impose on you? Or, to paraphrase Sondheim, don't we all require someone to sit in our chair, ruin our sleep, and make us aware of being alive? The novel, then, has moved thus far in a particular direction: from interiority and sickness with the Protestant Dr. John to exteriority and health with the Catholic M. Paul. Why, if so, does Lucy end up alone?

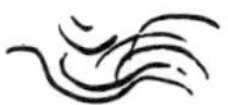

In their final scene together, M. Paul ushers Lucy into a pleasant house with a schoolroom attached. What he grants her is property with her name on it: a room of her own, financial security, a degree of autonomy. His preparations signify much more to Lucy than her own bourgeois ascendancy. "It was his foresight, his goodness, his silent, strong, effective goodness," she writes, "that overpowered me by their proved reality. It was the assurance of his sleepless interest which broke on me like a light from heaven." Surrounded by this proved reality of his affections, freed from having to search for signs of affection, Lucy closes out the novel with a pivot: "[M. Paul] was away three years. Reader, they were the three happiest years of my life. Do you scout the paradox? Listen."

The paradox consists in this: Lucy works diligently to cultivate her school, taking on more students, expanding her property, coming into possession of some capital. She attributes her material prosperity and personal contentment to a "relieved heart" whose "energies lay far away" — to the legacy of and hoped-for future with M. Paul. "The secret of my success did not lie so much in myself, in my endowment, any power of mine," she relays, "as in a wonderfully changed life, a relieved heart," for "the spring which moved my energies lay far away beyond seas, in an Indian island." The paradigm that Lucy describes is one of outward-facing solitude: while she plods away in healthy, satisfied employment, her inflowing sources of emotional energy "lay far away" and securely *outside* her person, with M. Paul in the West Indies. She lives autonomously, but that living is permanently mediated by an external force: her beloved is externalized into the general design of her life, and his absence is her sustenance. Unlike Lucy's prior, bereft freedoms, this freedom allows for more than precarity and loneliness. *Villette* puts forward this fusion of structural autonomy and emotional heteronomy, material independence and mental interdependence, as its horizon of ultimate possibility.

M. Paul imparts his last words to Lucy in a letter: "Remain a Protestant. My little English Puritan, I love Protestantism in you. I own its severe charm. There is something in its ritual I cannot receive myself, but it is the sole creed for Lucy." Lucy goes on to reflect that his Catholicism might in fact "be reckoned amongst the jewels" of his character. To end their relationship on this exchange is to insist that the Catholic and Protestant modes of the novel have indeed been vital to its central dynamic, indispensable to its central quest for selfhood and love. Rather than iron out their opposition, it indicates that Lucy and M. Paul have reached a tenuous equilibrium in and through each other, completed in each other's absence.

A final *deus ex machina* preserves the equilibrium indefinitely. Rather than tip the scales in a consummated union — *would* they have married? — Brontë pulls the narrative to an abrupt halt. Lucy intimates that M. Paul has died at sea, signaling his fate through apocalyptic language but refusing to say so outright. She deprives the reader of that certainty, cagily concluding on a negative image instead: "Here pause: pause at once. There is enough said. Trouble no quiet, kind heart; leave sunny imaginations hope. . . . Let them picture union and a happy succeeding life." A negative image is one the reader must hold in mind despite rationally grasping its untruth; it is like seeing double or going cross-eyed. By overlaying a seemingly tragic ending with its cheery obverse, Lucy "lets" us imagine a happiness that we cannot rid ourselves of, are unnervingly trapped in even as we grope in the dark to envision happiness's opposite. In this finale Lucy rather mercilessly unsettles hope for a happy ending, but also withholds the catharsis of conclusive tragedy, instead leaving her reader to flounder in the unknown. M. Paul's fate, and for that matter Lucy's, is left in the dark.

And what, if anything, remains of ecstasy? Lucy implicitly fails to experience a standard referent of ecstasy: sex. Whether the novel's swerve from the final implications of its marriage plot constitutes a tragic failure — or a kind of escape route — is left ambiguous. In either case, Lucy's implied virginity evokes the nuns that haunt *Villette*. Lucy is visited by a ghostly nun throughout the novel, revealed to be a practical joke played on her by a schoolmate's lover but nonetheless retaining its charge as a psychological double. And M. Paul's former beloved, we learn, had apparently died in a convent after forswearing him. Does Lucy then mysteriously duplicate the arc of the nun for herself — or is her seemingly celibate fate a decidedly Protestant mirror image of it?

More to the point, one might wonder, is M. Paul's assumed death by shipwreck a final step back, a final gesture of renunciation — that is, does he become collateral damage against which "Lucy Snowe" can hold fast to her full name and to all that entails in perpetuity? The repeated reverberation of "Lucy Snowe," like "Jane Eyre," imprints the maiden name firmly in the reader's mind, seeming almost subliminally to foreclose or complicate the possibility of marriage. And the thirst for a "freedom not to consent" may only go so far when one's freedom to consent faces up to real and solid limits: in Lucy's case, the prospect of marriage to a domineering man, one who might reasonably be expected to efface her too thoroughly. As it happens, Lucy's complete sarcastic quip before blacking out had been: "I might just now, instead of writing this heretic narrative, be counting my beads in the cell of a certain Carmelite convent." Though dripping with sarcasm, the phrase hints at a binary opposition between the convent — or, broadly speaking, a perceived Catholic subjugation — and the "heretic" composition of an autobiographical tale. If it is in his absence that Lucy pens her tale, perhaps the permanence of that absence clears way for the story: crudely, he dies so that she can write. Self-erasure here gives way to autobiography, the self's ultimate solidification.

The novel's interpretive possibilities are vast, however, and one might consider whether Lucy — and Brontë by extension

— has set up a hoax for the reader. Perhaps Lucy does eventually marry, but prefers in her autobiography to cultivate an aesthetic of opacity, to draw a closed circle around herself and her fate that no prying eye could possibly puncture. Lucy's "here pause: pause at once" is after all a statement of aesthetic intent: a declaration of a cutting-short, a freeze-framing, that can preserve the past and fossilize it in an eternal present. Lucy declines to publicly subject her relationship to the element of the historical, the everyday, or perhaps, the novelistic. It endures as the exceptional, the monumental, as the having-been of greatness, and it closes out with a bang and not a whimper. The frozen images of "wild ecstasy" on Keats's Grecian urn come to mind — those fair youths who, although they can "never, never" kiss, as a consequence "cannot fade" and are "for ever piping songs for ever new." Like the ecstatic moment sealed in silence, M. Paul's fate now lies outside the novelistic frame. These fissures are constitutive of the novel as much as they point outside it, gesturing outward to what cannot or will not be novelistically contained. If ecstasy endures, it is perhaps as this, as an aesthetic commitment to what will not be contained.

In Brontë's final novel, as in select spheres today, Catholicism becomes the arena in which questions regarding the value of selfhood, of expressive individualism, appear to work themselves out. Yet Brontë resists the easy conflations that all-too-often threaten to poison such discourses, and throws a wrench in our retroactive ideologizing, by presenting us with a tangled knot of paradoxes and not a thesis statement. While her protagonist pushes up against the demands of bourgeois selfhood — and often finds genuine psychological value in constraint, limitation, and obstacle — Brontë nonetheless suggests that not all constraints are created equal, that some exact costs we would not wish to bear. She must have grasped that the romance of unfreedom meant one thing in theory and quite another in practice. For she holds both in mind at once, honoring the psychological value of the former while seeming, though we cannot know for sure, to flee the implications of the latter. We close *Villette*, then, suspended in the fog of Brontë's ambivalence. The novel's abrupt and ambiguous climax is almost a confession on the part of its author: *I do not yet know how this ends.* Where, indeed, do such contradictory impulses lead? Lucy Snowe's existential drama is perhaps ours to live now.

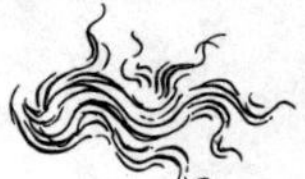

ROBERT RUBSAM

The High Art of Distance

"Art, of course, lives in history," said Elizabeth Hardwick. By which she meant that a novel emerges in its own time, and changes in its passage to our own. This — the likeness which is also an unlikeness, the unfamiliar familiarity — is the shock of reading classic literature, of literature even a generation or two removed from one's own. We understand that a novel is essentially a historical survivor, written in one moment, picked off the shelf in another, yet we want it also to enlighten us about our own lives, of which the author necessarily knew nothing. Astoundingly, they quite often do. And yet it is in those gaps, those absences, that the real excitement lives. We should not recognize ourselves, and yet we do. We should not be moved, but we are. And then we are offended, or struck, or in some other way expelled, and the gap expands, and the past and the work and the author come to seem the distant shore they really are.

We can visit, but not to stay.

I have a theory: the more we recognize in an era, a place, an artwork, the stranger its differences strike us. This is perhaps especially true for the novel, whose most familiar forms can be used to convey so much that we do not understand. "So much of a novel, after all," observes Hardwick, "is information, necessary fact that gives a floor of understanding from which the flights of inspiration are launched." Reading a novel from another country, another century, requires you to set a new foundation, plane a new floor — and to surrender yourself to the novel's "subtle time," that "spiritual and intellectual lengthening, extending like a dream in which much is surrendered and slowly transformed." Yet for even the most sympathetic reader, this process is never complete. Your surrender becomes a kind of suspension, slack or tense, between your time and the novel's, your era and the author's, communicating down the years like a current shooting down a wire. You connect, and you don't. You feel, you sense, you embrace, but always at a distance. There is always some gap.

Yet a reader's life, too, has its seasons. At a certain time in your life, you encounter a work written a certain time in the author's, and you understand, or you don't. The work, the reader, the writer are like dancers moving across the floor; all three must make a trio for the dance to continue. Thirteen years ago I first tried to read *The Savage Detectives*; but this past spring I read it at a sprint. All that intertextuality, all those fractured, puffed-up perspectives: I needed a decade-plus and hundreds of other books to begin to approach them. So, too, can a writer miss his or her moment, and be recovered later. Robert Walser's obsessive self-obscuring semi-fictions sing clearer in our deeply pessimistic age than during the course of his indigent life.

To say nothing of chance, when we are made to encounter the unexpected, and are made to change. In January 2017, I was twenty-five years old and in Melbourne, Australia. One day I was wandering north of the river when I passed a bookshop that was going out of business. I was with a friend then stationed in Okinawa and in a week I would fly to Tokyo, and so I picked up, at a deep discount, a slim Japanese novel called *Snow Country*.

Published in 1948, *Snow Country* tells the story of Shimamura, a young man from Tokyo, and his relationship with Komako, a geisha who serves a hot springs resort in the mountains. Shimamura is a cold man, ambivalent to the point of cruelty; in the first pages, he reflects that only a single forefinger remembers his lover. And yet again and again across the seasons he finds himself drawn away from his family, and back to Komako and the mountains. The novel proceeds as a series of piercing images: a woman's complexion melting into a snowy mirror, a train window in which the reflection of an eye is superimposed off a light burning deep in the mountains. Komako will not let go of Shimamura, who, whatever his apathy, cannot raise the strength to escape. It concludes suddenly, and with great violence: Shimamura arrives at the site of a fire, turns upward, and feels the Milky Way roaring down into his body.

It was a startling book, a vision of the novel as something both shaped and shattered. By chance, it was also my first encounter with the great Japanese writer Yasunari Kawabata. A master of compressed forms and oblique endings, Kawabata helped introduce modernism to Japan, and published a number of significant novels, as well as more than a hundred and fifty short and ultra-short stories. For this he was the first Japanese writer to be awarded the Nobel Prize in Literature. From his time to mine: I have been reading him ever since.

In the early 1920s, when he was a student at Tokyo Imperial University, Kawabata lived above a hat shop in the northeastern neighborhood of Asakusa. The neighborhood was then one of the liveliest and most Westernized in Tokyo, and the indifferent student preferred to wander the modern quarter, taking in the revues, going to the movies, and soaking in the public baths. He seemed determined to engage in all that was new and exciting, and at the expense of his studies.

Along with much of Tokyo and Yokohama, Asakusa was leveled in the Kanto earthquake in 1923. Viewing the ruins, the novelist Jun'ichiro Tanizaki reveled in the possibilities available for reconstruction in the Western style. "How marvelous!" he wrote. "Tokyo will become a decent place now!" Kawabata's building withstood the shaking, and he spent the following days wandering the wreckage, a jug of water and lunch in his backpack, writing down his observations.

In the first decades of the twentieth century, Japanese literature felt like a similarly cleared space. The autobiographical form known as the "I-Novel" was in decline, and a battle was being waged between the Marxist writers of proletarian literature and the modernists inspired by translations of Valery, Marinetti, and Durrell. Eminent writers such as Tanizaki and Ryunosuke Akutagawa argued in print about the future of literature. Would it be with Akutagawa's "pure" fictions, "close to poems in prose"? Or with Tanizaki's plotted works, "complicated things embellished with maximum intricacy"? Were the answers to be found in the Japanese and Chinese classics, or in Tanizaki's occidental fixations?

Kawabata and his cohort found themselves suspended between these positions. In 1924, he co-founded the literary journal *Bungei Jidai* with Yokomitsu Riichi, a fellow writer and the founder of the *Shinkankaku-ha*, the New Sensationalist School of writing. Heavily influenced by European modernism, the Sensationalists emphasized the significance of form over content, artefacts of detached observation, and the personification of objects and the natural world. Their stories are full of fragmented narratives, found documents, and streams of consciousness. "We have become quite weary with literature that is as unchanging as the sun that comes up from the east today exactly as it did yesterday," Kawabata wrote. "Our eyes burn with desire to know the unknown."

Though his English was middling, Kawabata attempted to read Joyce and Woolf, and his earliest stories were in a distinctly modernist vein, employing fragmented forms. "A Saw and Childbirth," first published in 1924, narrates a dream which begins in Italy, moves to the narrator's hometown, finds he has to urinate, and engages in battle with a woman holding a saw. Kawabata folds the act of interpretation into the narrating, asking again and again what is happening, and what it means. In the final lines, he lies in bed, reflecting (in J. Martin Holman's translation): "Somewhere would she bear someone's child?"

"The Dancing Girl of Izu," published in 1926, tells the story of a walking trip that Kawabata took across the Izu peninsula in 1918. When the narrative begins, the narrator is twenty years old, and has been on the road for several days. While climbing the Amagi pass, he reunites with a group of itinerant musicians who make their living performing at hot spring inns. He has already seen them twice before, and found his eye drawn by a young girl carrying a drum whom he believes to be about seventeen. The boy falls in with the group, traveling down the mountain and into Yugano. He tries speaking with the shy girl, and even dreams of inviting her to his room. Yet when he glimpses her coming out of the bath, he realizes that she is much younger than her dress had implied, and he is relieved. "I felt pure water flowing through my heart," he reflects. His affections can remain unrequited; he will not have to allow another into his life.

Such distance came easily to Kawabata. "For me," he wrote in 1934, "love, more than anything else, is my lifeline." And love for him was a history of loss. Born in Osaka in 1898, he was an orphan by the age of three, and by 1914 had lost his grandmother, his sister, and the blind grandfather who raised him. In 1922, in a story of the same name, he reflects on being christened "The Master of Funerals." His family life is retained as a series of fragments, each memory tied with a particular death. His parents exist as photographs on the family altar. He can only recall his sister as she appeared on the day of their grandmother's funeral, carried on a relative's back in white mourning clothes. The young man is so composed that he finds himself invited to the funerals of strangers. Yet his decorous behavior was never feigned, he writes. "Rather, it was a manifestation of the capacity for sadness I had within myself."

His first love was for a male high school student, and in the early 1920s he proposed to a young woman who broke off their engagement. Even his most passionate male characters tend to keep their distance from life: they recognize emotions, but do not seem to feel them. Shimamura's love draws him back to Komako, yet his apathetic treatment enrages her. In the novel *A Thousand Cranes* in 1952, an orphaned man named Kikuji drifts between various women, including his late father's mistress and her young daughter, with a nearly existential level of indifference, a ghost in his own life. Even Kawabata's happiest characters seem unwilling to act on their intuitions or feelings; when old Shingo hears a distant rumbling, in *The Sound of the Mountain*, he senses death. Yet this does not alter his conduct, and he proceeds through his family's many crises without acknowledging it. These men keep everything inside.

As an editor at *Bungei Jidai*, Kawabata helped to shape and to promote New Sensationalism and its tenets. Yet his own early work only lightly resembles that of his peers. There is a directness to the writing which heightens every elision. Rather than circling each absence, he lets them stand. Other than his interesting but unsuccessful modernist novel *The Scarlet Gang of Asakusa*, Kawabata incorporates these fragments directly into the form of his stories, implicitly presenting them as fissures within the psyche of his characters, rather than overtly in the jagged structure of the text.

"Dancing Girl" is built around precisely such withholding. We wait until the story is almost over to learn that the narrator has gone walking to overcome the "stifling melancholy" of orphanhood. Early on, the male musician reveals that his wife has lost two children, one by miscarriage, another born prematurely. Only some pages later are we told that the premature baby in fact died within the last couple of months, while the performers were still on the road. As they head south to Shimoda to commemorate the forty-ninth day since the baby's death, they talk freely, and without sentiment. "They said the baby was almost as transparent as water at birth, and it did not even have the strength to cry." Like the death of the narrator's parents, this tragedy rests always beneath the surface of the story, evoked through their conduct. His love for the dancing girl is not consummated, or even acknowledged. She dotes on him, but when the girl sees him off at the ferry, she refuses even to speak. When the boat sets off, he begins to sob, "a sweet, pleasant feeling," as though he might drain away, and "nothing would remain."

"Dancing Girl" and subsequent publications earned Kawabata substantial acclaim, and in the 1930s he moved from the avant-garde to the mainstream. He judged the inaugural editions of the Akutagawa Prize, and in 1934 he was appointed to the *Bungei Kondan Kai*, the Literary Discussion Group assembled by a former head of the Public Security Division of the Home Ministry. This was a period of increasing control within the arts: the literary fervor of the 1920s had given way to the increasingly militaristic and authoritarian 1930s, and many of his former rivals in the proletarian literary movement were jailed, tortured, and forced to make *tenkō*, a public rejection of their Marxist principles.

Given his frequent statements on behalf of artistic independence, Kawabata's cooperation with an organ of censorship and control might seem awkward. He published articles insisting on freedom of speech and the rejection of social norms, and when in 1935 the BKK chose not to award the significant Akutagawa Prize to the *tenkō* writer Shimaki Kensaku, he protested publicly. Yet he also seems to have used it to firm up his own place in the literary landscape, knocking down upstarts such as Osamu Dazai and achieving financial security. When an early version of *Snow Country* won that award in 1937, he used it to purchase a villa in the mountain town of Karuizawa.

Like all his novels, *Snow Country* was published serially, before being compiled into a revised text. Because it is such a slim, exacting novel, it would be easy to think of it as a perfectly conceived work. In the introduction to his translation, the great Edward G. Seidensticker compares it to a haiku. Yet this was never Kawabata's method. *Snow Country* was originally serialized between 1935 and 1937, but he returned to it in 1939 and 1940 and added a final chapter in 1947. Kawabata once remarked that it could have been broken off at any point — a harsh, fragmented quality that could describe all of his best stories.

His long works all began as short stories, often published without promise of future installments. Tanizaki theorized the Japanese novel as a work of architecture, requiring a carefully reinforced floor plan. Kawabata rarely thought ahead, writing on deadline for whatever newspaper or magazine would ask him, and essentially all of his major works were first published in installments, a common practice for Japanese writers at the time. Yet where Tanizaki used the extended gestation to construct a sturdy foundation, Kawabata leapt sharply from installment to installment, proceeding by non-sequitur, often skipping over major events to focus on stray details: the eye in the windowpane, the play of light on the Kamakura hills, the deep black of a camellia blossom. His practice was to "sound the overtones" of that first chapter, until the full harmony emerged, or he gave up; his career is full of abandoned works. They often end on a piercing image: the roaring Milky Way, the tea bowl broken across paving stones, the boy whose sorrow drains him dry. The effect is startling, and the lack of resolution lingers.

In his best books you sense him ranging across the course of a life, fusing his biography and the currents of his time into the thing called style. All those early deaths wounded Kawabata profoundly; and for all his philandering, you sense a man who held himself at a great distance from his own life. His characters, too, reside at a calculated remove from their own circumstances. *Snow Country* was based on an affair Kawabata had in the mountain hot springs town of Yuzawa, and he began writing the novel there, too. If it was anything like the fictional relationship, this affair must have been disappointing for all involved. Shimamura holds himself back from Komako, preferring to observe her from a distance so that he can keep from plunging into the warmth of real passion. He describes the world, so that he will not have to reach it.

One morning, Shimamura awakes to find his lover preparing herself in his frigid room. "The white in the depths of the mirror was the snow, and floating in the middle of it were the woman's bright red cheeks." He remarks on the "indescribably fresh beauty in the contrast," yet Shimamura is also reducing each element — the morning, the woman — down to their essence: blood and snow, red on white. In the process he is arranging them all within his own memory, perhaps hoping to step back from the scene and, like a man arranging flowers, to discover some harmony in it.

You see here Kawabata's distance, but also the way he privileges intensity of focus: when his characters notice something, the story reorients towards it, following their associations across space and time. This continues to the best of his late work. In *The House of the Sleeping Beauties*, in 1961, a not entirely impotent man named Old Eguchi visits the title's seaside establishment. In this place, old men spend the night beside beautiful young women who have been drugged to sleep. Night after night Eguchi returns, closely observing each girl's skin, her hair, the feeling of her toes, how her body smells. These observations lead him to remember his past, the first lover taken away by her family, an affair with a married woman, the camellia tree in the garden of a Kyoto temple he had visited with his youngest daughter.

In his hands, this free associative movement is clean, effortless. On the first night, the smell of the girl's breathing causes him to think of milk, which causes him to think of his grandchildren, which brings to mind two affairs from his own past: a geisha who could not stand the smell of his grandchildren, and then his own first love, from whose breast he had once drawn blood. Over only a handful of pages, Kawabata slips easily back and forth between Eguchi's present and past, conflating the scent of the sleeping girl and the sound of the waves below with his youthful flight from his family with the girl by his side. "The facts were different, but in the course of time Eguchi's mind had made them so." The loneliness of the character combines with the restlessness of the style: Eguchi can never remain with anyone; like the narrative, they are always passing on.

The effect is like a cold flame, an emotion held unsustainably in check. The women's bodies are described in steady, precise detail, and yet there is no familiarity to them: they might be statues or painted figures for all he can reach them. They exist, in an objective physical sense; but Eguchi can only access the women who exist in his own past, who become real in the course of his recollection. As in the late work of Kawabata's protégé Yukio Mishima, something from beyond the human world is required to pierce the veil, to touch them at all. In order for Shimamura to admit any deep emotion, he must allow the Milky Way to flow into him. The novel ends with a gesture, turning away from the human story to face something abstract, an ideal as pure and as violent as a mountain river.

There is a condescending idea that Kawabata's brevity, his aloofness, are somehow "quintessentially Japanese." But his work stands apart from his predecessors and contemporaries. Perhaps no one makes a better contrast than Osamu Dazai. Across a short but prolific career, Dazai mined his own dissolute life in a series of confessional novels and stories. These are stories of self-styled bohemians, many of them drug addicts, most alcoholics, who alternate between states of ecstasy and debasement. "I am the sort of person," confesses the narrator of *No Longer Human*, "who can forget even the name of the woman with whom he attempted suicide." Though he was once a Marxist, by the time of his brief fame in the late 1940s Dazai could more accurately be described as a nihilist. "Philosophy?" declares a character in *The Setting Sun*. "Lies. Principles? Lies. Ideals? Lies. Order? Lies. Sincerity. Truth? Purity? All lies." "There is something fundamentally cheap about such awareness of genius," Dazai writes elsewhere in the book. "Only a madman would read a novel with deference." In life and on the page, Dazai played the part of the brilliant clown, the man who writes his novel "clumsily, deliberately making a botch of it, just to see a smile of genuine pleasure on my friend's face — to fall on my bottom and patter off scratching my head."

Dazai believed that Kawabata hated his work — he was right — and believed that he had shut him out of the Akutagawa Prize in 1935. In response, he published an open letter mocking the older writer's work. "Does keeping small birds and watching dancers perform," he wrote, "constitute such an admirable life?" He accused Kawabata of feigning a cold, emotionless exterior, an obsession with essences and ideals rather than the brute facts of life. And Kawabata's works do conflate people with the weather, the landscape, and the seasons. In his Nobel lecture, Kawabata finds this same quality in the poetry of a Zen monk who, in "seeing the moon, becomes the moon." His novels are often grounded in rituals and traditional arts such as Gō, lending a refinement and a purity to human affairs. *A Thousand Cranes* filters its erotic tensions through the tea ceremony, imbuing each act of prostration and consumption with the significance of tradition. Even the most abject debasements take on their own cold beauty.

There is little beauty in Dazai, and no refinement. For his narrators, society's charades mask the real and unendurable agonies of existence, a performance which we bear only out of our own ignorance. As one character writes in his suicide note: "When I pretended to be precocious, people started the rumor I was precocious. When I acted like an idler, rumor had it I was an idler. When I pretended I couldn't write a novel, people said I couldn't write. When I acted like a liar, they called me a liar. When I acted like a rich man, they started the rumor I was rich. When I feigned indifference, they classed me as the indifferent type. But when I inadvertently groaned because I was really in pain, they started the rumor that I was faking suffering."

This clownish despair brought Dazai fame and success, but it was short-lived: he killed himself alongside a mistress in 1948. Yet in recent time Dazai has surged in popularity. His heightened emotionalism has found a following on TikTok, a perfect home for such piercingly direct statements as "learning is another name for vanity. It is the effort of human beings not to be human beings." Kawabata's work might be modern, but it is of a restrained modernity; Dazai overflows, rushing on into our own time, obsessed with the illusion of connection, the theater of confession. Kawabata's elusive, opaque fictions cannot compete in such an exhibitionist contest.

"I am one of the Japanese who was affected least and suffered least because of the war," wrote Kawabata in 1948. He joined several patriotic writers' associations, and was sent to Nagano prefecture to discuss literature with farmers. He wrote for newspapers in Manchukuo, and visited Mukden with other prominent Japanese writers. Unlike his old friend Yokomitsu Richii he did not become a rabid anti-Westernist, and he did not join the Pen Brigades sent abroad to write propaganda. "I was never caught up in a surge of what is called divine possession," he recalled, "to become a fanatical believer in or blind worshiper of Japan." He served as an air raid warden in Kamakura; he spent the blackouts reading *The Tale of Genji*. After the defeat, he declared that he would live only to maintain the traditions of Japan.

The postwar period was probably the most productive of Kawabata's entire life. In 1948 he became the fourth president of the Japanese PEN Club, and traveled to PEN congresses across the world to promote Japanese literature. He wrote frequently for newspapers, and serialized numerous novels simultaneously. In the ten years after 1945 he published a revised edition of *Snow Country* as well as *The Master of Go*, *A Thousand Cranes*, *The Sound of the Mountain*, and numerous "Palm of the Hand Stories." These post-war works deploy a simplified, refined version of his pre-war modernism to address traditional Japanese arts in a thoroughly Westernized context. Other writers suffered under the U.S. Occupation's Civil Censorship Detachment, which forbade, among other things, "Criticism of the Occupation Forces," "Third World War Comments," "Glorification of Feudal Ideals," and "Overplaying Starvation." But as under the military government of the 1930s and 1940s, Kawabata's personal remove and his quiet, private subject matter largely evaded scrutiny. Even *The Master of Go* is largely ambivalent in its symbolic depiction of Japan's defeat. Unlike in *The Setting Sun*, an aristocratic tradition simply slips away, too refined to insist on its own defense. The world had changed, and so should literature. Akutagawa's "pure" fiction must give way to something else.

"If there is to be a 'renaissance of literature,'" Kawabata wrote in 1935, "it will have to take place in works that are at once of pure literature and aimed at a mass audience." He applied this theory in earnest through the 1950s and 1960s, writing great quantities of "middlebrow literature" for the highest-paying major newspapers and magazines, long novels such as *Tokyo People* which remain to this day untranslated. For Kawabata's English-language admirers, this trove can seem more like a hoard, waiting for excavation. *The Rainbow*, an intermittently effective recitation of his core preoccupations, recently translated by Haydn Trowell, is the latest exhumation. Originally serialized in 1950–1951 in one of Japan's largest women's magazines, it tells the story of Mizuhara, an architect with three daughters by three women. Momoko, the eldest, and Asako, the middle child, live with him in Tokyo in the immediate aftermath of the war. Asako wants to find their missing sister, but Momoko is indifferent, caught up in a vicious romance with a teenage boy.

In works such as *The Master of Go*, the Japanese defeat is addressed indirectly, through a meditation on other subjects. Kawabata visited Hiroshima as a representative of PEN, and though he said that he would one day write a novel on the subject, he never did. *The Rainbow* is as close as he came. Five years before the novel begins Momoko was in love with Keita, a schoolboy and member of the kamikaze Special Attack unit. On their final night together, Keita made a mold of her breast from which to make a teacup to drink his last cup of sake before death. Realizing they might never see one another again, she gives herself to him, and he takes her virginity. She rejoices in the feeling, like "a flash of lightning in the overcast sky of her long love; a radiant, scorching cause of joy." His response is immediate. "'Ah,' he spat out softly, turning his back to her. 'Ah. How dull.'" He finds her pathetic, violated, and he dies in Okinawa without seeing her again. This is one of the few explicit references to imperial war-making in Kawabata's work, in part because he remained at as much of a distance as an ambivalently pro-Imperial writer could.

From 1942 to 1944, Kawabata commemorated the outbreak of the Pacific War in the Tokyo *Shimbun* newspaper, publishing articles on the writings of soldiers killed in action. "I have always grieved for the Japanese with my private grief," he wrote in 1948, "that is all." Wartime literature portrayed Japanese soldiers as brave recruits, solid men spreading enlightened Japanese culture across the Pacific. Yet Keita is an unsentimental depiction of a Japanese soldier, caught up in fear and self-loathing, a death in search of a purpose. Late in the novel, his father reflects: "The dead escape condemnation. But it's fine to put the blame on them."

Kawabata's serial plots are never terribly strong; they are propelled by thematic resonances rather than narrative drama. But *The Rainbow* is a particularly overextended beast. The plot is dictated by extensive coincidences, and despite being only a little over two hundred pages long, it is drawn far too thin. It is full of characters who do little but explicate their motivations, and at great length. Mizuhara is often present to deliver lectures on Japanese architecture, but does little else. Kawabata's best work is defined by reserve, a nearly perverse unwillingness to state the obvious. Here, however, characters talk and talk, expressing everything, suggesting nothing.

Asako is a particularly failed creation, prone to sudden distressed exclamations, as if incapable of thinking even five seconds into the future. Her virginity is contrasted with Momoko's bitter, wounded state, driven from a shattered love towards manipulative sex. This dichotomy recurs frequently in Kawabata's work. As others have remarked, he prized beauty, "fresh" beauty, above all things, with virginity signifying the ultimate in beauty. Asako, Momoko, the sleeping beauties: all are ideal women who cannot be touched. In the autobiographical *Letters to My Parents*, Kawabata declares: "I always fall in love with women who are in between a child and an adult in age." "I am all but moved to tears of gratitude that such a girl exists," he writes, "but I could never love her." His men keep their distance from such women, as if afraid of corrupting them.

Yet for all his devotion to the pure, Kawabata's virgins are often his worst characters, either fading into nothingness or remaining as symbolic foils to more complex women. Asako is not only weak, but passive; where Momoko pursues a series of destructive love affairs, her sister's one attempt at romance lands her in the hospital, before she disappears from the novel entirely. Whatever his moralizing intentions — such as his claim that *A Thousand Cranes* was written to illustrate "the vulgarity into which the tea ceremony has fallen" — his work becomes electric once his characters have been in some way compromised. I am thinking of Shimamura's apathetic philandering and Komako's stubborn love, the diverse lusts of young Kikuji and Old Eguchi. Without such stains and blemishes, Asako and her father are lifeless.

When we pick up the failed works of a major artist, we glimpse the hard limits of his or her artistic project, and with it their worldview, and the result can be disorienting. The outlook that gave us such beautiful insights also gave us a host of inconsistencies and contradictions. We might want to dismiss a disappointing work as minor, insignificant, or we might use it to demolish the writer's perfectly constructed canon from the inside. The flaws give the lie to the concept of brilliance; if they fail here, imagine where else their work might fall short. Yet it seems to me undeniable that such faults are essential components of an artist's worldview. Without them, we see the reflection, not the landscape. Kawabata's intuitions are not presented piecemeal; they arrive as a total worldview. A general allergy to plot created narratives driven largely by aesthetic associations. His profound emotional distance gave him a unique vantage on how passion ravages the mind. His apoliticism made him both the beneficiary and the critic of the imperial government and its militarist mentality. And he saw that the same impulses which seek to preserve purity wish even more to destroy it. This was not all conscious, yet it is expressed again and again across his oeuvre. In the work of a truly great writer, even the flaws cohere.

So it is in *The Rainbow*. In the final quarter, the focus narrows in on Momoko, and Kawabata achieves passages of immense power. The eldest sister becomes pregnant, and receives an abortion which neither her father nor Keita's seem willing to mention; even the novel describes it only as "the operation." Too weak to return home, she stays in Kyoto with Keita's father. Time begins to collapse, and the narration leaps from one reflection to another: her birth mother's suicide, the death of her first lover, the arsenic pill which her adoptive mother swapped out with sugar. How much of life turns on such small actions, she wonders, how much misery do we unknowingly perpetuate? Her furious heart is empty, and like a true Kawabata protagonist, she submits herself to the will of the world, unable to act upon her fury. Yet that rage is still there, like a taut string quivering at the heart of the novel, always ready to snap.

In the final pages, she is brought to meet her youngest sister, a geisha named Wakako, in a restaurant in the northwestern neighborhood of Arashiyama. As they are walking along the Oi river, she stops before a pool and sees a small tree reflected in the water:

> It was a web of fine branches, drawn clearly over the water. What kind of tree was it? Above the embankment, its intricate, delicate lines were difficult to distinguish among the surrounding foliage, yet they stood out perfectly on the surface of the river. It was as though she was staring not at a reflection but at a tree growing inside the water.

The world is clearer in reflection, as life is more vivid in art. Momoko goes off to see her sister. In the final moments she slides open a shoji screen, to hear the river's flow.

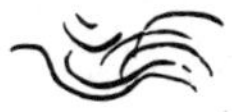

I have been trying to read Kawabata's works in his own time, but now I must write about him in mine.

In 2017, I took my copy of *Snow Country* from Melbourne to Tokyo. I read it quickly, incompletely. I remember feeling at a loss, held apart from the characters, both thrilled and disoriented by the conclusion. So over the next few weeks I found copies of *A Thousand Cranes* and *The Master of Go*, as well as books by Mishima and Endo, and I devoured them as I went. I read them in Nikko, across the mountains from the Yuzawa snow country. I read them in Kyoto, in a coffee shop in Arashiyama. And I read them in Kamakura, where, on April 16, 1972, Kawabata went to an apartment in Hayama and drew a bath. He unhooked the gas line — on purpose? by accident? — and died.

When I think back on that time, I remember being shocked by the suddenness of Kawabata's revelations: the roaring milky way, the broken tea bowl. I was young, I was in a foreign country, I was open to everything, like a house with all the windows flung wide. I took it all in, and reflected later. Several weeks later I came to Tsuwano, in the mountains west of Hiroshima. One night, I was eating a simple sushi meal by myself when a pair of men approached me. They were English teachers and were celebrating a colleague who was changing schools. Would I like to join them?

I spent that night with perhaps twelve other teachers, and after many drinks they asked what I was reading, and I told them. They didn't think much of Endo, Mishima was too patriotic, Kawabata far too old-fashioned. A middle-aged man from Izumo described him as a "classic" whom few people actually read. He wrote his email on a piece of paper and told me to write him. I folded the slip, put it in my pocket, and lost it on the way back to my room.

Their words stuck with me. I had spent so much time in Japan, had witnessed so much, yet what had I understood? Kawabata's books had surprised me, sure, but had I read them properly? What had I gained from them, really? Perhaps an openness to surprise, and to shock. Near the end of my trip, I arrived at the Koya-san temple complex in the mountains south of Osaka. It had snowed heavily, and during my days there tree branches snapped and roofs rumbled. I was walking alone through the Kongobu-ji when I came upon a small side room, its paneled walls bright with gold leaf. All my trip I had come across similar such artworks, and marveled at how the gilding set off the painted landscapes, abstract fields leafed across deeply detailed scenes. Yet I had not *seen* them. For as I stood there I saw, I really saw, that the screens formed a long landscape of mountains and waves, with a flock of cranes soaring across it all. I looked closer, and saw cloud patterns dimpling the edges of the gold leaf, and all at once I realized that the cranes had been scattered by the winds, separated in the field of clouds, calling to one another but lost, and lost forever, in this field of great beauty, and it was as if the light were blinding me, as if my body was collapsing, and a great wave of beauty and sadness flooded through me, a Kawabata feeling, a feeling I have not forgotten in all the years since.

"I AM AN AMERICAN DAY"

DIDI TAL

"In the huge gathering . . . there were, according to the official estimate . . . 1,250,000 persons. So far as available records indicated last night, this was the largest crowd that has ever assembled at a single point anywhere in the world." This *New York Times* report from May 1942 refers not to a military parade in Nazi Germany but to a celebration in New York City. "The magnet that drew this astonishing turnout to Central Park, where it filled out not only the five acres of the Mall but the thirteen acres of the sheepfold, was the local observance of 'I am an American Day,' which, by proclamation of President Roosevelt, was marked yesterday in hundreds of other American communities, great and small."

"I am an American Day" was a freshly instituted national holiday. It had started as a grassroots initiative before it was adopted by Congress and signed into law by President Roosevelt in 1940, and it was honored in small, local celebrations in cities and towns across the country, in schools and community centers, following special guidelines and utilizing educational materials that were put together by the Immigration and Naturalization Service under the Department of Justice. "Many desirable values result from such public ceremonies," the government's handbook from 1944 states. It continues, "The community ceremony lends dignity to the new citizenship status. Through the public ritual of oath or pledge, loyalty is cemented and the individual's feelings are stirred by group honors paid to the flag." "I Am an American Day" existed until 1952, when it was renamed "Citizenship Day," moved to September, and merged with "Constitution Day." But it was in its early days, the 1940s, that the occasion was freighted with public meaning and celebrated on a national scale. This was true also of the centerpiece of the celebration — large public naturalization ceremonies. In May 1942 in Central Park, forty-six thousand men and women became new American citizens and made this country their home. And the country welcomed them.

This little-known episode in the country's long relationship to immigration is full of contradictions. Jewish and political refugees fleeing death and persecution in Europe unavailingly tried to secure visas to the United States. At Ellis Island, just a few miles away from Central Park, people awaited deportation back to the European horror. America did not adjust its closed-door policy and its quota system in the face of mass statelessness and murderous oppression. And yet the naturalization numbers increased sharply. Fewer immigrants came in, but more people than ever before became new citizens. Those new Americans, many of them former refugees, became messengers of a new patriotism. As Americans by choice, they embodied the ideal of citizenship and loyalty.

Naturalization procedures were restructured to publicly express these messages. Up until the beginning of the twentieth century, naturalization was not a standardized process in the United States. It was performed in five thousand federal, state, county, and municipal courts across the country. Every court determined its own procedure, requirements, fees, and naturalization papers. In 1906, however, the Basic Naturalization Act established the Bureau of Immigration and Naturalization under the Department of Labor and provided a "uniform rule for the naturalization of aliens throughout the United States." This put in place a standard procedural framework that governed naturalization for most of the twentieth century. The authority to grant or to deny naturalization continued to be vested in the courts, but duplicates of every naturalization form had to be filed with the newly founded Bureau of Immigration and Naturalization in Washington, and standardized forms and fees were instituted.

In 1940, the Nationality Act transferred the Immigration and Naturalization Service from the Department of Labor to the Department of Justice. The act established requirement standards such as periods of residence, proof of good character, and special provisions for spouses of American citizens. It revised and detailed standardized guidelines for citizenship and its acquisition through birthright or naturalization, and it outlined the procedural framework for the process of naturalization. It also continued the United States' Asian exclusion policy in terms of naturalization rights, clearly stating that the right to become a naturalized citizen extends only to white persons, persons of African descent, and to races indigenous to the Western Hemisphere. The only exception to these exclusions were Filipinos who served in the United States Army.

Naturalization consisted of two steps, colloquially referred to as filing "first papers" and "second papers." Both were now made to take part in "open court." And, for the first time, the ceremonial and performative elements of naturalization were coded into legislation. Interestingly, the Nationality Act of 1940 also included a series of recommendations regarding the "education" — a euphemism for indoctrination — of prospective citizens and the public on the meaning of American citizenship. Henceforth the presiding judge was required to deliver a "patriotic address to new citizens." The larger celebratory occasions used their patriotic addresses to encourage enlistment and raise support in America's participation in the war. An "I Am an America Day" address by Judge Learned Hand in 1944 touched many and was printed in newspapers in following days under the title "The Spirit of Liberty":

> What do we mean when we say that first of all we seek liberty? I often wonder whether we do not rest our hopes too much upon constitutions, upon laws and upon courts. These are false hopes; believe me, these are false hopes. Liberty lies in the hearts of men and women; when it dies there, no constitution, no law, no court can even do much to help it. . . . in the spirit of that America for which our young men are at this moment fighting and dying; in that spirit of liberty and of America I ask you to rise and with me pledge our faith in the glorious destiny of our beloved country.

Between 1795 and 1952, a "Declaration of Intention" was the first step in attaining American citizenship. The language in both the 1906 and 1940 acts does not make a clear distinction between filing the declaration in terms of papers and making the declaration orally in front of a judge or a clerk. The material part of the declaration was a signed form complete with a pledge under oath to ". . . renounce absolutely and forever all allegiance and fidelity to any foreign prince, potentate, state, or sovereignty of whom or which at the time of admission to citizenship I may be subject or citizen." The text also included a clause on the commitment to organized government and a sworn oath to permanently reside in the United States.

The final stage of the ceremony, the oral oath of allegiance — the act of enunciating a commitment of loyalty in the company of witnesses and thus rendering that commitment binding — is a bit reminiscent of a marriage ceremony. Here, too, an individual binds themselves to another (or another entity) through the act of speech. Ever since the inception of naturalization policy in the newly founded United States of America, the transformation from non-American to American citizen required public language — the recitation of an oath. "I Am an American Day" celebrations from the early 1940s are, by far, the largest and grandest naturalization rituals in American history.

The largest of them was held in Central Park in 1944. In those festivities one and a half million people surged into the city to bear witness and promise loyalty. As in previous years, Mayor Fiorello La Guardia presided, and political speeches and musical performances accompanied the ceremony. Soldiers were in attendance, including veterans of World War I and even of the Civil War. Two years earlier, General Charles de Gaulle, then leading his occupied country from exile, was a surprise speaker at the event; he was invited by Mayor La Guardia to address the crowd over radio from London. "General De Gaulle told the gathering that millions of Frenchmen were placing their hopes of freedom in the efforts of the United States," the *Times* reported. It must have been quite a moment.

Enthusiasm for "I Am an American Day" waned after the war. By 1946, attendance at the Central Park festivities dropped to one hundred and fifty thousand, and the merriment hit a low point as well. The new Americans in the crowd listened while Mayor William O'Dwyer, who had been a distinguished soldier during the war, warned them not to import any "dangerous, foreign ideologies to the U.S." The robust patriotism of the war years was being drained by new Cold War anxieties, and immigrants bore the brunt of the new dread. The pomp and circumstance was replaced by foreboding. Was it inevitable that American pride would shrivel into fear as more and more newcomers found shelter within our borders? Is heterogeneity an inspiration or a threat? We are still asking ourselves that question.

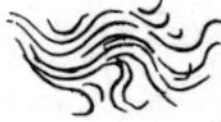

SEWN CLOSE TO PASCAL'S HEART

YAHIA LABABIDI

"Man is but a reed, the weakest in nature, but he is a thinking reed." The line appears halfway through Pascal's philosophical work, *Pensées* ("*Thoughts*"), quiet as a whisper, final as a verdict. In around a dozen words, he captures both our fragility and our strange dignity. This is Pascal's gift: the ability to distill what is vast into a sentence, and make the infinite startlingly present. To read him is to encounter a mind that recognized truth had to be lived, suffered, loved. His words carry the heat of a soul exposed to something greater than itself, whose whole being seems to burn through the page.

I discovered Pascal in my early twenties, like many do, through his profound and evocative collection of aphorisms. I had no religious education to speak of, and certainly no theology. Still, there was something in those complete fragments that reached past my youthful skepticism, addressing my inchoate longing. His voice seemed to emerge from the edge of two worlds: the measurable and the mysterious.

Pascal was born into the age of Richelieu and Louis XIV, when France trembled between the old certainties of faith and the new promises of reason. The Fronde civil wars of his youth taught him that human institutions, however grand, could crumble overnight. Perhaps this instability shaped his urgent spiritual seeking. When the ground shifts beneath your feet, you learn to look up.

He was a mathematical prodigy, reformulating geometry at twelve and inventing the mechanical calculator at nineteen to ease his father's tax duties. His work on probability theory laid foundations that would stand for centuries. But to remember only his genius is to forget his gravity. He also knew what it meant to live close to death. From childhood onward, he suffered from chronic stomach ailments and nervous disorders that grew worse with age. He lived only thirty-nine years, much of it in bodily misery. Yet from this wounded life came spiritual clarity. In one of his memorable petitions, he asks God to "teach us the proper use of sickness."

His mathematical precision never abandoned him, even in matters of the soul. Consider how he approaches the question of God's existence. Where others built elaborate proofs, Pascal offered what became known as his "wager." "Let us weigh the gain and the loss in wagering that God is," he writes. "If you gain, you gain all; if you lose, you lose nothing." Critics have dismissed this as cold opportunistic calculation, but they misunderstand. His wager was never meant to be a trick. He was trying to shake his reader out of indifference. If God exists, then eternity is at stake. If not, then nothing you love will last anyway. Rather than a syllogism, it was a cry from a man on the edge, pleading with others to look up before it was too late.

On the night of November 23, 1654, that cry was answered. Pascal experienced what he could only describe as fire, a torrent of divine presence that lasted two hours and changed everything. Here was a man who had spent his life measuring, calculating, proving, suddenly confronted with something that rendered his sophisticated vocabulary utterly inadequate. He wrote it down immediately in a text now known as the "*Mémorial*." It begins with a single word repeated: "Fire."

The word stands naked on the page, stripped of the elaborate reasoning that had defined his intellectual life. "God of Abraham, God of Isaac, God of Jacob, not of the philosophers and scholars." That last phrase reveals everything. His conversion was not intellectual; it was volcanic. The God he encountered was not the prime mover of Aristotle or even the necessary being of Aquinas, but the living God who spoke to prophets and burned in bushes.

What follows is perhaps even more telling. He sewed the document into the lining of his coat, near his heart, and carried it with him until his death. Think of it: this master of public discourse, this defender of doctrine, reduced to the wordless intimacy of a hidden document pressed against his chest. The gesture seems almost superstitious, deeply personal, at odds with his rationalist reputation. How does one return to mathematics after touching eternity? How does one debate theology after encountering the God who exists beyond all categories? Pascal lived the rest of his life in this tension, caught between the measurable reality he had mastered and the immeasurable mystery that had mastered him. The "*Mémorial*" was discovered by accident, stitched inside the fabric, long after the body had cooled: a final secret, a private fire that had never been extinguished.

Soon after his conversion, Pascal withdrew increasingly from Parisian society and became closely associated with the Jansenists of Port-Royal. These rigorously Augustinian Catholics believed in the absolute sovereignty of divine grace and the profound corruption of fallen human nature. Their theology suited Pascal's temperament perfectly. Where mainstream Catholicism often spoke of cooperation between human will and divine grace, the Jansenists insisted that salvation was God's work alone. Man could neither earn it nor resist it.

Pascal lived among them for extended periods, embracing their discipline of prayer and study. When the Jesuits attacked Port-Royal's theology, Pascal defended his friends in the *Provincial Letters* (1656–1657), a masterpiece of polemical literature that combined theological precision with devastating wit. He wrote under the pseudonym Louis de Montalte, crafting letters supposedly sent from Paris to a friend in the provinces. The device allowed him to appear as an innocent observer gradually discovering Jesuit moral casuistry. "I had thought that I was merely ignorant," one letter concludes. "But I find I have been deceived."

Yet even among the Jansenists, Pascal remained inward, solitary. He had tasted something no system could fully contain. The God of his "*Mémorial*" demanded more than correct doctrine. He demanded everything. Even Pascal's compassion bore the marks of his rigor: "We must have pity for one another," he writes, "but we must feel for some a pity born of tenderness and for others, a pity born of disgust." It is a hard saying, but not a cruel one, blending a sense of mercy with moral exactitude.

It is in the *Pensées*, unfinished and fragmentary, that his genius remains most alive. He died before they could be completed, leaving behind bundles of notes written on scraps of paper, organized by theme but never synthesized into a single argument. What survives is not a book but a soul in pieces. There are no conclusions, only openings. "Man is neither angel nor beast," he writes. "And the misfortune is that he who would act the angel acts the beast." The line lasts because it is true. We recognize ourselves, caught between pride and appetite, and feel in his words both judgment and mercy.

What makes Pascal enduring is not only what he believed, but how he spoke. Where Descartes built systems and Spinoza constructed geometries of the emotions, Pascal worked in lightning strikes of insight. "The heart has its reasons which reason knows nothing of." "We run carelessly to the precipice, after we have put something before us to prevent us seeing it." "The eternal silence of these infinite spaces frightens me." Each sentence carries the weight of a meditation, the clarity of a mathematical proof, the urgency of a man who knew the soul could be lost.

Perhaps, Pascal is a master of brevity because he lived with the pressure of death and the presence of the divine. When time is short and eternity is long, every word matters. His fragments read like prayers in disguise; they subtly invite us to kneel, arguments that double up as psalms. Even his opponents recognized the force of his prose. Voltaire, no friend to Christianity, remarked that, "One must agree that Pascal was a man of an extraordinary eloquence. His style is like his thought — original, profound, often sublime." Likewise the combative aetheistic Nietzsche, who admitted: "I have a predilection for Pascal."

Maybe what draws us to Pascal across the centuries is his refusal to choose between reason and faith, between the life of the mind and the life of the spirit. He shows us that a thinking person need not abandon thought to believe, nor abandon belief to think clearly. His God was encountered not despite his mathematics but through it, not in opposition to his learning but in its depths.

Even his silences speak. In the fragments, there are notes to himself, lists of themes, broken beginnings. They remind us that the greatest truths are not always delivered whole. Sometimes they come as fire in the night, stitched close to the heart, hidden until we too are ready to see. Sometimes they arrive as a whisper. He shows us what it looks like to think with one's whole being. His legacy is not a system but an example: the spectacle of a brilliant mind undone by love, remade by grace, and given back to the world as a gift.

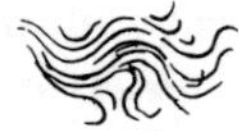

IN TEHRAN UNDER FIRE

FATEME KARIMKHAN

It was still early in the war. After four days of internet blackout — and, God knows, testing countless VPNs — I finally reached a stable enough connection to check my email. The last one was from a prestigious university in New York, where I was scheduled to begin my Ph.D. in the upcoming academic year. They had asked why I hadn't confirmed my admission yet, warning that if I delayed any further, I might lose my spot. I responded politely that these nights I can't sleep from the sounds of Israeli rockets landing right and left across my city, and that during the day, I'm constantly trying to make sure the many people I know across town are still alive. News that someone two oceans away was thinking about my fall plans felt like a comforting distraction. But truthfully — even if I had not been under rocket fire — the new travel restrictions against Iranian citizens would have made it impossible to attend that program anyway. I typed up a version of these sentiments, hit send, and then I stared at my phone screen, watching the VPN wheel spin, waiting for the email to leave "draft" status and finally be sent. The wait, of course, wasn't short. As with all attempts at action during the days Tehran lost to war, it dragged on.

I'm not the only one who, in those black days, stopped thinking about the future or set aside carefully made plans. After the first wave of Israeli attacks on Iran — which mainly targeted western parts of the country and densely populated cities such as Tehran, Isfahan, and Tabriz — many others, too, collapsed under the weight of seeing mangled bodies or even just images of bombed-out homes on TV screens and social media.

Naturally, the fears of the future felt very real. They were triaged in a sort of macabre sliding scale. Immediate fears: where will the next missile land? who will it kill or render mourners? Near-future fears: what happens if food and medicine shortages hit? And more distant ones: when will this war end, and under what circumstances? And if it ends, will ordinary people — social, cultural, political actors — have any right to live? And if so, who will protect them?

For years, Iranians have feared becoming the next Syria or Afghanistan. In those days, more than ever, that fear breathed down our necks. Still, what most occupied Iranians — day and night — wasn't what might happen in ten days or ten years. We were most occupied with counting the dead while dreading the next strike.

And it was not only the fear of death. It was also the fear of losing the last means of connection, solace, and sanity — the internet, which had become a lifeline during the COVID-19 pandemic's isolation. In the days we lost to war, it became common to begin sentences with *If I die during internet blackout* . . . Audio recordings, snapshots of handwritten wills, Telegram notes — these were shared openly online, often with heartbreaking directness.

A father told his child to seek out help with funeral arrangements. A mother, in a voice message to her daughter living abroad, said, "If we die, make sure you request reparations — maybe it'll make your life easier." Another young woman, addressing the unborn child she was due to deliver in four weeks, wrote: "If I die, I want you to know I never thought I'd be giving birth to you in a war. Had I known this would happen, I might have chosen not to bring you into the world."

Many just didn't want to be forgotten. For younger left-leaning Iranians, this sentiment was particularly inflected with memory of the mass of faceless fatalities in Gaza, so many of whom were killed by Israeli airstrikes and then forgotten. In the younger generation's digital pleas to be remembered, they invoked the memory of Fatima Hassouna, a Palestinian photojournalist and artist from Gaza, born in 1999 and tragically killed on April 16, 2025, in an Israeli airstrike that also took the lives of ten of her family members. She achieved international recognition for her powerful documentation of civilian life during the Gaza war, especially after foreign journalists were barred from entering the region. Young Iranians' online wills began with "Don't let us become numbers," referring to how the names and stories of those killed in Gaza have often been lost. Except for a few, most are remembered simply as part of a rising death toll — hundreds more each day — rather than lives, dreams, and human histories. This was the fate that these young Iranians feared.

They were right to dread a similar oblivion. In the first ten days of the war that began with Israel's attack on June 13, at least 400 people were killed. Despite relentless efforts by journalists and citizens, fewer than a hundred of them have been named, and about half as many photos have been made public. The fear of dying and becoming a statistic is painfully real. But there's another, quieter fear: of leaving lives unfinished.

My mother, a woman in her early fifties, who left Tehran at my insistence during the bomb-filled days, told me as she departed, "I hope if someone must die, it's us old folks. You're still young. You haven't lived. You have so much left to do." I joked: "Out of a population of ninety-two million, around 935 people have been killed in under two weeks. The daily odds of dying are one in several million. You're more likely to die from cancer than from a missile." She didn't find it funny. And she was right. There's not much to laugh about in war.

A few weeks before the sirens started, Nazli, a close friend of mine, had told me she'd been diagnosed with a rare, untreatable cancer. Her doctor had bluntly told her that she likely had two years to live. Even as someone who has spent much of her adult life studying death, the news was hard for me to hear. I didn't want to respond with hollow comfort. I couldn't decide what to say. After the shock passed, my mind kept circling the same question: if I were in her position, what would I worry about most? An unlived life? An unfulfilled love? A long, raw intimacy never granted? My family? The pets and plants I care for? Probably all of that and more.

Sometime after she shared the news, I emailed her: "Sudden death robs us of one thing — time. Time to fully form ideas and complete projects. If there's anything that needs time — unfinished research, a puzzle not yet solved, something that needs building — I'll do it. I'll give you my time, now or after you're gone."

We always think that we have plenty of time until we are suddenly — it always feels sudden — disabused of that illusion. During the first days of the war, with forced closures and the internet down, even with long days ahead of me, I had no time. The hours couldn't be filled with reading. Even writing the shortest lines — even describing the weather — became impossible. After a few days of staring at my laptop and writing nothing, I gave in and wrote a letter to my publisher. It included final drafts of some texts with necessary edits, as well as a portion of a book I had been writing about the protests in Iran in 2022, with a note stating: "If I don't finish it, the introduction explains the concept — I hope someone else can complete it later." I felt lighter.

But there is a category of creation that cannot be delegated. And I was in the middle of such a project: a half-finished novel. I've been working on it for over five years. When I look at its pages, the weight of its incompleteness sits on my shoulders. The plot is straightforward, but a novel can't be handed off to someone else. There's a not-so-famous Iranian author, who is also a renowned writing teacher, who says, "Every writer's duty is to write one great love story and then die." And this novel, full of ellipses and question marks, is mine. My one great love story. Still unfinished.

On the Sunday that fighter jets and missiles bombed Tehran more than twenty times, my resistance to writing a will on social media finally broke. I typed: "If I get killed, some of my translations will be published eventually; the unfinished book on 2022 will remain, and a half-written novel I haven't been able to add a single line to in days will remain unfinished."

To friends who asked how I was doing after the Sunday attacks, I repeated the same silly calculation about cancer vs. war. I even laughed. But later I realized what I'd missed in my conversation with my sick friend — what is missing from the will-writing culture — is this: the deepest fear is not the absence of a future. That is inevitable, war or no war. What haunts us — my friend back then and I now — is the absence of the present. The days that could have been spent writing, creating, and loving — are now swallowed up by endless explosions.

War doesn't steal our future — it steals our present. Not our becoming, but our being.

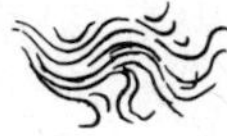

CELESTE MARCUS

The Revolutionary Synagogue: Notes of a Grateful American

Pedro Alvares Cabral was the first human being in recorded history to have been on four continents. He set foot on each of them — Europe, Africa, America, and Asia — in a single year, 1500, which was the same year that he led the first extensive European exploration of the northeast coast of South America. He "discovered" what we know today as Brazil in April of that year, and wrote home to King Manuel I notifying him of Portugal's brand new territory, theirs by virtue of the authority vested in him by the King and his interpretation of the divine will. Cabral sailed on from Brazil, but he left behind the seeds of what would become the first robust Jewish community on the American continent. Among Cabral's crew was a man who went by the name João Faras. Faras was an astronomer, astrologer, physician, translator and — most importantly for our purposes — he was a member of the community of

Portuguese Jews who had been forcibly converted to Christianity by the King of Portugal just a few years after the Spanish expulsion.

Cabral's men had reached what would become Brazil on April 21, but Faras remained on a boat offshore for six days — he had developed an irritation which made it impossible for him to walk. On the twenty-eighth of that month, finally upright and capable of studying the stars to determine location, Faras and two assistants set up a wooden astrolabe on the beach and attempted to establish the altitude of the midday sun. After some days of study, he drafted a letter to King Manuel I, which included a sketch of the stars which make up the southern hemisphere. He explained with apologies to the king that, due to his lame leg, he could not identify the precise height of the stars, but he did identify a new constellation, which we now know as the Southern Cross.

The king to whom that letter was addressed was the very same monarch who, on December 5, 1496, demanded that all his Jewish subjects leave the country. The following year this edict was rescinded and Jews were prohibited from fleeing the country and instead forced to convert to Catholicism. These decrees were issued just four years after the Jews of Spain had been forced from their homeland due to King Ferdinand's and Queen Isabella's genuinely world-altering antisemitism — in fact, Manuel issued the decrees in order to satisfy the Spanish monarchs, to whose daughter Manuel was attempting to marry off his son. There were few options for relocation for Spanish Jews in 1492 — England and France had already instituted country-wide bans (in the aftermath of expulsions) against Jews in 1290 and 1306 respectively. Many countries that did not ban Jews wholesale prohibited Jews from owning land and required Christian oaths for vassals under the feudal system. The easiest place for them to go was Portugal, and many of the Jews who were tormented by Manuel's oppression were originally from the Spanish Jewish community that had just been violently dispersed. Scholars judge from João Faras' weak Portuguese and preference for Spanish that he was likely among these Jewish Spaniards. In the intervening years, Faras had become a "converso," or hidden Jew — living publicly as a Christian but privately as a Jew — and so he and his descendants must have remained for as long as the Portuguese maintained control of Brazil.

Jewish responses to the inquisition differed. Some, like Faras, chose to stay in Spain or Portugal, convert to Catholicism, and brave the anti-Semitism which stalked them even after baptism. Rumors swirled that the "new Christians" practiced Judaism in secret, adulterating Catholic purity with atavistic practices. Many chose to leave the Iberian peninsula altogether, and some part of that group travelled north to the newly independent Dutch provinces, which permitted Jewish immigration and Jewish practice. In this period Jewish fate was overwhelmingly determined by the governing power's caprice, which often swung between prejudice and avarice: prejudice because anti-Semitism is a weed that flourishes under every sun and avarice because the Jews repeatedly proved themselves lucrative residents, and in the host countries, money-lust rivaled xenophobia in ubiquity and its power. There was not a single state which granted Jews rights because it understood that Jews were *owed* rights. The best Jews could hope for were privileges granted by opportunistic and self-regarding leaders. Privileges could only be acquired and maintained for as long as the governing authority could be persuaded that the deal was a good one. (Authoritarian dealmakers can be like that.)

The Dutch accepted the Jews because the Jews promised wealth and they made good on that promise. The Muslim rulers of Spain had permitted Jews to participate in trade and business, and for the Jews it was a more or less benevolent period, but when the Christians came and the Jews were eventually forced to flee they carried their business acumen on the road with them and, more importantly, they brought connections to the many Jewish businessmen who had been dispersed by the Inquisition and were now scrounging for residence in port cities around the world. The Jews in exile constituted a kind of international business network owing to their relations with each other. By 1600 most of the discriminatory laws that were enforced in other European countries were either not on the books in Amsterdam or ignored there. When, in the early seventeenth century, the Dutch West India Company dispatched ships to conquer territory across the ocean, some of these prospering Jews went with them. They met the community that João Faras' had helped found when they got to South America.

The descendants of João Faras and his community lived as crypto-Jews for generations. In the years after they first arrived in the new world, the conversos flourished financially, so much so that Adam Smith observed in *The Wealth of Nations* that

> The Portuguese Jews, persecuted by the inquisition, stript of their fortunes, and banished to Brazil, introduced, by their example, some sort of order and industry among the transported felons and strumpets by whom that colony was originally peopled, and taught them the culture of the sugar-cane. Upon all these different occasions, it was not the wisdom and policy, but the disorder and injustice of the European governments, which peopled and cultivated America.

Note that Smith referred to them as "Portuguese Jews" — it seems those Jews who converted learned what so many have had occasion to discover: antisemites don't want Jews to be Jews, but they don't want them to be anything else either. Wealth did not gain the Jews toleration, and these Jews knew nothing like the religious freedom that their brothers and sisters enjoyed in Amsterdam — the conversos in Brazil would continue to live in "hiding" for one hundred and thirty years. But apparently hiding was not enough. Between 1593 and 1595 an Inquisitional Commission was established in Olinda, in the port of Recife in Brazil, where conversos were tried and arrested. When the court was dismantled, Jew-monitoring was taken over by the local bishop.

All this changed in 1630, when the Dutch West India Company wrested control of Brazil from the Spanish. They had come to

South America with a specific interest in the cultivation of sugar cane, a trade dominated by the conversos, as Adam Smith noted. The Dutch brought with them members of the powerful Jewish community in Amsterdam, and also the freedom and toleration which was the law of the land back home.

Thus began the first openly practicing Jewish community in the Americas. This is where we started. It was, for a time, the freest Jewish community in the world. Less than ten years after the Dutch arrived, Brazilian Jewry built the first American synagogue, Kahal Kadosh Zur Yisrael, in Recife, which was responsible for maintaining a school and a cemetery for the community. For twenty years it seemed that true freedom was possible as a way of life. But it was too good to last — in 1649 the Portuguese instigated a war to win control of northern Brazil, which they managed to do within six years. After victory they instructed the conquered that the Jews, like the Dutch, had three months to pack their things and go.

Most of the Jews returned to Amsterdam, some went to Curaçao, Surinam, and Barbados, and twenty-three boarded a ship called the *Saint Catherine* bound for New Amsterdam, a Dutch colony in North America known today as New York City. Their welcome was not warm. Peter Stuyvesant, the director general of New Netherland, began a campaign against the Jews which would last for the rest of his time in office. Stuyvesant met the twenty-three Jews at the dock and tried to prevent their disembarking. He wrote home to his superiors in Amsterdam hectoring that the Jews were "deceitful," "very repugnant," and "hateful enemies and blasphemers of the name of Christ," who ought to be made to depart lest they "infect and trouble this new colony." He also warned that granting the Jews liberty would force the Dutch Reform community to do the same for "Lutherans and Papists." (Intolerance is paradoxically inclusive.) Perhaps Stuyvesant had in mind the revolutionary liberal colony recently founded in Rhode Island by the radical Roger Williams, who had written a charter for the city which promised that no one would be "in any wise molested, punished, disquieted, or called in question for a difference in opinion in matters of religion." This goodwill in Rhode Island did indeed extend to Lutherans and Catholics and it would eventually include Jews. Some of the Jews living under Dutch protection in Barbados, Surinam, and Curaçao got word of the freedoms offered in a faraway place called Providence and ventured there as early as 1658.

The Dutch West India Company (which included Jews among its founders and its directors) was not especially interested in protecting its Jewish subjects, but neither was it swayed by Stuyvesant's warnings of a pollutant Jewish mass. His superiors had more pressing concerns involving their pocketbooks: a group of Spanish-Portuguese Jewish merchants in Amsterdam had sent the company a letter outlining several reasons why the Jews should be granted entry in New Amsterdam, and prime among them was that "many of the Jewish nation are principal shareholders" of the company itself. The leadership was convinced, and instructed Stuyvesant likewise. Yet the conditions they demanded were a far cry from the freedom these Jews had grown accustomed to in Recife: they were permitted to travel, trade, live, and remain in New Netherland only so long as "the poor among them shall not become a burden to the company or to the community, but be supported by their own nation." And they were prohibited from practicing their religion in public. These Jews had plenty of experience with precisely this form of religious practice: clandestine and implicitly shameful.

The first documents that spurred on the Enlightenment which rattled Western culture and altered the course of modern history were written in the early seventeenth century, roughly concurrent with settlement in the New World. The proto-liberalism that they espoused was in part the breakthrough accomplishment of the legacy of Amsterdam, particularly the revolutionary thinking of one of Amsterdam's Jewish sons, Baruch Spinoza. These were the ideas that eventually culminated, almost two centuries later, in this thunderous sentence: "We hold these truths to be self-evident, that all men are created equal, that they are endowed by their Creator with certain unalienable Rights, that among these are Life, Liberty and the pursuit of Happiness." A rather spectacular historical irony was about to play out: whereas the Enlightenment was kindled an ocean away, it came to fruition nowhere with greater force than the country that would blossom out of Colonial America, the country whose promise was sealed in the Declaration of Independence.

A miracle in Jewish history, in sum, was about to take place. The name of the miracle was the United States of America. The attainment of American independence from Great Britain marked the creation of the only polity in human history that Jews, along with all other human beings on the planet, were considered the just recipients of rights which were owed them purely by virtue of their humanity. These rights were not a charter or a privilege, they were axiomatic.

But there was a problem. By the time of the first Jewish settlement in Colonial America, the ideas that would coagulate into the rich soil from which the possibility of political liberalism would eventually spring were only just beginning to form and were certainly in their infancy in the New World. Anti-Semitism was an early import with which Jeffersonian ideals would have to contend. Peter Stuyvestant was early in his legislation of antisemitic laws — Jews in New Amsterdam were prohibited from purchasing land, serving in the guard (they were forced to pay a tax in lieu of guard duty), voting, holding public office, engaging in retail operations, and trading with the Native Americans — but New Amsterdam was hardly an outlier in terms of codifying antisemitism in the New World. The Catholic community of Maryland instituted a ban on Jewish settlement years before any Jews ever moved there. After Roger Williams' death, Rhode Island became an inhospitable home to its Jewish residents and the Jewish community that had flourished there shriveled. Even in Pennsylvania, which had been founded by the Quaker William Penn as a "holy experiment" of religious tolerance, Jews had no citizenship rights before the revolution — Penn's founding charter required all voters and public office holders to profess faith in Jesus Christ. And to some of the Enlightenment thinkers who laid the groundwork for the earth-shaking intellectual revolution consecrated in the American Declaration of Independence, Jews were not obviously worthy of any rights or privileges at all. Thomas Paine — the Voltaire of America in this respect, too — violently opposed both Christianity and Judaism, but believed that Christianity could be unlearned whereas Judaism was biological, and that Jews had to be cured of their Judaism or they would endanger enlightened society.

In this social pre-Enlightenment and pre-American context, the few Jews of North America who arrived before America's founding followed the pattern of settlement that Jews had repeated in most of their new host countries — they settled primarily in major port cities and worked within the established international, and then national, network of Jewish merchants. Newport, Philadelphia, Charleston, and Savannah became centers of Jewish life, and insofar as Jews enjoyed the hospitality of their Christian hosts; "tolerated guest" was the highest status to which Jews could aspire. And here again they relied on their financial success for their security.

The New World did not extend rights to its Jews until long after Jewish settlement first began. This, despite the fact that the idea of "rights" as such, the idea that a person could be owed anything, as a matter of right, by the state and its governing officials, was percolating in the American intellectual welter. The stirrings of egalitarian idealism were beginning to be felt. Those ideas did not come to the fore until the American Revolution. And the American Revolution was also a revolution in Jewish history.

By the time the Revolutionary War began, one hundred years after a Jewish community settled in New Amsterdam, the Jewish population in North America had swelled to about a quarter of a million people. That Jewish community, which lived through the years of war, was the first Jewry to see a country founded with the promise of a place in it for all people, and so for them, too. (I hasten to add that the new republic was, as a matter of principle and practice, kinder to them than to its black population.) Descendants of that early New Amsterdam community, Shearith Israel, were still living in New York when British fleets approached New York Bay in 1776. Half of them, led by the cantor Gershom Mendes Seixas, fled first to Connecticut and then to Philadelphia three years after the British vacated that city in 1777. Seixas managed to snatch one of the congregation's two Torah scrolls, lovingly referred to as "the revolutionary Torah," and took it with him to his father-in-law's home in Stratford, Connecticut. A few years later he and his flock moved to Philadelphia at the invitation of a congregation called Mikveh Israel, which would become America's first permanent Jewish congregation.

When the patriot Jewish refugees of New York, led by Seixas, arrived in Philadelphia, the Jewish population of the city had about tripled in size. Israelite patriots from Richmond, Charleston, Savannah, Lancaster, and Easton had already come to the city fleeing the British. These Jews had come, while other residents stayed behind, because they believed in the Revolutionary project, in the philosophical premise of freedom and democratization. As two Philadelphian Jews put it in 1782, American Jews had "fled here from different parts for refuge" and arrived there to reconstitute the fledgling Mikveh Israel congregation on March 24 of that year as a "revolutionary synagogue," which is how that congregation is described by the contemporary congregation of Mikveh Israel. The move to the City of Brotherly Love was symptomatic of deeply held commitments to the possibility of a country founded on the ideals of the Enlightenment, a possibility that was at that point in the war far from certain to come to fruition.

Jewish American patriots understood from the first that the Enlightenment had implications for how modern Jews ought to relate to their own religion. The first recorded meeting of Mikveh Israel mimicked Jefferson in declaring independence for American Jewry. These Jews claimed that the Philadelphian Jewish community that they were replacing had enjoyed "no right or legal power," since it was founded only according to the custom of ordinary and familiar congregations and not as a conscious group of free rights-bearing individuals. But now, the document declared, the group must "bind ourselves one to the other that we will assist to form a constitution and rules for the good government of the congregation" in order to "promote our holy religion and establish a proper congregation in this city." This declaration formally united two traditions for the first time: Judaism and liberalism. The alchemy of that precious admixture altered the course of human history. (It became the civil religion of American Jewry for a long time, and like all civil religions it came to be taken for granted and in need of refreshment. In our time it may be gravely in crisis.)

The affecting thing about the Jewish kindling to the new American dispensation is that Jews were championing their claim to rights about which they did not yet feel completely secure. In the matter of democracy they were rather like Nahshon, the Israelite at the Red Sea whose faith was so great that he dove into its waters before Moses parted them. Before the war was over, the freedom that Jefferson described was very young and (as we would say) aspirational. The Jewish patriots were taking a great risk in throwing their lot in with the revolution: it was not at all clear in 1782 that freedom from Britain would come, or that if it did it would bring with it rights for all citizens regardless of religion. In fact, the same year that the Jews of Mikveh Israel drew up their constitution, they also bought a plot of land to build their first synagogue on a street called Sterling Alley, which happened also to house a church belonging to a German Reform Congregation. The church complained: they did not want their community polluted by Jewish proximity. The Jews had a choice: they could adjudicate the case in court, or they could placate the bigots by buying a new plot of land a safe distance away with money they hardly had to spare. They chose not to bet on the American courts and found another location. In April 1782 it was not at all clear that a Philadelphian court would honor a Jewish community's right to erect a synagogue wherever it pleased.

The principles were sterling, but it was a struggle. Religious rights were not quite an existential certainty for American Jews, but they were prepared to fight for the American promise. The next year the patriot Jewish congregation in Philadelphia, with Seixas at its helm, petitioned the state of Pennsylvania to formally alter the religious oath required by all elected officials so that Jews would not be prohibited from running for public office; the Pennsylvania Council of Censors considered and then tabled the request, but news about the petition was printed in three newspapers at the time favorably reporting the Jewish cause — it was a salient social issue, and the Jews were on the liberalizing side of it. When the war ended, many states heeded Seixas' plea and rescinded their test oaths of their own accord. As the Jews who had been holed up in Pennsylvania returned home after the war, the states that accepted them back *all* dropped their test oaths: Georgia, South Carolina, Pennsylvania, Delaware, and New York lost their test oaths by 1792. Virginia, which had not been a Jewish center before the war, got its first synagogue shortly after victory was declared; its test oath had been abolished in 1786 in the extraordinary Virginia Stature of Religious Freedom, drafted by Thomas Jefferson and husbanded into law by the like-minded James Madison. All this was not, to put it mildly, the familiar Jewish experience of the exile.

In the last decade and a half of the eighteenth century, the laws of state constitutions, and the freedoms owed to all citizens of the newly won country, were in far greater flux than we may realize. True, the Constitution of the United States, and the amendments to it, forbade the federal government to make laws establishing religion or limiting the freedom of religious expression, and it prohibited religious tests for federal offices — but much discretion was still left up to the states. Some states enforce blue laws — laws which prohibit work on Sundays, the Christian Sabbath — to this day, and blue laws were used in the early decades of the country to coerce working class Jews to abandon Jewish practice. Blasphemy laws, always the spear point of illiberalism, were in place in many states into the nineteenth century as well. The federal Constitution of 1787 allowed all states to decide for themselves who could and could not vote — the ideas which would make up the country's legal skeleton had not yet calcified into shape. In New Jersey, for example, the state legislature amended the state constitution in 1790 to formalize a right that had already been in practical operation. It added the phrase: "he or she" in a clause regarding enfranchisement: ". . . no person shall be entitled to vote in any other township or precinct, than that in which he or she doth actually reside at the time of the election." It thus made explicit a property-owning woman's right to vote, which that state had considered implicitly secured through an ambiguity in its original constitution. And seven years later, the state removed a different phrase regarding property ownership after which the number of women voters increased dramatically, as did the number of voters amongst free people of color. And so it remained in the state until 1807.

The Jews were among the scrappy minorities eager to secure for themselves the rights which were not yet clearly stipulated and honored by all. The Jews of New York immediately took advantage of that state's decision, in 1784, to automatically recognize all religious societies that applied for incorporation. The New York congregation Shearith Israel was incorporated that very year, thus securing the same legal benefits and status as churches in the state. The same legal benefits: almost a secular salvation.

The quarter of a million Jews who benefited from the birth of political liberalism in those early years was a fraction of world Jewry. At that time the largest plurality of the Jewish population — roughly one million people — was concentrated in Eastern Europe and Russia. After the partition of Poland in the final decade of the eighteenth century, at about the time that America's Jews were reaping the first fruits of American liberalism, Jews in Russia were restricted to a large region known as the Pale of Settlement, established in 1791, essentially an enormous ghettoized community in which Jewish life was governed by strict Russian laws. This geographical sequestration remained in force for over a hundred years (it was dissolved shortly after the abdication of Nicholas II during the Russian Revolution). In Russia there had been no Enlightenment, even if Voltaire and the "enlightened despot" Catherine the Great voluminously corresponded.

But in the late eighteenth century and early nineteenth century, the new liberal dispensation began to make itself known to Europe's Jews. The phenomenon known as "emancipation" was born, with all its mighty imperfections, first in Austria with a proclamation by the emperor in 1782. In France, the French Revolution and then the rule of Napoleon allowed Jews to become full citizens of the state and annulled the laws requiring that the Jews live in a ghetto and enacted other liberalizing measures, which were extended to the countries that Napoleon conquered. (There were also outbursts of anti-Semitism among the revolutionaries, and Napoleon also enacted some reactionary measures against the Jews. Progress is never unalloyed, especially for Jews.) As is well known, the phenomenon known as "emancipation" also led to the phenomenon known as "assimilation," with its many psychological agonies and social anxieties. Liberalization came to be rightly seen as a threat to tradition; the founder of Habad Hasidism, in Russia in 1812, wrote that "should Napoleon be victorious, wealth among the Jews will be abundant and the glory of the children of Israel will be exalted, but the hearts of Israel will be separated and distanced from their father in heaven. But if our master [Czar] Alexander will triumph, though poverty will be abundant and the glory of Israel will be humbled, the heart of Israel will be bound and joined with its father in heaven." This same plot — the joy of liberalization and the fear of liberalization — would later play out in the years of the great immigration to America, when millions of Jews who never experienced it before came to the shores of a liberal order.

And there were other liberalizing developments for the Jews — for example, the creation and distribution across borders of a Jewish press. This innovation in Jewish life created the possibility for there to exist such a thing as a global Jewish community. Jewish newspapers detailing the goings-on of local Jewish life was soon enhanced by a more ambitious Jewish journalism designed to disseminate news of Jewish communities in far-flung parts of the world. The first known Jewish newspaper produced by and for Jewish readers was the *Gazeta de Amsterdam*, which was printed in Spanish for the converso Dutch community in the Dutch capital. Between 1835 and 1840 eighteen Jewish newspapers were founded in five different countries. Over the following five years, their number increased by fifty-three in thirteen different countries. The circulation of news and opinions strengthened the new liberal muscles.

Scholars argue that a single event catalyzed this steep rise: the Damascus Affair. In 1840, thirteen members of the Jewish Syrian community in Damascus were accused of kidnapping and murdering a Catholic priest and his servant and draining their blood to bake matza — the blood libel that had haunted Jews throughout the medieval period, but the global Jewish community was shocked to discover that the old antisemitic trope still had currency in the modern period, and that in a city as cosmopolitan and significant as Damascus, political and religious leaders could permit — indeed, sanction — such a thing. The French Consul in Damascus, Ulysse de Ratti-Menton, supported the libel, and ordered an investigation in the Jewish quarter. Ratti-Menton swayed the governor of the city, who also happened to be the son-in-law of Muhammad Ali, the viceroy of Ottoman Egypt who governed Ottoman Syria at that time.

The accused were imprisoned and violently tortured until they confessed to the crime. Some were forced to convert to Islam on penalty of death. Others were sentenced to death. Some number of the seven prisoners who were forced to confess died during the interrogations. At the same time state authorities kidnapped sixty-three Jewish children and held them hostage until the entire Jewish community collectively confessed and also brought proof of the murder forward. Bones were unearthed somewhere in the Jewish quarter on the basis of which Ratti-Menton and Sharif Pasha declared that this was "proof" of the ritual slaughter, and more Jews were arrested on charges of abetting the murderers. Christians and Muslims in the city united to unleash violence on their Jewish neighbors. A synagogue in a suburb of the city was pillaged and desecrated.

One of the arrested was a man named Yitzchak Picciotto. His brother, Eliyahu, happened to be the Austrian consul in Aleppo. It was thanks to him that world Jewry was made aware of the catastrophe. Dissolve to American Jewry. Then numbering about fifteen thousand, the Jews of the United States protested the murders in six different cities. For the first time in American Jewish history, Jews demonstrated on behalf of their own interests and exercised influence in foreign policy — they pressured President Van Buren to protest, and the United States consul in Egypt did so at the President's bidding. As Hasia Diner, the historian of American Judaism, put it,

> For the Jews, the Damascus affair launched modern Jewish politics on an international scale, and for American Jews it represented their first effort at creating a distinctive political agenda. Just as the United States had used this affair to proclaim its presence on the global scale, so too did American Jews, in their newspapers and at mass meetings, announce to their coreligionists in France and England that they too ought to be thought of as players in global Jewish diplomacy.

At the same time, the most powerful Jews in the world — among them Moses Montefiore in England, the Rothschild family, and the lawyer Isaac-Jacob Adolph Cremieux who went on to serve as the Minister of Justice in France — questioned the integrity of the investigation. The pressure worked, and the Syrian authorities were forced to lift the death sentence for those who had not succumbed to torture.

The Jewish press came into being in part because the Damascus Affair made clear how uneven the quality of life for Jews was depending on where and under whose authority they lived. Suddenly it was possible for Jews in Cincinnati to know that a Jewish child had been secretly baptized, kidnapped, and forced to be raised as a Catholic in Rome — as happened in 1858 in the infamous Mortara Affair. And when pogroms started rolling through the Pale of Settlement at the end of the nineteenth century, Jews were aware that in a place across the ocean called America it was possible to assert one's right to live wherever one pleased, to vote, to buy land, and to bring a violent antisemite to court with the confidence that the court was tasked to rule in a wronged Jew's favor. And so it made sense that between 1880 and the start of World War I approximately two million Eastern European Jews came to America. By 1914, when Congress squeezed Lady Liberty's arms shut after the start of World War I, the American Jewish population had swelled to 2,349,754 — more than all of the Jewish population in Austria-Hungary — according to the American Jewish Yearbook.

The Declaration of Independence changed Jewish history and it changed Jewish identity. Suddenly Jews possessed a sense of possibility that was not delusional and not limited to messianic redemption. Democracy promised nothing less than to sever the old equation between exile and suffering; and whereas antisemitism has never been expunged from American life, and has recently become more prominent in American life, it generally did not express itself violently. (That is why the Tree of Life massacre and the subsequent violent assaults on Jews in America were so terrifying.)

America is not the only modern revolution in Jewish history, not the only experiment in rejecting the unjust terms of Jewish existence in the violent diaspora. The same dissatisfaction with the oppressive reality that led to the emigration of millions of Jews, that awakened a new sense of historical agency in the exiled Jews, issued also in the other great experiment: the restoration of Jewish sovereignty in the land of Israel, the creation of a Jewish state. You might say that America and Israel, democracy and self-determination, are the two competitors for the Jewish future. Yet it is important to be clear that there are many differences between these two dispensations, and the ways in which these respective states are different are intensely significant for their respective citizenries. The United States is blind to chosenness, or Chosenness. No people who live inside it are esteemed or despised as essentially other in the eyes of the state. Neutrality about difference, and a skepticism about historically and biologically inherited privilege, is a corollary of the American system. America was a nation founded on the principle that all people are equal: there are no exceptions in this all-encompassing proposition.

But Israel — and in this sense Jews are no different from every other ethnically defined nation — was conceived as a Jewish state, whatever the definitions and the difficulties of such a conception. As in all other nation-states, such a definition is a secularized version of Chosenness. When the Jews lost their state the first and then the second time, they were forced to reckon with the plight of every minority in an alien state, in an exile, up until the founding of America: the people who belong, the majority, are held to be historically and sometimes even ontologically better than the people who do not. The state of Israel sought to modify the ugliness of this deep distinction by introducing democracy into the bargain, and making an explicit promise of complete equality to all; but still it lives within the old European framework of a majority and a minority, which, when the minority reaches a size that frightens the majority, has always led to violence. Even as Israel promised equality, it promised favoritism. Is a liberal ethnically-based state a contradiction in terms? Whatever the situation in theory, in practice the government that presides in Jerusalem today certainly thinks so. Netanyahu and his fevered cronies have drowned the possibility of real democracy in blood. Israel promised equal rights to all citizens. In this, it has failed.

So here I am, even in these days, to praise America, and what it has done for the Jews, and why. And to implore my fellow Jewish Americans to remember what we owe American liberalism, what it cost us in life and in pain to get here, and what it will cost us if the dream of American liberalism is allowed to wither. Before the United States, no country had ever accepted liberalism as the groundwork upon which to build a polis and to justify itself. And certainly no liberal society ever made the next essential breakthrough that America did, which was to add pluralism — the recognition of the blessings of difference and of the axiomatic rights of groups as well as individuals — to its public philosophy as a corollary of liberalism.

The magnitude of the struggle that we face in America now is owed precisely to the high moral bar that a liberal order sets for itself. The practice of political liberalism is always incomplete, always asymptotic, because there will always be citizens and non-citizens. The promise of universal equality will always be denied full fruition, and so, in some sense, liberal states are hypocritical by definition. (The moral revolution that is America long ago committed a genocide on its own ground.) Yet there are worse things than stubbornly aspiring to justice, especially when one prefers it to come from below rather than from above. Not doing so is far worse. Better to fail trying to institutionalize equality than to build a political framework on the premise that like should favor like. Tribalism is a constant seduction, but that does not make it a good. And tribalism in a heterogeneous society may quickly become an evil.

The commitment of American Jews to America was well founded. We need to remember this now, as everything is shaking, and as so many of our brothers and sisters link arms with the cruel reactionaries destroying the American Revolution and offer them "antisemite" as a useful spin-word for fascism. The Declaration of Independence is indeed based on, and necessitated by, self-evident truths. It would be a terrible delinquency to shut our eyes to its promise.

LEON WIESELTIER

The Cheeseman

A little lectionary:

Every human being, no matter how slightly gifted he is, however subordinate his position in life may be, has a natural need to formulate a life-view, a conception of the meaning of life and its purpose. — KIERKEGAARD

The world has become "infinite" for us all over again, inasmuch as we cannot reject the possibility that it may include infinite interpretations. — NIETZSCHE

A man's vision is the great thing about him. Who cares for Carlyle's reasons, or Schopenhauer's, or Spencer's? A philosophy is the expression of a man's intimate character, and all definitions of the universe are but the deliberatively adopted reactions of human characters upon it. — WILLIAM JAMES

The anarchy of the philosophic systems is one of the most effective reasons for continually renewed skepticism. Historical consciousness of the limitless variety of philosophic systems contradicts the claims of each of them makes to universal validity and this supports the skeptical spirit more powerfully than any systematic argument. — DILTHEY

Worldviews can engage in controversy, but only rigorous knowledge can decide, and its decision bears the stamp of eternity. — HUSSERL

The ever more exclusive rooting of the interpretation of the world in anthropology which has set in since the eighteenth century finds expression in the fact that man's fundamental relation to beings as a whole is defined as a worldview. It is since then that this term has entered common usage. As soon as the world becomes picture the position of man is conceived as a worldview. Within this, man fights for the position in which he can be that being who gives to every being the measure and draws up the guidelines. — HEIDEGGER

From the father the child has a right to demand a view of life, that the father really has a view of life. — KIERKEGAARD

If I want to have a worldview, then I must view the world. I must establish the facts. The smallest fact from the connection between the soul and hormonal balance gives me more perspectives than an idealistic system. But the facts are not finished, they are hardly even begun. A worldview that waits for facts believes in progress. — MUSIL

The schoolboy believes his teacher and his schoolbooks. — WITTGENSTEIN

The most practical and important thing about a man is still his view of the universe. We think that for a landlady considering a lodger, it is important to know his income, but still more important to know his philosophy. We think the question is not whether the theory of the cosmos affects matters, but whether, in the long run, anything else affects them. — CHESTERTON

Lavoisier makes experiments with substances in his laboratory and now he concludes that this and that takes place when there is burning. He does not say that it might happen otherwise another time. He has got hold of a definite world-picture — not of course one that he invented: he learned it as a child. I say world-picture and not hypothesis, because it is the matter-of-course foundation for his research and as such goes unmentioned. — WITTGENSTEIN

Principles, guidelines, models, and limitations are storehouses of energy. — MUSIL

A person, to be a person, must have a worldview. — THE CHEESEMAN

A person, to be a person, must have a worldview: I was a very young man when the cheeseman unexpectedly addressed those words to me. The setting was completely unphilosophical. The words from across the counter startled me: was it possible not to have a worldview? Certainly not where we were, where I was growing up, which was a thicket of convictions. I was raised in a neighborhood of verities, Brooklyn, New York 11235. The streets flowed with answers. I was always already in possession of a worldview and could not even picture the emptiness of the opposite condition. I never met a nihilist. The worldview that held me in its grip, sometimes too tightly, was not anything that I had chosen: I was born into it and was systematically schooled in it. We are all born into a worldview; we receive it, we do not invent it; we are not Prometheans who begin *ex nihilo* and operatically create the terms of our selves and our world.

The most pressing business for a thinking mind is what to do about what it already believes. Credence must be earned by more than fidelity, which is not an intellectual virtue. The intellectual melodrama of my youth was whether I could find a way to assent to what had been bequeathed to me, to accept it not only as mine but also as true. Would I want it to be mine if it was false? I have intense feelings of affection for what my ancestors believed, because they believed it and I am their son, and for what their beliefs, true or false, enabled them to achieve (a belief system need not be true to issue in beauty and goodness, or to strengthen the spirit under duress); but neither filial duty nor the stewardship of tradition requires that we adopt the errors or the illusions of those who preceded us.

The vindication of a worldview that we did not elect must be accomplished in a manner that is spiritually richer than a mere reconciliation with facts, with the accidentals of one's birth. Decades later I came to cherish this sentence at the beginning of *The Guide of the Perplexed*: "certainty should not come to you by accident." Accident had to be elevated into necessity, which could then be celebrated as luck. But I was taught to begin with the feeling of luck, which had the unpleasant implication that everyone who was unlike me was unlucky, when of course they all ardently believed in their own luck, too. Chosenness, specialness, distinctiveness, uniqueness: irony does not flourish in the hothouses of self-love. In their insistence upon our own possession of the only truth, my rabbis outwitted themselves: their confidence about truth was designed to unburden us of the obligation, or the need, for a critical examination of first principles, but instead it seduced some of us in its direction. What was it that they did not want me to know? How can one live in the kingdom of truth and not use one's mind? What is truth if not the harvest of examination and reflection? I suppose there are two kinds of people, those whose minds are started by a claim to truth and those whose minds are stopped by a claim to truth.

So the inherited scheme that makes the world constantly meaningful is only the start of a life in beliefs. Passive assent brings no glory to what is assented to. The clarification of conviction should be a matter of personal honor for an individual; otherwise he has no bragging rights for what he believes. I do not mean that we must become a population of philosophers, but surely we must all cop to a strain of doubt, a bout of obscurity, a run of uncertainty, even if it has passed or we have mastered it. There is no shame in human finitude. The important point is that beliefs are paltry things without their reasons. A weak faith is one in which there are more beliefs than reasons. (A "heretic in the truth" is how Milton acidly described the man who holds a correct opinion without knowing why.)

The history of received intellectual frameworks, even before the legendary convulsions of modernity, has been turbulent and wounding. Do not think for a second that it was not ever thus, that people in the fourteenth century harbored no doubts and posed no objections: that is the escapist fantasy of reactionaries. Wholeness — the seamless fitting together of all that is human, and then of all that is human with the cosmos — was never for creatures such as ourselves; or to borrow the current cliché, it is, however ennoblingly, forever aspirational.

A society of perfectly contented and perfectly coherent people has never existed. I cannot believe that there ever lived a completely integrated individual; and if there did, then the thoroughgoing absence of alienation in such a person should be regarded as a flaw, as a disorder. Moreover, nothing provokes a doubting mood as much as a claim to certainty. And a culture of certainty is not only edifying, it is also asphyxiating. A final completion of the search for what is really the case is not a human option. The history of ideas and the history of religions demonstrate that all the traditions that solemnly instruct us never to change have themselves changed, to a greater and lesser degree, with greater and lesser integrity. Rabbi Akiva was one of Moses' most illustrious successors as a teacher of the law, but there is an astonishing midrash which describes Moses visiting Rabbi Akiva's classroom in the first century — sitting in the eighth row, the midrash adds with wanton hermeneutical imagination — and not comprehending a word that was being said. When Moses hears Akiva tell his students that what he has just taught them is the law that was given to Moses at Sinai, he is reassured. It is the very definition of a tradition to be transmitted, handed down, passed on — which is to say, to make accommodations for its survival. Every tradition that prides itself on its rigidity but has made it all the way to us is clearly deceiving itself in this regard. Traditions are inheritances that must continue to be inheritances, and this is not possible without a capacity for honorable adaptation.

The continuity of tradition demands a measure of discontinuity, carefully and knowledgeably managed, with a clear assessment of historical circumstances and intellectual flexibilities. This, the distinction between bending and breaking, between developing and dissipating, is not easy: too much discontinuity is as lethal to tradition as too little discontinuity. Going into the future with only the old is as stupid as going into the future with only the new. But if you live according to a tradition, if you love it with all your heart, but you do not pass it on, you have betrayed it.

It is not fulfilled only by your own practice of it. It was not created just for your own enjoyment of it. What I cherish must not end with me; or so I must resolve.

> What thou lovest well remains,
>   the rest is dross
> What thou lov'st well shall not be reft from thee
> What thou lov'st well is thy true heritage . . . .
> Here error is all in the not done,
> all in the diffidence that faltered . . .

The enterprise of perpetuation is not only a matter of having children and educating them adequately. It is also a matter of building and sustaining institutions, those allegedly soulless entities without which the most poetical accomplishments of the human soul would not stand a chance against time. In a free society, certainly, there is no excuse. But in our free society an excuse is desperately needed, because here we doom traditions with ignorance and indifference; here we have more important things to do.

Precisely because the acquisition of a worldview seemed moot to me, like settled business, and precisely because I inhabited a universe of previousness, the notion that a worldview is somehow lacking, and therefore an obligation, something for which I was responsible, was odd to me. The cheeseman saw the woolen yarmulke on my head; he knew that I was not wanting in an encompassing scheme; and yet he pronounced his admonition. And thereby he shook the settledness of things. The sufficiency of the received, one of the dogmas of my upbringing, would no longer suffice. And if one must have a worldview, then which worldview? Even without a familiarity with the shock that anthropology delivered to the West in the eighteenth century, I knew that there were many pictures of the world on offer. They were everywhere. I lived not only among synagogues but also among churches, though I left the neighborhood before it included mosques. Inside those churches and mosques, no doubt, they wrestle with the same problem of the threat to the validity of belief that is posed by the multiplicity of beliefs. A church down the street from a synagogue always thickens the plot. A sense of exclusiveness invites a siege mentality.

The cheeseman made belief seem less like an inheritance — a marvelous consequence of genealogy — and more like a task. In the matter of the most profound commitments, there was suddenly the suggestion of a choice. This was a little alarming: wasn't the purpose of a patrimony, and of loyalty to it, to relieve me of choice? Moreover, I was quite sure that I was thoroughly unequipped for such a decision. (It was not until many years later that I understood that obedience, too, is a choice. The thing about voluntarism is that you can check out but you can never leave.) Yet there I was, on Brighton Beach Avenue, experiencing the vertigo from which modern Western thought has never recovered: the recognition, vexing and then intoxicating and then vexing again, that there are many pictures of the world and that all of them are held to be true by the people and the communities who espouse them. What did the diversity of fervently championed truths say about the possibility of truth? Maybe my view is correct and your view is incorrect, and there the story ends. No, too simple. But why too simple? Somebody must be wrong! My head, loyally and disloyally, swam.

This teaching — my early induction into the arcadian anxieties of a philosophical existence — did not take place in a classroom. It took place in an appetizer, which is what we called a delicatessen that did not serve meat, so as to respect the ontology of the Jewish kitchen. And my tutor was not, professionally, a teacher. His job was to run the cheese counter in Mr. Haber's market on Brighton Beach Avenue in Brooklyn. The cheeseman was slightly stooped, balding, soft spoken, with a heavy accent and a gentle smile. I never saw him without his white apron. He stood behind a weathered cutting board that bordered a long refrigerated counter with a glass window that displayed the rows of culinary delicacies. (The appetizer was well named.) He handled the blocks and the wheels expertly, slicing them with a ruthless wire that he manipulated with the dexterity of a craftsman. The slices fell gracefully onto a waiting sheet of wax paper, which he then folded speedily and with geometrical precision. And all the while he talked and he taught. He cautioned me about hollowness and shallowness; as I stared at the sturgeon, he worried me about nothingness.

His accent was the tell. This was not supposed to have been his fate. Like almost all the adults I knew when I was growing up, the cheeseman was a displaced and disrupted individual. He was living his second life in his second world, because his first life in his first world had been annihilated. When the Germans invaded Poland, he was a graduate student in philosophy, and a Jew, at the university in Warsaw. Those were good years for philosophy in Poland, a flourishing era of logicians and phenomenologists. He devoted himself to the advanced study of Kant. It was at the cheese counter that I first heard the word "Kant." But it was all blown to bits by the war. He never told me how he survived it, or which of its many hells he endured, but like Mr. Haber, and like my parents, he was "a survivor" — which is to say, he had a spirit more powerful than history. His mind emerged intact from an apocalypse. He had carried philosophy with him. He never abandoned it. Did it abandon him?

Years later I wondered whether philosophy, or the philosophical attitude, had stood him in good stead during the atrocities. I prayed that it had. For philosophy can surely serve as an instrument of human perdurability, though you would not know it from the philosophy departments. I pictured him starving and thinking, hiding and thinking, running and thinking, weeping and thinking. But I wondered also about the limits of mental detachment in the face of catastrophe. Elias Canetti once remarked that during the war he did not save Goethe but Goethe saved him. It is a *geistliche* sentiment, but I wonder. Aren't there circumstances in which the equilibrium of a philosophical mind is not merely impossible but also suicidal? What are abstractions in a world on fire? What is an idea compared to a crumb of bread?

Should reflection upon existence teach interest or disinterest, and *in extremis* which is wisdom?

In any event, he made it out alive, and Mr. Haber, a man of such bountiful kindliness he could have been mistaken for a simpleton, gave him work. When the cheeseman discovered that one of his regular customers, a young man whose mother sent him frequently to his counter with the same order was eager to hear what he had to say, he was delighted to instruct the lad. He cut the cheese and discoursed on philosophy. I had the impression that he cut the cheese more slowly in those pedagogical moments, so that we would have more time for the seminar. I developed the habit of doing my errands at hours when the store might be less crowded and he could elaborate more fully, in his heavy accent, on his themes.

O those accents! They are almost all gone now. It is a commonplace of the literature of American immigration that the children were often ashamed of how their parents sounded, but for me it was Mozart. The accents were proof that everything that we were told about a vanished world had been exactly so. Not that I doubted it, not at all; but the accents were a sensual link, the actual sound of their world audible in my world, so that I sometimes felt almost as if I could travel backward along the accents, like traversing a rope stretched over a hideous drop, to the time and the place before the extermination of my people was attempted. I love refugees: these people of the before and the after, they gave me life. Refugees are the aristocrats of human fragility. They know more than we do, even if their knowledge is not power. In shul there were moments when the sound of those accents was almost too much to withstand, as when, in the afternoon prayer on Yom Kippur, old broken-down Mr. Frost sobbed as he prayed: "Do not cast us aside in our old age, as our strength wanes do not forsake us . . ." I never saw the cheeseman in shul: a philosopher. Mr. Haber was there often.

I hope that we will one day come to see the folly of our acceptance of disruption as an ideal of life. I refer not only to the Darwinism of the technologists: owing in part to their successes, a much wider social and cultural prestige has been conferred upon a cataclysmic view of change. (Is arrogance the condition of innovation or its consequence?) The only thing that we seem to produce in larger quantities than data is disrupted lives. In our romance of shattering we have come to scorn the shattered. If you have known shattered people, then you will think twice about all the shiny advanced rubbish about the virtue of hastiness, the idolatry of the will, the worship of the macro. After all, a dissatisfaction with contemporary conditions can take many forms and have many consequences: there are myriad ways to manage necessary and justified change, and heartlessness is not a requirement of progress, even if there will always be "losers." Cataclysmic change is always sloppy change and always cruel change. I am so sick of living in the rubble of my culture and the rubble of my politics. Isn't destruction exciting? Cataclysmists are pathologically at peace with human costs. To the social breakdowns that preceded them they add the social breakdowns that they devise, and the population of broken people grows. A new electorate! Like all revolutionaries they are vandals, except that they enjoy the further conceit of having circuitry on their side, as if science makes a moral difference. And now we have a government that looks down from its morally moronic stratosphere and gleefully breaks people. The viciousness is not a by-product of the policy, the viciousness *is* the policy.

The population of broken people grows beyond our borders, too. In 2024, according to the Population Division of the United Nations Department of Economic and Social Affairs, the global number of international migrants was 304 million people, or 3.7 percent of the world's populations. These immense movements of human beings are all attempts to escape varieties of horror and danger; nobody, except the rich, uproots themselves recreationally. There is an unprecedented amount of vulnerability and instability, of homelessness and statelessness, in our world — disruptedness is a dark norm, and we must therefore take the trouble, and not only in southwest Texas, to understand disrupted people, people who will never know what the Stoics called a smooth flow of life, fractured and fissured people, *people who need help*. They are not alien, they are hurting. All hurting people are alien, I suppose, if you are fine; but wellbeing can itself be a myopia. In their indifference to the most elementary human considerations, it is the nativists who are the aliens. Syria is an entire nation of disrupted people, and the contemporary *locus classicus* of the savagery of disruption is Gaza. Cleansings and expulsions are nothing other than disruption as an instrument of war. I am not ranting. I am shocked again by all this damage, which in a certain light coheres as an era. And I am recalling the cheeseman and what he represented, the sweet obscure contemplative man whom they failed to kill, who for the rest of his exiled days could aspire to nothing better than the rent and the attempted mastery of his own memories. Healing must not be confused with happiness. There is no return from disruption, there is only the arduous labor of creating yet another life. Did the cheeseman have a family? There was something isolated about him, the halting tone of the solitary. When he stood before me and talked about moral theory, I heard justice but saw injustice. You cannot pretend to be familiar with the world unless you know post-catastrophic people. The man was a living monument to the futility of the categorical imperative.

"Kant" was not the only word I first heard at the cheese counter. "Descartes" was another. As he cut through a brick of muenster one afternoon, he explained the cogito, and more generally the question of certainty. "Imagine a man suspended in space", he said. "There is no wind, no light, no sound, no external stimulation of any kind, nothing that could be registered by his senses. How would he know that he exists?" All around me the wrinkled Jews of Brighton Beach were fussily buying herring and rye bread and seltzer. ("The plebeian bubbly," as Irving Howe delightfully called it.) My aproned teacher continued: "He would know that he exists because he is thinking. Thinking!" The squares of muenster were piling up on the wax paper. "And not only would it. He would know it with certainty." The cheeseman's eyes were hot. For emphasis he would sometimes come out from behind the display case that separated him from his customers, wiping his hands on his apron, and give me the intellectual climax again. "Thinking!" "Certainty!" I stalked his every syllable. When he handed me the artfully packaged cheese — all those tucked-in angles, muenster made mathematical — I knew that the lesson was done. Years later I learned that the story of the floating man was Avicenna's invention, and that Descartes' argument was somewhat more complicated, and somewhat less persuasive, than my teacher's version of it. Perhaps he had a more sophisticated account that he could have provided but there was another customer waiting behind me, and maybe she was getting cranky. I wouldn't have blamed her. Still, it was he who gave me the gift of the problem of doubt. It was at the cheese counter, in a hundred afternoons of provisions, that I acquired the conviction that the stakes in matters of belief are high.

In those years, before the Russian Jews arrived, Brighton Beach was a tired place, populated largely by retired workers from the garment industries in New York. The avenue was a block away from the sea, and they had come there for the beauty and the breeze, they were not floating men, and for the boardwalk, which was a stupendous incubator of community, particularly on summer nights, when the heat in the uncooled dwellings drove them outside to the shore beneath a Yiddish moon. (Later the Russians would bring their balalaikas.) Mr. Haber's establishment was one of a series of storefronts on the ground floor of one of the many low, glum apartment buildings that sometimes seemed as hunched and as weathered as the people who inhabited them. (The camera recently panned past Mr. Haber's block in *Anora*, which was set in these homely streets.) Beyond the appetizer, a few steps past our Sunday night deli, was a movie theater called the Oceana, where I began my education in American cinematic kitsch. There was no Antonioni in my Brooklyn. And further up the avenue was the elevated subway, which regularly overwhelmed the neighborhood with its nasty screeching noise and sent sparks falling to the unignited street below. The din of the train was the soundtrack for my tutorials.

Along with "Kant" and "Descartes," I heard "Leibniz." Even in my undeveloped state I recognized that there was something unbearable about a survivor teaching theodicy. I do not mean that the cheeseman had found comfort in his own mind for his own suffering. I never knew him well enough to take the measure of his wounds. Had he uncovered, for his own adversity, what Leibniz called a sufficient reason? But there he was, the pounded man expatiating upon the idea of the best of all possible worlds. When he explained the Leibnizian idea of God, I was reminded of what little I knew of Maimonides. (The cheeseman never discussed Jewish philosophy.) I remember him insisting that Leibniz's optimism was derived not inductively, as a conclusion to be drawn from experience, but rationally. The world *has* to be this way — reason says so; and never mind the testimony that he himself could have given that the world is not this way. The cheeseman was certainly an expert on the frustration of the rational by the real. But at the same time he was an ardent exponent of reason. He adored it. Its concepts were stations on a magical journey away from spurious magic. In the company of reason the ordinariness of his surroundings melted away and an antique grandeur was recovered. I am embarrassed to recall that I did not adequately appreciate his reverence for reason. I was an adolescent reading Nietzsche, who is very bad for adolescents, and more generally I had fallen under the spell of existentialist paperbacks. I believed that reason was the problem; I was a hormonal fool. Reason, unlike logic, is not for the young.

What did the cheeseman mean by a worldview? I cannot say for sure. He almost certainly did not have in mind the organizing apparatus of the mind, the operating systems of categories and conceptual schemes that make experience legible: the cheese did not come with a side of epistemology. He preferred to impart to me moral and metaphysical ideas. He failed to warn me that all these ideas may not go together even when the individual pieces seemed proven and right. I had the impression that he was telling me, instead, to choose among philosophical packages; and for a young man packages are more exciting than pieces. Packages can make you feel brilliant. Yet perhaps he was not at all recommending a package, as if slices of thought could be neatly joined together like slices of cheese: the skeptical and even playful tone of his little lectures belied a young man's hope for a single answer to all the questions. He was not preaching dogma, or any variety of mental convenience. He was soft, but he was strict, as if to say: young man, there is no haven from complication. A worldview, in his account, or in my understanding of his account, was not an evasion of intellectual labor. It was an invitation to intellectual labor. He was advising me of a duty. I sometimes associate the stirrings of my mind with the smell of smoked fish and pungent cheese.

A worldview is certainly a package, because it purports to be comprehensive, and sometimes even totalistic. The advantage of its scope is that it equips you for every contingency. It anticipates every confusion and every surprise. For this reason, whatever its intellectual merits, it has an undeniable psychological utility. "A *Weltanschauung*," Freud wrote in an undelivered lecture not long before he fled Vienna, "is an intellectual construction which solves all the problems of our existence uniformly and on the basis of one overriding hypothesis, which, accordingly, leaves no question unanswered and in which everything that interests us finds its fixed place." In subsequent years such unifying and simplifying explanations came to be most commonly described as ideology, and associated with tyrannical political systems, though they may tyrannize just as easily over an individual mind in an open society as over an entire society in a closed one. When ideology is thwarted by the openness of a society, it often curdles into conspiracy theory.

Modern philosophy, mainly in Germany, includes something known as "*Weltanschauung* philosophy," which was largely the creation of Wilhelm Dilthey, the heir of Vico, whose immortality is owed to his prescient and extended defense of the humanities against the natural sciences. Dilthey classified and inventoried the many types of *Weltanschauungen*; it was his tribute to the natural diversity of the human mind. (The term *Weltanschauung* was coined, but not developed, by Kant in the *Critique of Judgement* in 1790.) Dilthey was one of those thinkers who, after Nietzsche, the self-styled "psychologist", was happy to collapse philosophy into psychology, and so he shrank from calling a worldview a philosophy. In an especially provocative remark, he declared that "worldviews are not products of thought." For this reason, worldviews are felicitously "undemonstrable and indestructible." The origin of worldviews, in his telling, was to be found in human need: "the formation of worldviews is determined by the will to stabilize the conception of the world." Americans might describe this as the will to closure. One way to preempt spiritual crisis is to remove foundational concepts from the teeming domain of the mind — to hold them with intellectual immunity, as it were.

But where in the hierarchy of intellectual virtues does stability belong? What is the mortal terror in inconsistency? Yet it was the unphilosophical, or even anti-philosophical, character of worldviews that lent them to the purposes of culture, I mean culture defined in the anthropological sense, as the given outlook of a community or a society or a nation, the sum of its assumptions and its axioms — the spirit of an age. Indeed, all that is required to come into possession of a worldview is to speak a language. (God, said Nietzsche, is in our grammar.) Thus Karl Mannheim seized upon Dilthey's remark to emphasize the irrelevance of "theory" to the creation of a *Weltanschauung*. Philosophy, he observed, is "merely one of its manifestations." In his account, a worldview is "the basic impulse of a culture" that manifests itself in all the culture's expressions, high and low, and represents the "global unity" that runs through the entirety of a way of life in all its material and non-material aspects and knits them together. Hegel strikes again! Mannheim's objective was not psychology but sociology — more specifically, the sociology of knowledge, which was invented by Marx but codified by Mannheim a hundred years later.

We might even say that a worldview is a degraded form of philosophy, an intellectualization of what we now like to call a habitus, a polished collection of doctrines with no rough edges, easy to swallow, allergic to paradox, bored by variations, of no intellectual distinction, handy for the education of children and the advancement of demagogues, a social asset, perfect for nothing more ambitious than a personal identity. Foremost among the attractions of identity is that it confers intellectual invulnerability. It takes guts to keep allowing ideas in; such porousness can be mistaken for vacuity, when in fact it represents a stubborn determination to keep checking the merits of one's ideas, because justification is the work of a lifetime. In 1938, in an essay called "The Age of the World Picture," Heidegger declared that "all great philosophy culminates in a worldview." He did not mean it as a compliment. He wished to secure the superiority of philosophy, especially as he construed it. Yet as a factual matter — and he was always insulted by the grubby concern ("positivism") with facts — Heidegger was himself in the worldview business, and his statement is false: there are great philosophies that cannot be in this way reduced. Their difficulty and their depth make them impossible to package and useless to cultural and political programs — as Heidegger's own doctrine of Being should have been, except that the phenomenologist-turned-mystagogue found a way to place Being at the service of the Führer. When a way to grovel is sought, a way to grovel is found. Is there anything more poisonous than identity made ontological? (Heidegger had a Romanian contemporary named Constantin Noica, a metaphysician who also lived in the woods and also sided with the fascists, who wrote a tome with the risible but chilling title *The Romanian Sense of Being*.) The closer one studies worldviews, the more facile they seem, and the more sordid their history.

Can we agree that there is no such thing as the spirit of an age? There are many spirits in any age. The impulse to dissolve and to merge, the lust for oneness and for sameness, the entire Parmenidean enterprise, has had an awful blinding effect. Monism is sublimely satisfying, but it leaves out too much. Empiricism, before it is magnified into a philosophy and enters the lists, may be just a fancy term for alertness, for the scruple about paying the requisite attention. The issue is the philosophical and even spiritual significance of the details. We have been taught, especially under the influence of the social sciences, that knowledge advances by means of subsuming the particulars, by means of generalizations, but so, too, does ignorance. Common features are not always more revealing than uncommon features, and the unification of a manifold is not always the surest method of grasping it. Enter art.

The love of one thing may be owed to the fear of many things. The rampant variability of reality must be desperately brought under control. Unfortunately the pluralists, whose fundamental intuition against the monists seems unimpeachable, get too rattled by the task and go too far. They believe that the only way to relieve the pressure of the diversity and the opacity of the world is to surrender the possibility of objectivity altogether and to confine assertions of meaning and truth to the more lenient realm of subjectivity. Philosophical claims, they rule, will henceforth be regarded as self-expressions. And how they have prospered in America! William James was so convinced that serious thought was entirely an activity of personal temperament that he concluded that philosophy consists of "a few main types" — "cynical characters take one general attitude, sympathetic characters take another," and so on. Argument is usurped by personality. Cogito ergo sum? He *would* say that!

Dilthey's conclusion that the historical multiplicity of worldviews leads inexorably to relativism is similarly overwrought and unfounded. Why, in the end, can one view out of a thousand not be the true one? Why does it matter that a true opinion is surrounded by many false ones? Why is critical reasoning helpless before a large field? Shouldn't it, in the name of its purposes and its methods, relish the challenge? Or is the anxiety about philosophical commitment political — that the rational justification of one position among others would be disrespectful or hegemonic? But the respect that we owe other believers — though not other beliefs — must be apparent long before the exercise of criticism begins; it must always be prior. I respect many people whose views I hold to be nonsense. (Evil nonsense, however, makes cordiality much harder.) There is something immature about being scared of other people's philosophical choices; it is like being scared of other people's happiness. And it is even more abject to be afraid of choice itself. The wounded pride of the eighteenth century — the rudeness of its discovery that what Hamlet told Horatio was correct, there *are* more things — is not enough of a reason to give up on truth; the anthropological revelation demanded only an expansion of the search for it. Anyway, the Western thinkers who were so unnerved by the existence of natives and aboriginals were never going to seriously consider their views of the world. (A few lines after his remark about cynical and sympathetic philosophies, James declared that "the thought of very primitive men has hardly any tincture of philosophy.") The plenitude of philosophies and worldviews means only that people everywhere have been contemplating difficult questions and ultimate realities, and that is not bad news. We must tread carefully here, because from the truth that nobody can believe everything the lie that nobody can believe anything may quickly follow. The history of ideas is not the meal, it is the menu.

The cheeseman's insistence that I gain a worldview may have been his way of teaching me the belief in belief, and his successive presentations of the philosophers may have been his way of suggesting that one day I would have to make a choice. And so it may not have been a worldview after all that he was commending to my attention, if a worldview is a summary of prevalent but unexamined beliefs, an arrangement of platitudes, a perquisite of membership in a culture, a badge of belonging. Whether by means of heritage or contagion, people usually hold the picture of the world that is held by people like themselves, but the cheeseman was not prodding me to select a conformity. He wanted me to stretch, not to wallow.

I came away from the appetizer also with another treasure: a lasting impression of one man's *amor intellectualis*, and therefore with the notion that thoughtfulness is an essential element of dignity. It would be hard to exaggerate the cheeseman's dignity. His circumstances never levelled him. All of his dreams had been destroyed, except his dream of understanding; and that dream could be realized anywhere, even in a small food shop in a distant corner of the world. He had suffered, but he had not lived stupidly. The cheeseman was the first genuinely philosophical individual I ever encountered, the first one who exemplified — or modelled, as we would say — the intrinsic satisfaction of serious thought. In this way he prepared me for my low and stupid age. He gave me a course in the experience of mental independence. It is unlikely that he had many people with whom he could explore the contents of his educated and energetic mind, and it pleases me to imagine that our conversations may have relieved his loneliness. I hope I helped. All hail the solitariness of the thoughtful! And the master whose name I never knew.

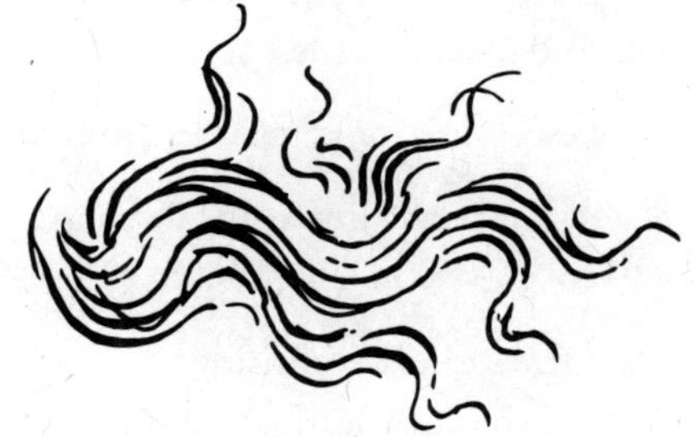

CONTRIBUTORS

JACKSON ARN is an art critic in New York.

DAVID GREENBERG is a professor of history and of journalism and media studies at Rutgers University and the author most recently of *John Lewis: A Life*.

RYAN RUBY is the author most recently of *Context Collapse: A Poem Containing a History of Poetry*.

JULIA KIESERMAN is a doctoral student at New York University. She writes about security and privacy issues.

VANESSA GARCIA is a writer, a journalist, and a visual artist.

HENRY OLIVER is a fellow in the Emerging Scholars Program at the Mercatus Center at George Mason University.

CASS R. SUNSTEIN is the Robert Walmsley University Professor at Harvard Law School and the author most recently of *On Liberalism: In Defense of Freedom*.

JAMES P. RUBIN served as a top adviser to two secretaries of state, Madeleine Albright and Antony Blinken, and as the chief spokesman of the State Department from 1997 to 2000. In the Biden administration he was Special Envoy and Coordinator of the Global Engagement Center at the Department of State.

JOHN BERRYMAN, who died in 1972, won the Pulizer Prize for poetry in 1965 for *77 Dream Songs*.

MICHAEL WALZER is professor emeritus at the Insitute of Advanced Study and the author most recently of *The Struggle for a Decent Politics: On "Liberal" as an Adjective*.

PAUL REITTER, who recently translated Marx's *Capital* with Paul North, is ASC Distinguished Professor of Germanic Languages and Literatures at Ohio State University.

PAUL NORTH, who recently translated Marx's *Capital* with Paul Reitter, is the Maurice Natanson Professor of German at Yale University.

MYLES ZAVELO is a writer from New York City.

ANNA BALLAN is a Ph.D. student at Yale University.

ROBERT RUBSAM writes fiction and nonfiction.

DIDI TAL is a doctoral student in the Department of Germanic Languages at Columbia University where she studies the history of immigration.

YAHIA LABABIDI is an Egyptian-American poet and the author most recently of *Palestine Wail*.

FATEME KARIMKHAN is an Iranian journalist, essayist, photographer, and sociologist. She lives in Tehran.

CELESTE MARCUS is the executive editor of *Liberties*. Her book *Chaim Soutine: Genius, Obsession, and a Dramatic Life in Art* was recently published by Public Affairs.

LEON WIESELTIER is the editor of *Liberties*.

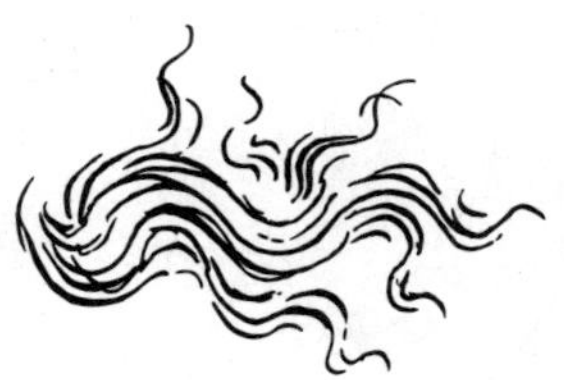

The insignia that appears in the pages of *Liberties* is derived from details in Botticelli's drawings for Dante's *Divine Comedy*, which were executed between 1480 and 1495.

Liberties mourns the passing of
of our friend and contributor

ALFRED BRENDEL

maestro.

JOIN IN OUR WORK

***Help ensure the future of* Liberties**

Liberties: A Journal of Culture & Politics features essays from award-winning writers, significant scholars, the next generation's rising talents, and poets from around the world. There's a reason why cultural warriors, political leaders, opinion makers, and engaged citizens from across the political and cultural spectrum read and cherish *Liberties*. Through this quarterly in-print publication, new weekly online content, podcasts, vodcasts, and in-person events, *Liberties* champions liberal democracy and the humanities.

As a matter of principle, *Liberties* does not accept advertising or other funding sources that might influence our independence.

We look to our readers and those individuals and institutions that believe in our mission for contributions — large and small — to support this not-for-profit publication.

If you are interested in making a donation to *Liberties*, please contact Bill Reichblum, publisher by email, `bill@libertiesjournal.com`, or by phone, `202-891-7159`.

`libertiesjournal.com`.

SUBSCRIPTIONS

There's Nothing Artificial about Our Intelligence

Surprise your intellectually curious friend with a gift that keeps on giving — a subscription to *Liberties.*

Scan this QR code or go to libertiesjournal.com/subscribe to make a present of groundbreaking essays, criticism, and commentary. *Liberties* brings together leading thinkers exploring ideas that matter for our culture and our politics.

Subscriber benefits include choices of in-print, all digital access, new monthly online content, invitations to in-person salons and other events, and weekly emails of the latest in the global world of *Liberties.*

Professional discounts available for active military; faculty, students, and education administrators; government employees; and those working in the not-for-profit sector.

Printed in Canada.

Liberties: A Journal of Culture and Politics is distributed to booksellers in the United States by Publishers Group West; in Canada by Publishers Group Canada; and internationally by Ingram Publisher Services International. It is available by annual subscription and by individual purchase from bookstores and online booksellers.